EXPLORERS AND EXPLORATION

Marshall Cavendish
New York • London • Singapore

Marshall Cavendish
99 White Plains Road
Tarrytown, New York 10591-9001

www.marshallcavendish.com

© 2005 Marshall Cavendish Corporation

Consultants: Ralph Ehrenberg, former chief, Geography and Map Division, Library of Congress, Washington, DC; Conrad Heidenreich, former historical geography professor, York University, Toronto; Shane Winser, information officer, Royal Geographical Society, London

Contributing authors: Dale Anderson, Kay Barnham, Peter Chrisp, Richard Dargie, Paul Dowswell, Elizabeth Gogerly, Steven Maddocks, John Malam, Stewart Ross, Shane Winser

MARSHALL CAVENDISH
Editor: Thomas McCarthy
Editorial Director: Paul Bernabeo
Production Manager: Michael Esposito

WHITE-THOMSON PUBLISHING
Editors: Alex Woolf and Steven Maddocks
Design: Ross George and Derek Lee
Cartographer: Peter Bull Design
Picture Research: Glass Onion Pictures
Indexer: Fiona Barr

ISBN 0-7614-7535-4 (set)
ISBN 0-7614-7546-X (vol. 11)

Printed in China

08 07 06 05 04 5 4 3 2 1

Library of Congress Cataloging-in-Publication Data

Explorers and exploration.
    p. cm.
  Includes bibliographical references (p.) and index.
  ISBN 0-7614-7535-4 (set : alk. paper) -- ISBN 0-7614-7536-2 (v. 1) -- ISBN 0-7614-7537-0 (v. 2) -- ISBN 0-7614-7538-9 (v. 3) -- ISBN 0-7614-7539-7 (v. 4) -- ISBN 0-7614-7540-0 (v. 5) -- ISBN 0-7614-7541-9 (v. 6) -- ISBN 0-7614-7542-7 (v. 7) -- ISBN 0-7614-7543-5 (v. 8) -- ISBN 0-7614-7544-3 (v. 9) -- ISBN 0-7614-7545-1 (v. 10) -- ISBN 0-7614-7546-X (v. 11)
  1. Explorers--Encyclopedias. 2. Discoveries in geography--Encyclopedias. I. Marshall Cavendish Corporation. II. Title.

  G80.E95 2005
  910'.92'2--dc22

                    2004048292

ILLUSTRATION CREDITS

Cover: Buzz Aldrin on the surface of the moon, 1969 (Peter Newark's American Pictures).

color key	time period
▬▬▬	to 500
▬▬▬	500–1400
▬▬▬	1400–1850
▬▬▬	1850–1945
▬▬▬	1945–2000
▬▬▬	general articles

CONTENTS

TIME LINE   **804**

GLOSSARY   **808**

RESOURCES FOR FURTHER STUDY

    BIBLIOGRAPHY   **814**

    PLACES TO GO   **817**

    RESOURCES FOR YOUNGER READERS   **820**

    INTERNET RESOURCES   **822**

LIST OF MAPS   **824**

INDEX OF MAPS   **825**

THEMATIC INDEXES

    BIOGRAPHICAL INDEX   **830**

    GEOGRAPHICAL INDEX   **836**

    INDEX OF SCIENCE AND TECHNOLOGY   **845**

COMPREHENSIVE INDEX   **851**

TIME LINE

AFRICA

c. 500 BCE
Hanno of Carthage sails down the African coast.

c. 245 BCE
In Egypt, Eratosthenes of Cyrene calculates the polar circumference of the earth.

c. 146–170
Working in Alexandria, Egypt, Claudius Ptolemy produces the *Almagest* and the *Guide to Geography*.

1355–1356
Having spent thirty years traveling to almost every Muslim country in the world, Ibn Battutah returns home to Morocco and dictates his memoirs.

1419
Henry the Navigator begins a program of African exploration.

1430
Cheng Ho sails from China to East Africa.

1488
Bartolomeu Dias rounds Africa's southern tip.

ASIA

334–323 BCE
Alexander the Great marches his army from Greece to India.

c. 138–125 BCE
Zhang Qian forges the Silk Road.

c. 100 BCE
The rudder is invented in China.

c. 250
The magnetic compass is invented in China.

399–414
Faxian makes a remarkable overland journey, along Silk Road routes, from China to India and back.

618
Under the Tang dynasty, use of the Silk Road becomes far more frequent.

645
Hsüan-tsang returns to China after traveling to southern India.

1246
John of Piano Carpini crosses central Asia to Karakorum.

1259
Under Kublai Khan, the Silk Road flourishes.

1271–1295
Marco Polo travels from Venice to China and back.

1368
After the inward-looking Ming dynasty comes to power in China, the Silk Road begins to decline.

1430
Cheng Ho returns to China with African animals.

1497–1498
Vasco da Gama sails from Europe to India by way of the Cape of Good Hope.

1596–1597
Willem Barents spends a winter on Novaya Zemlya.

1583–1610
Matteo Ricci, an Italian, lives and travels in China, a country considered closed to foreigners.

AUSTRALIA AND THE SOUTH PACIFIC

CENTRAL AND SOUTH AMERICA

1498
By landing in present-day Venezuela, Christopher Columbus becomes the first European to set foot on the South American mainland.

1500
Pedro Álvares Cabral lands in Brazil.

1507
Martin Waldseemüller's world map is the first to use the name America.

1513
Vasco Núñez de Balboa sights the Pacific.

1533
Francisco Pizarro conquers the Incan Empire.

EUROPE

c. 500
Boats with lateen (triangular) sails ply the Mediterannean.

c. 865
Floki Vilgerdarsen reaches Iceland.

c. 985
Erik the Red colonizes Greenland.

1154
The Arab geographer al-Idrisi produces a world map for King Roger II of Sicily.

c. 1180
The magnetic compass is first used in Europe.

c. 1410
Ptolemy's works, translated into Latin for the first time, become widely read by European scholars.

1492
Ferdinand and Isabella sponsor Christopher Columbus.

1494
The Treaty of Tordesillas divides the New World between Portugal and Spain.

1519–1522
Ferdinand Magellan captains the first fleet to sail around the world.

1569
Gerardus Mercator produces the map projection that still bears his name.

1580
Francis Drake completes the first British circumnavigation of the world.

1788
The African Association is founded in London.

1806
Mungo Park is killed on the Niger River.

1828
René-Auguste Caillé reaches Timbuktu.

1853–1856
David Livingstone crosses Africa and discovers the Victoria Falls.

1857–1858
John Hanning Speke correctly identifies Lake Victoria as the source of the Nile.

1874–1877
Henry Morton Stanley crosses Africa from east to west along the Congo River.

1728
Vitus Bering discovers that Asia and America are separated by a narrow stretch of water (later named the Bering Strait).

1866–1868
Francis Garnier explores the Mekong River.

1879
Nikolay Przhevalsky gets to within 125 miles (202 km) of Lhasa, Tibet. Adolf Nordenskiöld completes the Northeast Passage.

1894–1897
In her sixties, Isabella Lucy Bishop travels to China and Korea.

1904
Francis Edward Younghusband leads British troops into Lhasa.

1923
Gertrude Bell founds Iraq's archaeological museum in Baghdad.

1933
An airplane flies over Mount Everest.

1953
Edmund Hillary and Tenzing Norgay make the first known ascent of Mount Everest.

1605
Willem Jansz lands on the Cape York Peninsula, in northeastern Australia.

1642
Abel Tasman discovers Van Diemen's Land (Tasmania) and New Zealand.

1699–1701
As captain of the *Roebuck*, William Dampier surveys the northwestern coast of Australia and parts of New Guinea.

1766–1768
During his circumnavigation of the world, Philip Carteret discovers and names twenty Pacific islands.

1768
Louis-Antoine de Bougainville visits Tahiti during his circumnavigation of the world.

1768–1771
On his first Pacific voyage, aboard the *Endeavour*, James Cook charts the coasts of Australia and New Zealand.

1798–1799
Matthew Flinders circumnavigates Tasmania.

1801–1803
Matthew Flinders circumnavigates Australia.

1836
HMS *Beagle*, captained by Robert Fitzroy and carrying Charles Darwin, crosses the Pacific Ocean.

1860–1861
Robert O'Hara Burke and John Wills cross Australia on foot from south to north but die on the return journey.

1947
Thor Heyerdahl crosses the Pacific Ocean on the *Kon-Tiki*.

1616
Willem Schouten and Jakob Le Maire sail around Cape Horn.

1799–1804
Alexander von Humboldt and Aimé Bonpland collect a vast amount of scientific data relating to the geography, climate, and wildlife of South America.

1835
During HMS *Beagle*'s circumnavigation of the world, Charles Darwin collects specimens in the Galápagos Islands.

1602
The Dutch East India Company is founded.

1733–1741
Vitus Bering's Great Northern Expedition maps the northern and eastern coasts of Russia.

1749
In a bid to prevent scurvy, the British navy begins issuing lime juice to sailors.

1783
The Montgolfier brothers pioneer balloon flight.

1830
The Royal Geographical Society (RGS) is founded in London.

1845–1862
Alexander von Humboldt publishes *Kosmos*.

1863
Édouard Lartet and Henry Christy discover prehistoric artifacts in French caves.

1910
Louis Blériot becomes the first person to fly across the English Channel in an airplane.

1940
Prehistoric cave paintings are found at Lascaux, in central France.

NORTH AMERICA

1000
Blown off course while heading for Greenland, Leif Eriksson almost certainly lands on Newfoundland.

c. 1009
Snorri Thorfinnsson, the son of Thorfinn Kalrsefni and Gudrid, is the first child of European descent born in the Americas.

1492
Christopher Columbus sails west across the Atlantic and reaches the Caribbean.

1497
John Cabot sails from England to Newfoundland and explorers the cod-rich waters and adjacent coastline.

1513
Juan Ponce de León explores Florida.

1519–1521
Hernán Cortés conquers the Aztecs.

1524
Giovanni da Verrazzano sails up the eastern coast of North America.

1528–1536
Álvar Núñez Cabeza de Vaca travels overland from Florida to Mexico City.

1534
Jacques Cartier claims New France (Canada).

1585
An English colony is established at Roanoke Island.

1598
Juan de Oñate establishes colonies in present-day New Mexico.

1608
Samuel de Champlain founds Quebec.

1609
Henry Hudson discovers New York harbor.

1608–1629
Champlain establishes the French hold on New France (Canada).

1664
New Amsterdam is taken by the English and renamed New York.

1673
Louis Jolliet and Jacques Marquette explore the Mississipi River almost to its mouth.

1682
René-Robert Cavelier de La Salle claims the Mississippi for France.

THE OCEANS

c. 570
Brendan the Voyager allegedly travels across the Atlantic Ocean.

c. 1280
The first European sea chart, the Carte Pisane, is drawn up.

c. 1450
A quadrant is first used at sea.

c. 1480
Marine astrolabes are used for the first time by Portuguese navigators.

1492
Searching for Cathay (China), Christopher Columbus crosses the Atlantic Ocean and comes upon the New World.

1511
The Portuguese gain control of the sea route to the Spice Islands.

1513
Juan Ponce de León discovers the Gulf Stream.

1519–1522
Ferdinand Magellan sails from the Atlantic to the Pacific through the Strait of Magellan; one of his ships, the *Victoria*, goes on to make the first circumnavigation of the world.

1611
Hendrick Brouwer discovers the Roaring Forties, a wind system.

1641
The Dutch conquest of Malacca ends Portuguese control of the spice trade routes.

1661
Robert Boyle proposes a systematic exploration of the world's oceans.

THE POLES

c. 130
As part of his *Guide to Geography*, Ptolemy draws a world map that includes Terra Incognita ("unknown land"), a huge southern continent.

1520
Ferdinand Magellan sights land to the south of South America as he travels from the Atlantic Ocean into the Pacific.

1578
Francis Drake discovers that Tierra del Fuego, the land seen by Magellan, is an island.

1596
Willem Barents discovers Spitsbergen.

1607
Henry Hudson travels to within 577 miles (929 km) of the North Pole.

1642
During his journey across the southwestern Pacific Ocean, Abel Tasman finds no southern continent.

SPACE

c. 129 BCE
Hipparchus completes his star catalog.

c. 150
In his thirteen-volume *Almagest*, Claudius Ptolemy describes the position and movements of the Sun, Moon, stars, Earth, and five other known planets (Mercury, Venus, Mars, Jupiter, and Saturn).

1543
Nicolaus Copernicus puts forward the theory that the earth moves around the sun.

1609
Galileo points a telescope upward and studies the stars.

1687
Isaac Newton describes the laws of motion and the force of gravity in *Principia Mathematica*.

1700–1702
Eusebio Francisco Kino proves that California is not an island.

1728
Vitus Bering discovers that no land bridge joins Asia to America.

1775
Daniel Boone leads settlers into Kentucky.

1778–1779
James Cook searches for a northwest passage from the western end.

1793
Alexander Mackenzie becomes the first European to cross the North American continent.

1792–1795
George Vancouver surveys the west coast of North America.

1805
Meriwether Lewis and William Clark reach the Pacific.

1824
Jedediah Strong Smith discovers that the South Pass offers a route for wagons; soon thousands of settlers are traveling the Oregon Trail.

1845
John Franklin is lost while searching for the Northwest Passage.

1869
John Wesley Powell makes a remarkable boat journey along the Colorado River. A railroad running from the east to the west coast of the United States is declared open.

1903
Orville and Wilbur Wright make the first powered flight.

1906
Roald Amundsen completes the Northwest Passage in the *Gjøa*.

1931
Louise Arner Boyd leads a scientific expedition to study the glaciers along Greenland's northeastern coast.

1725
Luigi Fernando Marsili publishes *Histoire physique de la mer* (Physical history of the sea).

1759
John Harrison's chronometer, a clock that tells time accurately at sea, enables navigators to calculate longitude.

1766–1769
Louis-Antoine de Bougainville circumnavigates the globe.

1853
The world's first public aquarium opens in London.

1870
Jules Verne describes submarines in *Twenty Thousand Leagues under the Sea*.

1872
During a circumnavigation of the world, HMS *Challenger* carries out the first scientific study of the world's oceans and seabeds.

1943
Jacques Cousteau and Émile Gagnan invent the Aqua-Lung.

1956
The Silent World, Jacques Coustea's color film of marine life, captivates audiences.

1978
NASA's *Seasat* satellite maps the surface of the world's oceans.

1985
Robert Ballard explores the wreck of the *Titanic*.

1991–2000
European Remote-Sensing Satellite (ERS-1) studies the world's oceans.

1772–1775
On his second Pacific voyage, James Cook circumnavigates Antarctica and finally disproves the myth of a large southern continent.

1820
Fabian Gottlieb von Bellingshausen sights Antarctica.

1893–1896
Fridtjof Nansen attempts to drift to the North Pole.

1897
Salomon August Andrée attempts to reach the North Pole by balloon.

1911
Roald Amundsen reaches the South Pole.

1912
Having reached the South Pole, Robert F. Scott and his team perish on the return journey.

1916
After an extraordinary Antarctic boat journey, Ernest Shackleton rescues his stranded men.

1926
Lincoln Ellsworth, Roald Amundsen, and Umberto Nobile fly to the North Pole aboard the airship *Norge*.

1769
James Cook observes the transit of Venus from the South Pacific island of Tahiti.

1781
William Herschel discovers the planet Uranus.

1846
The planet Neptune is seen for the first time.

1957
The first satellite, *Sputnik 1*, is launched.

1961
Yury Gagarin becomes the first person in space.

1968
Pictures of the earth from space are seen live on television.

1969
Neil Armstrong walks on the moon.

1995
The Global Positioning System is declared complete and fully operational.

1997
Sojourner lands on Mars.

1998
The first module of the International Space Station is launched.

2001
Mir, the Russian space station, is taken out of service after fifteen years of operation.

2003
After the loss of *Columbia*, NASA suspends the space shuttle program indefinitely. After eight years in orbit around Jupiter, the *Galileo* probe finally disintegrates in the planet's atmosphere.

2004
The Mars exploration rovers *Spirit* and *Opportunity* investigate the surface of the red planet.

GLOSSARY

adobe A mixture of silt and clay, dried in the sun, used to make reddish brown bricks for building.

aerial sextant A navigational instrument used to determine the location of an aircraft relative to the earth's surface.

aeronautics The study and practice of travel through the air.

aft At or near the stern (rear) of a ship.

alloy A metal made of a mixture of two or more other metals; bronze, for example, is an alloy of copper and tin.

altitude Height above the surface of the earth.

amber A fossil resin of yellow-orange color.

amidships Toward the part of a ship midway between the bow (at the front) and the stern (at the rear).

anchorage A place suitable for anchoring a ship.

anthropology The study of human beings, especially in relation to their society and culture.

Aragon With Castile, one of the two powerful Spanish kingdoms of the late Middle Ages (Aragon and Castile were united in 1479).

Arikara A member of an American Indian people that lived in circular dome-shaped earth lodges along the upper Missouri River.

asteroid A small celestial body, usually a piece of rock.

asteroid belt A region of space between the orbits of Mars and Jupiter where large numbers of asteroids are found.

astrolabe An instrument used to determine the position of the sun, moon, stars, and planets.

atmosphere The layer of gasses around a planet.

atoll An island consisting of a circular belt of coral with a central lagoon.

aurora borealis An atmospheric phenomenon that causes streaks of colored light to appear in the night sky above the northern polar region.

Aztec A member of a people who ruled a large empire in central and southern Mexico during the fifteenth century, before the arrival of the Spanish conquistadores.

ballast A heavy substance carried on board ships, balloons, and submersibles that improves the stability or controls the ascent and descent of a vessel.

barometer An instrument that measures changes in atmospheric pressure.

barometric pressure A measurement of the pressure of the earth's atmosphere, which changes according to the weather.

bathyscaphe A diving vessel for deep-sea observation that is lowered by a cable from a ship.

bathysphere A spherical deep-sea observation vessel.

bearing The relationship of one point to another on the earth's surface. The bearing of point *B* from point *A* is the angle between the lines *AB* and *AN*, where *N* is any point due north of *A*.

bends Decompression sickness caused when nitrogen bubbles form in the body's tissues.

black hole A hypothetical point in space of zero volume and infinite mass; the gravitational pull of a black hole is so strong that no object or light can escape from it.

botany The branch of biology dealing with plants.

botulism A serious form of food poisoning caused by eating preserved food that has been contaminated with botulinum organisms.

bowsprit A long wooden post that projects forward from the front of a ship.

braggart A loud and arrogant boaster.

buccaneer Name given to English, French, or Dutch sailors who attacked and raided Spanish and Portuguese ships and colonies in the New World.

caliph Title used in various Islamic empires for leaders who traced their descent to the prophet Muhammad.

caravel A small, fast Spanish or Portuguese ship with lateen (triangular) sails.

cartography The science and art of mapmaking.

carvel-built Referring to the hull of a ship constructed by fitting planks to a preconstructed frame and making the surface level by caulking the gaps.

catamaran A ship or boat that has two hulls and is therefore difficult to capsize.

caulk To stop and make watertight, for example, the gaps between the planks of a ship or cracks in a window frame.

celestial Of or relating to the skies, stars, and heavens.

cholera An infectious, often fatal, disease that causes severe vomiting.

Cholulan A member of an American Indian civilization that flourished around modern Puebla in central Mexico and was probably closely connected to the Aztecs.

chronometer A clock capable of keeping accurate time on board a ship. The name derives from two Greek words: *chronos* (time) and *metron* (measure).

clinker-built Referring to the hull of a ship constructed of overlapping planks.

coal-tar naphtha A waste product of the tar-making process.

cog A clinker-built, square-rigged, wide transport ship of the Middle Ages, the first to include a rudder in place of a steering oar.

collier A small ship whose job was to transport coal.

colony A settlement or entire country governed by and owing allegiance to a mother country, which may be some distance away.

Comanche A member of a Native American people who lived by raiding and hunting buffalo on the southern Great Plains.

comet A celestial body that follows a highly eccentric orbit around the sun; many comets trail a tail of dust behind them when they near the sun.

conquistador The Spanish word for "conqueror"; specifically, any of the soldiers, explorers, or settlers who, in the wake of Columbus's discovery of the Americas, helped to establish the Spanish presence in Central and South America during the sixteenth century.

continental shelf The area of the ocean floor closest to land.

corona The outermost part of a sun's atmosphere.

corvette A small eighteenth-century warship, usually with one main deck and one tier of cannon.

crane A large long-legged bird.

creditor One who lends money or to whom money is owed.

Cree A member of a major group of Algonquian peoples that once inhabited a vast swath of Canada stretching from Hudson Bay west as far as the Great Slave Lake.

Crusade One of several Christian military expeditions, especially in the eleventh, twelfth, and thirteenth centuries, whose purpose was to regain the Holy Land from the Muslims.

curragh An open leather boat with no keel and made of animal skins stretched over a wooden frame; used by the Celts of Ireland and Scotland during the Middle Ages.

delta An often triangular area at the mouth of a river, where the sediment (rocks, gravel, and other material carried by the current) laid down has caused the river to split into channels.

dhow A light yet strong wooden ship, with triangular sails and a short mast, used by medieval Arab traders.

dodo A large flightless bird, like a turkey, that lived on the island of Mauritius but is now extinct.

doldrums Ocean region near the equator where calms, sudden storms, and light, unpredictable winds predominate.

dowry Property a woman brings to her husband when they marry.

draft The depth that the submerged part of a vessel lies beneath the water.

ducado A Spanish monetary unit, equivalent to 1.33 ounces (37.6 gm) of gold; also known as a ducat.

dysentery An infection that causes severe diarrhea.

ebony A dark, hard, heavy wood.

electromagnetic radiation Energy waves (including visible light, radio waves, and X rays) produced by periodic variations in the electric and magnetic fields of their source. Electromagnetic radiation is dominant on an atomic level but can extend over large distances.

electromagnetic spectrum The range of all known wave energy in the universe, including visible light, invisible light (such as infrared and ultraviolet), and radio waves.

encomienda The medieval Castilian landholding system, involving forced labor and tribute, especially as transferred to New Spain.

Enlightenment An intellectual movement of eighteenth-century Europe that rejected traditional social, political, and religious arrangements and ideas in favor of new ones more closely based on logic, reasoning, and scientific observation.

entrepreneur A person who, often at some risk, sets up a business.

equinox A twice-yearly event, usually occurring around March 22 and September 22, when the sun crosses the celestial equator and day and night are of equal length.

evangelical Christianity A form of Christianity whose adherents believe in the sole and literal authority of the Bible.

expeditionary force A group of explorers, usually army or navy officers.

extraterrestrial Referring to something whose origin is somewhere other than Earth.

feudal Referring to a system of political and social organization that prevailed in medieval Europe, according to which a commoner was obliged to serve a lord in return for protection and, usually, the right to farm land.

fiber-optic cable A cable containing many thin, flexible, transparent fibers, often used to carry telecommunications.

fjord A narrow inlet of the sea surrounded by high cliffs.

folklore The body of traditional tales, customs, and art forms preserved, often orally, among any given people.

forage Food for cattle and horses such as grasses and hay, usually found or carried by travelers.

ford A place where a river is shallow enough to be crossed.

fore At or near the front of a ship.

foundry A factory where metals, usually iron, are smelted and moulded into shape.

Franciscan A member of one of the Roman Catholic religious orders of men or women founded by Saint Francis of Assisi in 1209 or an offshoot of one of those orders.

frequency A mathematical property (the number of oscillations per second) that distinguishes one form of wave energy from another.

frieze An ornamental sculptured band on a building or piece of furniture.

frostbite A medical condition in which skin and underlying tissues freeze. If blood circulation is not restored to the affected area, frostbite degenerates into gangrene.

gabardine A smooth, hard-wearing twilled cloth.

galleon A large wooden sailing ship used for warfare and commerce, especially by the Spanish during the fifteenth and sixteenth centuries.

gangrene A condition, caused by loss of blood supply to an area of the body, that causes the flesh to rot.

geology The study of the origin and structure of the earth.

geostationary Referring to the orbit of a satellite whose altitude and velocity are such that the satellite remains over the same point of the earth's surface as the earth spins.

glacier A large body of ice that moves slowly down a valley. As a glacier moves, it erodes rocks and soil.

gonfalonier In a medieval Italian republic, a chief magistrate.

gradient A slope, expressed as the rate of ascent or descent in relation to the distance covered.

gravity The fundamental physical force that one object exerts on another. The size of an object is the primary factor governing the gravitational force it exerts.

greenhouse effect The rise in temperature of the surface and lower atmosphere of the earth or another planet caused by a high presence in the atmosphere of carbon dioxide, which traps reflected heat.

grid A network of parallel lines intersecting at right angles to produce a series of identical squares.

hajj The pilgrimage to Mecca that Islam requires all its adherents to make once in their lifetime.

hemisphere Half of a sphere; specifically, a half of the earth.

heresy A religious belief that runs counter to an official teaching of a church or, for that matter, to a dominant opinion in a society or state.

hidalgo A member of the lower Spanish nobility.

hold The interior area of a ship where cargo and the crew's food stores are generally carried.

hydrography The study of seas, lakes, and rivers, especially the charting of tides or the measurement of river flow.

hypothermia Dangerously low body temperature caused by prolonged exposure to cold.

Iberian Peninsula The southwestern part of the European landmass that includes Spain and Portugal.

iceberg A floating mountain of ice; an iceberg is formed when a slab of ice breaks off a glacier (a frozen river) as it reaches the sea.

Inca A member of a people who ruled a large empire in northwestern South America from the thirteenth century until the sixteenth, when it fell to the Spanish conquistadores.

Inca Road The main north-south highway of the Incan Empire, which stretches some 4,350 miles (7,000 km) from Colombia to Chile at altitudes between 3,300 and 14,750 feet (1,000–4,500 m).

incumbency The period of time during which an official position, such as the presidency of a country, is held.

Indian agent A U.S. government official who served as a link with a particular Indian tribe.

intendant A senior official in New France who was in charge of economic affairs and represented the governor in his absence.

Inuit A member of a people living in Greenland and northernmost. *Inuit* is the plural of *inuk,* which means "person" in the Inuit language.

iron pyrite A mineral that looks similar to gold but has no value; also known as fool's gold.

isthmus A narrow bridge of land connecting two larger landmasses.

Jesuit A member of a Roman Catholic religious order known for its educational and missionary work.

keel The V-shaped backbone of a ship.

keelboat A shallow, covered riverboat, generally used for freight, that is usually rowed or towed.

lateen A rig with a triangular sail hung from a yard fixed diagonally to the mast.

latitude Measurement of a point on the earth's surface north or south of the equator.

league A distance equal to three miles.

log A written record of a journey; especially, the written record of a ship's daily progress.

longitude Measurement of a point on the earth's surface east or west of a given prime meridian.

Louisiana Territory The land west of the Mississippi River, encompassing the drainage basins of the Missouri and Arkansas Rivers, purchased by President Thomas Jefferson from France in 1803.

magnetic storm A major disturbance in the earth's magnetic field.

magnetosphere A layer that surrounds a celestial object (such as Earth), that is dominated by the objects's magnetic field, and within which highly charged particles are trapped.

magnet stone A naturally magnetic iron ore, also called magnetite.

malaria A fever caused by a parasite transmitted by the bite of the female anopheles mosquito.

Mandan A member of a Native American people related to the Sioux who lived along the Missouri River between the Heart and Little Missouri Rivers.

mantle The area below the earth's surface and above the core.

Maya A great civilization of southern Mexico, at its height around 800 CE.

meltwater Water that swells a river after the melting of snow and ice in mountainous regions near the river's source.

merchant marine A nation's commercial ships, as opposed to those used for military purposes. The merchant marine is in some nations privately owned and in others controlled by the government.

meridian An imaginary line, running from the North to the South Pole, used to indicate longitude.

meteorology The study of the weather, especially as a means of forecasting future weather conditions.

micrometeorite A tiny piece of space debris.

midshipman Temporary rank held by young men training to be naval officers.

militia An army unit formed of citizens, such as those used in early U.S. history by state governments.

Milky Way The galaxy of which Earth and its solar system are a part.

missionary One who works, usually in a foreign country, to spread a religious faith (especially Christianity) and to give humanitarian assistance.

missionary school School formed by Christian missionaries, in the Americas, China, or elsewhere, to teach the native inhabitants Western culture and Christian values.

mission hospital Hospital built and run by a Christian church group; its aims were to heal the sick and spread Christianity.

module A self-contained unit, as of a spacecraft.

monopoly Total control over the sale of a good or service in a given area.

monsoon A wind in southern Asia that blows from the northeast in winter and from the southwest in the summer, when it is accompanied by heavy rains.

Moor A member of a Muslim people of mixed North African, Berber, and Spanish descent who ruled a progressively smaller area of Spain from the tenth century through the fifteenth.

mountain man A man who worked as a hunter and trapper in the Rocky Mountains in the first half of the nineteenth century, before American settlers moved into the West.

multispectral scanner A remote-sensing device that contains several sensors, each equipped to detect and receive signals from a particular band of the electromagnetic spectrum.

mutiny A revolt against authority, especially of a ship's crew against its officers.

negative An image captured on chemically treated film or on a glass plate, with light and dark areas reversed, from which multiple positive photographic images may be produced.

Norse Referring generally to the people of Scandinavia (Norway, Sweden, and Denmark), especially during the years 790 to 1100.

oceanography Scientific study of the oceans.

orbit An object's regularly repeated path around a star or planet.

Oregon Trail A two-thousand-mile (3,220 km) path from Missouri to western Oregon, used from 1841 to the 1880s by thousands of settlers moving west.

Osage A member of a Native American people that lived on the central Great Plains.

Ottoman Empire Empire of the Turks in western Asia and southwestern Europe, ruled from Istanbul from 1453 to 1922.

outback The wild inland territory of Australia.

Pacific Northwest The region of the present-day states of Washington and Oregon.

parallel An imaginary line, circling the globe parallel to the equator, used to indicate latitude.

patent A government license giving an inventor the exclusive right to make or sell an invention for a specified time.

patron Someone who financially supports another person or a project.

Pawnee A member of a Great Plains Indian people that lived in earth lodges along the Platte River, raised crops, and hunted buffalo.

peninsula A long, narrow piece of land that juts into the sea or a lake.

philology The scientific study of the history of languages and their relationship to one another, especially based on an analysis of texts.

pilgrim One who travels to visit a holy place.

pillage To plunder a place, that is, to remove, often violently, everything from it of material value.

pinnace A light sailing ship, often used to carry provisions or messages from one ship to another or from ship to shore.

pioneer The first person to attain a given goal, such as a feat of exploration, the settlement of a new territory, or the invention of a new technology.

pirogue A small boat, much like a canoe.

planisphere A representation of all or part of the spherical earth on a flat surface.

polygamy The practice of having more than one spouse.

portage The carrying of boats overland from one waterway to another.

pressure ridge A layer of ice forced up into a block by the pressure of surrounding ice.

prevailing wind The wind that predominates in a given area or at a given time.

prime meridian An imaginary line that runs from the North to the South Pole through Greenwich, England, and marks zero degrees longitude.

principality A state ruled by a prince.

privateer A privately owned ship hired by a government to attack and raid the ships of another country; also, a crew member of such a ship.

projection A method of displaying the curvature of the earth on a flat surface so that its physical features can be seen in true relation to one another.

propeller A spiral-shaped shaft driven by the engine to power a ship forward.

Quaker A member of the Society of Friends, a Christian sect founded in England in the seventeenth century that advocates a simple form of worship with no creeds, clergy, or formal church structure.

quartz A mineral of silicon dixode that takes a variety of forms, including gemstones, sandstone, and quartz sand (used in the manufacture of glass and ceramics).

radar A piece of technology, consisting of a radio transmitter and receiver, that emits radio waves and analyzes their echoes in order to identify and locate nearby objects or geographical features.

radar mapping A procedure for mapping an irregular surface from a distance or through obstacles, such as cloud or ice, by sending out radio waves and analyzing the returning echoes.

radiate To emit energy in the form of particles or rays.

reconnaissance A preliminary survey to gain information; during armed conflict, the gathering of information on the movement and position of an enemy.

Reconquista The centuries-long Spanish campaign to drive out the Moors, the descendants of the Muslims who had conquered Spain in the eighth century.

recoup To receive an amount of goods or money equivalent to an amount lost.

reflector A telescope that focuses light from distant objects through the use of mirrors.

refractor A telescope that focuses light from distant objects through the use of glass lenses.

relativity The theory, first proposed by Einstein, that equated matter and energy by means of the speed of light, which Einstein believed was constant.

Renaissance A cultural movement that began in the fourteenth century in Italy and lasted into the seventeenth. The Renaissance was marked by a flowering of artistic and literary achievement and a resurgence of interest in the values of ancient Greece and Rome.

saga An Icelandic literary form, dating from between 1100 and 1500, whose purpose was to praise the heroic deeds of historic or legendary figures and demonstrate the correct and honorable way to behave.

samurai A member of the warrior class in Japan that was dominant until the late nineteenth century.

Sanskrit An ancient language of the Indian subcontinent, considered the root of many modern European and Asian languages.

satellite An object, natural or artificial, that orbits a planet.

scurvy A serious disease caused by lack of vitamin C; its symptoms include bleeding and sponginess in the gums.

Sea of Tranquillity (In Latin, Mare Tranquilitatis) An area of the moon's surface, sometimes visible from the earth as a dark spot in the moon's northern hemisphere. *Apollo 11*'s lunar landing module, the *Eagle*, landed in the southwestern part of the Sea of Tranquillity on July 20, 1969.

seaworthy Referring to a ship that is strong and sturdy enough to be used safely for a sea voyage.

seismic Relating to earthquakes or other vibrations of the earth's crust.

sextant An instrument used by seafarers and explorers to measure the height of the sun or a star above the horizon and thus give an estimation of one's latitude.

sheikh Chief or leader of a group of Arabs.

Sherpa A member of a Tibetan people living in the Himalayas who provide support for mountain climbers and served the British army during the Second World War.

Shoshone A member of a Native American people who lived by hunting and gathering in the Great Basin region and the northern Rocky Mountains.

Sioux A member of a Native American people that lived on the northern Great Plains and as far east as southern Minnesota.

Skraeling A Norse word, meaning "wretch" or "ugly person," used to describe the native North Americans the Icelandic settlers encountered.

sled A vehicle with runners instead of wheels that transports people and goods over snow-covered terrain or ice.

sloop A small, light, one-masted warship that usually carried between ten and eighteen cannons.

solar flare A sudden and intense burst of radioactive energy from a small area of the sun's surface.

solar system A group of celestial bodies that are held by the magnetic attraction of the star they orbit.

solar wind The flow of radioactive particles from the sun.

solstice The time during summer and winter when the sun is vertically above the point that represents its farthest distance north or south of the equator. In the Northern Hemisphere the summer solstice is reached around June 21, and the winter solstice around December 22.

sonar A system that uses sound waves to detect objects underwater.

space probe An unmanned exploratory spacecraft.

spar Any of the tapered wooden poles used in the rigging of sails.

spruce beer A concoction, made from the boiled and fermented leaves and twigs of the American spruce (a tree of the pine family), that proved particularly effective at preventing scurvy during the exploration of North America.

stade An ancient unit of length used by Greek and Roman surveyors; the standard length of a stade is generally assumed to be six hundred feet (965 m), though many variations exist.

stratosphere A layer of the earth's atmosphere that starts at about 26,000 feet (8 km) above the Poles and about 55,000 feet (17 km) above the equator and extends upward to around 165,000 feet (50 km).

sultan Title of a secular Muslim ruler, especially of the Ottoman Empire.

sundial An instrument that shows the time of day according to the shadow cast by a pointer known as a gnomon.

sunspot An area of the sun's surface, one associated with strong magnetic activity, that appears darker because it is cooler than the surrounding area.

synthesis The combination of several concepts or compenent parts into a single entity.

tack To direct a ship into the wind along a zigzagging course by repeatedly adjusting the direction of the bow and the angle of the sails.

Taino A member of a Caribbean people native to the Greater Antilles (Puerto Rico, Hispaniola, Cuba, and Jamaica).

taxonomy Classification of plants and animals according to the natural relationship between them; also the study of different methods of classification.

terrestrial Of or relating to the earth.

thermal imaging A process for producing an image of an object or area of terrain using a special type of camera that is sensitive to minute differences in the heat that is emitted; an especially useful technique for taking pictures at night or in the absence of light.

tidal bore A high wall of water that rushes up certain narrow rivers during exceptionally high tides.

Tlaxcalan A member of an American Indian people native to an area of east-central Mexico around Tlaxcala.

topography The physical features of an area, such as mountains, valleys, and streams; also, the study and mapping of such features.

Totonac A member of an Indian people native to an area of east-central Mexico.

trading post In North America, a settlement where European traders and Native American hunters exchanged goods for furs.

transit In astronomy, the passage of a planet across the face of the sun as viewed from the earth.

treason The crime of acting to overthrow or kill the monarch or government of the state to which the criminal owes allegiance.

trigonometry The branch of mathematics concerned with the properties of triangles.

Tuareg A member of a nomadic people native to the central and western Sahara Desert region of North Africa.

typhoid A severe infection that causes a rash and stomach pains.

ultraviolet A form of short-wavelength radiation.

viceroy Ruler representing the authority of a king or queen in a colonial territory.

Viking A term, from a Norwegian word meaning both "pirate" and "warfare," used generally to refer to a Scandinavian (someone from Norway, Sweden, or Denmark) during the years 790 to 1100; especially, any of the Norse raiders who plundered the coasts of western Europe in that period.

vulcanized rubber Rubber that has been treated with chemicals at a very high temperature to increase its usefulness.

water clock An instrument that measures time by the dripping of water from one container into another.

Wichita A member of an American Indian people native to the Great Bend area of the Arkansas River in present-day Kansas.

wind drift instrument An aerial navigation instrument that calculates the extent to which wind force is causing an aircraft to drift off course.

wind vane A simple device that indicates the direction in which the wind is blowing.

yard A spar crossing the mast to which sails are fixed.

RESOURCES FOR FURTHER STUDY

All Internet addresses were functional and accurate as of July 2004.

BIBLIOGRAPHY

GENERAL

BOOKS

Benedict Allen
Faber Book of Exploration
London: Faber and Faber, 2002.

Simon Berthon and Andrew Robinson
The Shape of the World: The Mapping and Discovery of the Earth
Chicago: Rand McNally, 1991.

Felipe Fernández-Armesto
The Times Atlas of World Exploration
New York: HarperCollins Publishers, 1991.

Robin Hanbury-Tenison
The Oxford Book of Exploration
New York: Oxford University Press, 1993.

Geoffrey J. Martin and E. Preston
All Possible Worlds: A History of Geographical Ideas
New York: Wiley & Sons, 1993.

Milbry Polk and Mary Tiegreen
Women of Discovery: A Celebration of Intrepid Women Who Explored the World
New York: C. Potter, 2001.

Fernand Salentiny
Encyclopedia of World Explorers
London: Dumont Monte UK, 2002.

Bertha Sanford
Quests for Spices and New Worlds
Hamden, CT: Archon Books, 1988.

Carl Waldman and Alan Wexler
Who Was Who in World Exploration
New York: Facts on File, 1992.

JOURNALS

Terrae Incognitae
The journal of the Society for the History of Discoveries, published annually since 1969. Its research papers and book reviews encompass the discovery and mapping of the earth since ancient times.
www.sochistdisc.org

AFRICA

BOOKS

Richard F. Burton
The Lake Regions of Central Africa
New York: Dover Publications, 1995.

Robin Hallett, ed.
Association for Promoting the Discovery of the Interior Parts of Africa: Records of the African Association, 1788–1831
New York: T. Nelson, 1964.

Mungo Park
Travels into the Interior of Africa (1799)
London: Eland, 1983, 1954.

JOURNALS

The Journal of African Travel Writing
A biannual journal whose mission is to present and analyze accounts of past and contemporary African travel; publishes scholarly articles, true narratives, primary historical sources, fiction, and poetry. For more information, visit
www.unc.edu/~ottotwo/index.html

ASIA

BOOKS

Charles Allen
Duel in the Snows: The True Story of the Younghusband Mission to Lhasa
London: John Murray, 2004.

Ed Douglas
Tenzing: Hero of Everest, a Biography of Tenzing Norgay
Washington, DC: National Geographic, 2003.

Vivian Fuchs and Edmund Hillary
The Crossing of Antarctica: The Commonwealth Trans-Antarctic Expedition 1955–1958
New York: Greenwood Press, 1968.

Edmund Hillary
The View from the Summit
London: Doubleday, 1999.

James Legge, trans.
A Record of Buddhistic Kingdoms: Being an Account by the Chinese Monk Fâ-Hien of His Travels in India and Ceylon (A.D. 399–414) in Search of the Buddhist Books of Discipline
New York: Dover Publications, 1991.

Ma Huan (J. V. G. Mills, trans.)
The Overall Survey of the Ocean's Shores [1433]
Cambridge: Hakluyt Society, 1970.

Milton E. Osborne
River Road to China: The Search for the Sources of the Mekong, 1866–1873
New York: Atlantic Monthly Press, 1996.

Donald Rayfield
The Dream of Lhasa: The Life of Nikolay Przhevalsky (1839–1888), Explorer of Central Asia
Athens: Ohio University Press, 1976.

Sanjay Subrahmanyam
The Career and Legend of Vasco da Gama
New York: Cambridge University Press, 1997.

Teresa Waugh, trans.
The Travels of Marco Polo: A Modern Translation from the Italian by Maria Bellonci
New York: Facts on File, 1984.

AUSTRALIA AND THE SOUTH PACIFIC

BOOKS

John Cawte Beaglehole
The Life of Captain James Cook
Stanford, CA: Stanford University Press, 1974.

Tim Bonyhady
Burke and Wills: From Melbourne to Myth
Balmain, NSW: David Ell Press, 1991.

Ian Cameron
Lost Paradise: The Exploration of the Pacific
Topsfield, MA: Salem House, 1987.

John Dunmore
Who's Who in Pacific Navigation
Honolulu: University of Hawaii Press, 1991.

Richard Hough
Captain James Cook
New York: W. W. Norton & Co., 1995.

Charles Christopher Lloyd
Pacific Horizons: The Exploration of the Pacific before Captain Cook
New York: AMS Press, 1977.

Alan Moorehead
Cooper's Creek
New York: Harper & Row, 1963.

CENTRAL AND SOUTH AMERICA

BOOKS

Marc Aronson
Sir Walter Ralegh and the Quest for El Dorado
New York: Clarion Books, 2000.

William Brooks Greenlee, trans.
The Voyage of Pedro Álvares Cabral to Brazil and India, from Contemporary Documents and Narratives
St. Clair Shores, MI: Scholarly Press, 1972.

Hammond Innes
The Conquistadors
New York: Knopf, 1969.

Charles Nicholl
The Creature in the Map: A Journey to El Dorado
New York: W. Morrow and Co., 1996.

William H. Prescott
History of the Conquest of Peru
New York: Modern Library, 1998.

Michael Wood
Conquistadors
Berkeley, CA: University of California Press, 2000.

EUROPE

BOOKS

Jack Beeching, ed.
Richard Hakluyt: Voyages and Discoveries; the Principal Navigations, Voyages, Traffiques, and Discoveries of the English Nation.
Baltimore: Penguin Books, 1972.

Gertrude Bell (Rosemary O'Brien, ed.)
The Desert and the Sown: The Syrian Adventures of the Female Lawrence of Arabia
New York: Cooper Square Press, 2001.

Felipe Fernández-Armesto
Ferdinand and Isabella
New York: Taplinger, 1975.

Richard Milner
Charles Darwin: Evolution of a Naturalist
New York: Facts on File, 1994.

Gerhard Friedrich Müller (Carol Urness, trans.)
Bering's Voyages: The Reports from Russia
Fairbanks: University of Alaska Press, 1986.

Christopher Ralling
The Kon-Tiki Man: An Illustrated Biography of Thor Heyerdahl
San Francisco: Chronicle Books, 1991.

Peter Edward Russell
Prince Henry "the Navigator": A Life
New Haven: Yale University Press, 2000.

Peter Sawyer, ed.
The Oxford Illustrated History of the Vikings
New York: Oxford University Press, 1997.

Rebecca Stefoff
Vasco da Gama and the Portuguese Explorers
New York: Chelsea House Publishers, 1993.

CD-ROMS

World of the Vikings
Drawing on material found in places from Newfoundland to Constantinople, this CD-ROM's multimedia version of the Viking story is based on the work of over fifty museums and research institutions, led by the National Museum of Denmark and the York Archaeological Trust. Find out more at
www.worldofthevikings.com

The Renaissance Explorers: A Voyage to the New World
This CD-ROM teaches students about life aboard a fifteenth-century ship as it surveys the history of exploration from Marco Polo to Walter Raleigh, with emphasis on the voyages of John Cabot. Activities include taking measurements with an astrolabe, provisioning a vessel, and exploring a 3-D re-creation of Cabot's ship, the *Matthew*. Available at
www.cambridgeeducational.com

NORTH AMERICA

BOOKS

John Logan Allen, ed.
North American Exploration
Lincoln: University of Nebraska Press, 1997.

Stephen E. Ambrose
Undaunted Courage: Meriwether Lewis, Thomas Jefferson and the Opening of the American West
New York: Simon and Schuster, 1996.

John James Audubon
Birds of America
San Diego: Laurel Glen, 1997.

Anthony Brandt, ed.
The Journals of Lewis and Clark (abridged)
Washington, DC: National Geographic Adventures Classics, 2002.

Tony Coulter
Jacques Cartier, Samuel de Champlain, and the Explorers of Canada
New York: Chelsea House Publishers, 1993.

James Delgado
Across the Top of the World: The Quest for the Northwest Passage
New York: Checkmark Books, 1999.

Lyman C. Draper (Ted Franklin Belue, ed.)
The Life of Daniel Boone
Mechanicsburg, PA: Stackpole Books, 1998.

Felipe Fernández-Armesto
Columbus
New York: Oxford University Press, 1991.

Ann Gaines
John Wesley Powell and the Great Surveys of the American West
New York: Chelsea House, 1992.

William H. Goetzmann and Glyndwr Williams
The Atlas of North American Exploration: From the Norse Voyages to the Race to the Pole
New York: Prentice Hall General Reference, 1992.

Donald S. Johnson
Charting the Sea of Darkness: The Four Voyages of Henry Hudson
New York: Kodansha International, 1995.

Jared Stallones
Zebulon Pike and the Explorers of the American Southwest
New York: Chelsea House Publishers, 1992.

CD-ROMS
Oregon Trail: A Complete History
The companion to an award-winning Web site, this CD-ROM provides hours of educational material. Text that examines the people who traveled the trail and the places they visited is backed up with photographs, maps, pictures, real-life stories, and a wealth of period documents. Available to purchase at **http://www.isu.edu/%7Etrinmich/ storecdrom.html**

THE OCEANS

BOOKS
Jacques-Yves Cousteau, with Frédéric Dumas
The Silent World
Washington, DC: National Geographic Society, 2004.

Lorraine Jean Hopping
Jacques Cousteau: Saving Our Seas
New York: McGraw-Hill, 2000.

Nancy Smiler Levinson
Magellan and the First Voyage around the World
New York: Clarion Books, 2001.

Dava Sobel
Longitude: The True Story of a Lone Genius Who Solved the Greatest Scientific Problem of His Time
New York: Walker, 1995.

Derek Wilson
The Circumnavigators
London: Constable, 1989.

THE POLES

BOOKS
Alan Gurney
Below the Convergence: Voyages toward Antarctica, 1699–1839
New York: Norton, 1997.

Roland Huntford
Scott and Amundsen: The Last Place on Earth
New York: Modern Library, 1999.

Fred L. Israel and Arthur M. Schlesinger, eds.
Robert E. Peary and the Rush to the North Pole: Chronicles from National Geographic
Philadelphia: Chelsea House Publishers, 1999.

John Maxtone-Graham
Safe Return Doubtful: The Heroic Age of Polar Exploration
New York: Scribner, 1988.

Beekman H. Pool
Polar Extremes: The World of Lincoln Ellsworth
Fairbanks: University of Alaska Press, 2002.

Lisle A. Rose
Assault on Eternity: Richard E. Byrd and the Exploration of Antartica, 1946–1947
Annapolis, MD: Naval Institute Press, 1980.

Michael H. Rosove
Let Heroes Speak: Antarctic Explorers, 1772–1922
Annapolis, MD: Naval Institute Press, 2000.

Richard Sale
Polar Reaches: The History of Arctic and Antarctic Exploration
Seattle: Mountaineers Books, 2002.

Joanna Wright, foreword
South with Endurance: Shackleton's Antarctic Expedition 1914–1917: The Photographs of Frank Hurley
New York: Simon & Schuster, 2001.

SPACE

BOOKS
Peter Ackroyd
Escape from Earth (Voyages through Time)
New York: DK Pub., 2003.

Giancarlo Genta and Michael Rycroft
Space, the Final Frontier?
New York: Cambridge University Press, 2003.

Nigel Henbest and Heather Couper
DK Space Encyclopedia
New York: DK Pub., 1999.

Carolyn Collins Petersen and John C. Brandt
Hubble Vision: Further Adventures with the Hubble Space Telescope [2nd ed.]
New York: Cambridge University Press, 1998.

Donald K. Slayton with Michael Cassut
Deke!: U.S. Manned Space: From Mercury to the Shuttle
New York: Forge / St. Martin's Press, 1994.

Thomas P. Stafford with Michael Cassut
We Have Capture: Tom Stafford and the Space Race
Washington, DC: Smithsonian Institution Press, 2002.

Carole Stott
DK Eyewitness Guides: Space Exploration
London: Dorling Kindersley, 1997.

Mark Voit
Hubble Space Telescope: New Views of the Universe
New York: H. N. Abrams / Smithsonian Institution / Space Telescope Science Institute, 2000.

John Zukowsky, ed.
2001: Building for Space Travel
New York: Harry N. Abrams, 2001.

CD-ROMS
The NASA Museum
This set of eight interactive CD-ROMs gives students of space exploration the opportunity to relive NASA missions through hours of video and audio clips, meet astronauts, tour space stations and spacecraft, and experience spaceflight simulations. Produced by High-Tech Productions; for more information, visit **www.hightechscience.org/nasa_museum. htm**

PLACES TO GO

NORTH AMERICA

UNITED STATES

CALIFORNIA
Marin History Museum
1125 B Street
San Rafael, CA 94901
415-454-8538
Collections relating to the history of Marin County include exhibits on Francis Drake (who anchored nearby in 1579), the Spanish mission at San Rafael, and Louise Arner Boyd, a local heroine.
www.marinhistory.org

Maritime Museum of San Diego
1492 North Harbor Drive
San Diego, CA 92101
619-234-9153
An impressive collection of historic ships, including the world's oldest active ship, the *Star of India* (built in 1863). The museum has exhibits on maritime history, commerce, and exploration.
www.sdmaritime.com

CONNECTICUT
Mystic Seaport
75 Greenmanville Avenue
Mystic, CT 06355
888-973-2767
Highlights of this forty-acre museum include replica nineteenth-century ships and buildings, galleries celebrating life at sea, and a shipyard where the art of wooden shipbuilding is preserved.
www.mysticseaport.org

DISTRICT OF COLUMBIA
The Library of Congress
101 Independence Avenue, SE
Washington, DC 20540
202-707-5000
The reading rooms of the world's largest library give access to electronic and published material on almost any subject. The library stages regular exhibitions of prized items from its vast collection.
www.loc.gov

National Air and Space Museum
Sixth Street and Independence Avenue, SW
Washington, DC 20560
202-357-2700
This museum maintains the largest collection of historic air- and spacecraft in the world. Items on display include the original Wright brothers' flyer of 1903, the *Apollo 11* command module, Charles Lindbergh's *Spirit of Saint Louis,* and a lunar rock sample.
www.nasm.si.edu

National Museum of American History
14th Street and Constitution Avenue, NW
Washington, DC 20650
202-633-1000
All aspects of American history are covered here, including the gradual exploration and settlement of North America by Europeans, the emergence of the United States, and the construction of the railroads.
www.americanhistory.si.edu

National Museum of Natural History
10th Street and Constitution Avenue, NW
Washington, DC 20560
202-633-1000
This branch holds several collections related to scientific exploration, especially exploration sponsored by the Smithsonian itself. Displays of specimens are reinforced by maps of the journeys.
www.mnh.si.edu

FLORIDA
John F. Kennedy Space Center
KSC, FL 32899
321-867-5000
Located close to NASA's launch headquarters at Cape Canaveral, the Kennedy Space Center's numerous displays tell the dramatic story of the United States space program, past, present, and future.
www.ksc.nasa.gov

KANSAS
Kansas Museum of History
6425 SW Sixth Avenue
Topeka, KS 66615-1099
785-272-8681
Several of this museum's displays document the early exploration of Kansas, particularly along the Santa Fe and Oregon Trails.
www.kshs.org

KENTUCKY
Fort Boonesborough State Park
4375 Boonesboro Road
Richmond, KY 40475
859-527-3131
This reconstruction of the fort built in 1775 by Daniel Boone is complete with blockhouses, cabins, and period furnishings.
www.state.ky.us/agencies/parks/ftboones

MARYLAND
Chesapeake Bay Maritime Museum
Navy Point
P.O. Box 636
St. Michaels, MD 21663
410-745-2916
A waterfront site whose displays explore and interpret the indigenous and Anglo-American history of a major maritime regions.
www.cbmm.org

MICHIGAN
Mackinac State Historic Parks
P.O. Box 873
Mackinaw City, MI 49701
231-436-4100
Six living-history parks and museums commemorate the history of the Straits of Mackinac, center of the Great Lakes fur trade and starting point for many explorers and surveyors of the northern United States.
www.mackinacparks.com

MINNESOTA
Runestone Museum
206 Broadway
Alexandria, MN 56308
320-763-3160
Home not only to the Kensington Runestone but also to a replica Viking ship and exhibits related to Norse history and early pioneer life.
www.runestonemuseum.org

MISSOURI
Missouri History Museum
Lindell and DeBaliviere
Saint Louis, MO 63112-0040
314-746-4599
The history of Saint Louis, gateway to the west, is a major theme of this museum, which holds the Louisiana Purchase transfer document.
www.mohistory.org

NEBRASKA
The Museum of the Fur Trade
6321 Highway 20
Chadron, NE 69337
308-432-3843
Located at the site of a trading post, this museum traces the history of the North American fur trade and the lives of those who took part in it.
www.furtrade.org

NEW YORK
South Street Seaport
19 Fulton Street
New York, NY 10038
212-732-8257
A restored enclave of historic buildings and numerous small maritime museums. Several historic vessels are moored at the adjacent jetties.
www.southstseaport.org

OKLAHOMA
Gilcrease Museum
1400 North Gilcrease Museum Road
Tulsa, OK 74127-2100
918-596-2700
In its comprehensive collection, the Gilcrease has much that relates to the discovery, expansion, and settlement of North America, especially the western frontier.
www.gilcrease.org

OREGON
End of the Oregon Trail Interpretive Center
1726 Washington Street
Oregon City, OR 97045
503-657-9336
Exhibits present the history of Oregon's immigrants from the east, from the arrival of the first fur traders to the coming of the railroads.
www.endoftheoregontrail.org

TEXAS
Museum of the Coastal Bend
Victoria College
Victoria, TX 77901
361-582-2511
This museum tells the story of the first European arrivals in Texas, which begins with the establishment by La Salle of Fort St. Louis.
www.museumofthecoastalbend.org

VIRGINIA
The Mariners' Museum
100 Museum Drive
Newport News, VA 23606-3759
757-596-2222
A permanent Age of Exploration gallery chronicles explorations of the fifteenth through eighteenth centuries. Visitors can examine reproductions of books and navigational instruments.
www.mariner.org

CANADA
Canadian Museum of Civilization
100 Laurier Street
P.O. Box 3100
Station B
Gatineau, Quebec J8X 4H2
819-776-7000
Canada's renowned national museum contains a wealth of artifacts, maps, and artworks that document the discovery, exploration, and settlement of New France and the emergence of the Canadian nation.
www.civilization.ca

Hudson's Bay Company Archives
Archives of Manitoba
200 Vaughan Street
Winnipeg, Manitoba R3C 1T5
204-945-4949
The Hudson's Bay Company's extensive records—which comprise explorers' journals, ships' logs, maps, letters, photographs, and accounts of life in more than five hundred trading posts—were deposited in Manitoba in 1974 and made available to the public in 1975.
www.gov.mb.ca/chc/archives/hbca

L'Anse aux Meadows National Historic Site
P.O. Box 70, St.-Lunaire-Griquet,
Newfoundland A0K 2X0
709-623-2608
Discovered in 1960, this famous Viking settlement has been excavated and reconstructed; a visitor's center gives an interpetation of the site.
http://collections.ic.gc.ca/vikings/

MEXICO
Museo de la Ciudad de México (Museum of Mexico City)
Pino Suárez Street, 30
Mexico City
(+52) 915 522 99 36
The history of Mexico City is the theme of this museum, with considerable space given over to pre-Columbian Tenochtitlán and the arrival of the conquistadores.
www.arts-history.mx/museos/mcm/indice1.html

EUROPE

UNITED KINGDOM
National Maritime Museum and Royal Observatory
Greenwich
London SE10 9NF
(+44) 020 8858 4422
The world's largest maritime museum is sited at the prime meridian (0° longitude). Its collection encompasses art, maps, manuscripts, ship models and plans, and navigational and astronomical instruments.
www.nmm.ac.uk

Scott Polar Research Institute
University of Cambridge
Lensfield Road
Cambridge CB2 1R
(+44) 01223 336540
This institute has a museum and library that hold artifacts, paintings, drawings, photographs, film, and written material relating to all parts of the polar regions and those who have worked there.
www.spri.cam.ac.uk

British Library Map Library

96 Euston Road
London NW1 2DB
(+44) 020 7412 7702
The major cartographic collection of the British Isles comprises over four million atlases, maps, globes, printing plates, books, and other cartographic material dating from the fifteenth century to the present day. Eighteenth-century America is especially well represented.
www.bl.uk/collections/maps.html

Royal Geographical Society
(with the Institute of British Geographers)

1 Kensington Gore
London SW7 2AR
(+44) 020 7591 3000
The world-renowned RGS archives hold over two million maps, photographs, books, artworks, artifacts, and documents that tell the story of five hundred years of geographical discovery and research.
www.rgs.org

Hereford Cathedral

5 College Cloisters
Cathedral Close
Hereford HR1 2NG
The Cathedral Church of St. Mary the Virgin and St. Ethelbert the King, parts of which date from the eleventh century, houses the Hereford *mappa mundi* (c. 1300), the world's finest surviving medieval map.
www.herefordcathedral.org/mappa.asp

OTHER EUROPEAN COUNTRIES

Bibliothèque Nationale de France (National Library of France)

58 Rue de Richelieu
75002 Paris
FRANCE
(+33) 01 53 79 59 59
Among the many significant items held by the French national library's maps and plans department are the 1375 Catalan Atlas and over four hundred medieval portolan charts, including the Carte Pisane.
www.bnf.fr/site_bnf_eng/index.html

Istituto e Museo di Storia della Scienza
(Institute and Museum of the History of Science)

Piazza dei Giudid, 1
50122 Florence
ITALY
(+39) 055 265 311
Highlights include the Medici collections of mathematical and astronomical instruments, around five thousand rare scientific texts, and a siginifcant collection related to the life and work of Galileo.
www.imss.fi.it/index.html

Nederlands Scheepvartmuseum (Netherlands Maritime Museum)

Kattenburgerplein 1
1018 KK Amsterdam
(+31) 020 52 32 222
NETHERLANDS
The glories of Dutch maritime history are represented by the Netherlands Maritime Museum's collections. Berthed permanently at a jetty outside is a replica of the Dutch East Indiaman *Amsterdam*.
www.scheepvaartmuseum.nl/index_ns.htm

Museu de Marinha (Maritime Museum, Lisbon)

Praça do Império
1400-206 Lisbon
PORTUGAL
(+ 351) 213 620 019
Lisbon's Marine Museum has over 17,000 items, including around 30,000 photographs and 1,500 drawings and ships' plans.
www.museumarinha.pt

Archivo General de Indias (General Archive of the Indies)

Avenida de la Constitución, 3
41071 Seville
SPAIN
(+34) 954 500 530
The holdings of the Indies Archive document Spain's relationship with its overseas colonies in the New World and elsewhere.
www.mcu.es/archivos/jsp/plantillaAncho.jsp?id=61

Museo de América (Museum of the Americas)

Avenida Reyes Católicos, 6
28014 Madrid
SPAIN
(+ 34) 915 492 641
The major repository for pre-Columbian artifacts brought back from North, South, and Central America by early Spanish colonizers.
www.geocities.com/museo_de_america

AUSTRALIA

Bligh Museum of Pacific Exploration

P.O. Box 154
Sandy Bay, 7006, Tasmania
(+61) 03 6293 1117
Located on Bruny Island, southern Tasmania, in a bay visited at various times by Abel Tasman, Tobias Furneaux, James Cook, and William Bligh, this small museum dedicated to the history of Pacific exploration displays historical maps, documents, paintings, and artifacts.
www.southcom.com.au/~jontan/index.html

Australian National Maritime Museum

2 Murray Street
Darling Harbor NSW 2009
(+61) 02 9298 3777
Built close to the site of Australia's first European settlement at Sydney Cove, the country's most visited maritime museum preserves Australia's aboriginal and postcolonial maritime heritage in a number of galleries and aboard several historic vessels.
www.anmm.gov.au

Western Australian Maritime Museum

Victoria Quay
Fremantle, WA 6160
(+61) 08 9335 8921
Exhibitions in two buildings focus on Dutch East India Company shipwrecks discovered off the coast of Western Australia and on the region's maritime endeavors. The museum also offers visitors the chance to explore a decommissioned submarine.
http://www.museum.wa.gov.au/default.asp?et=2&ei=37

RESOURCES FOR YOUNGER READERS

BOOKS

A for Antarctica
Jonathan Chester
Berkeley, CA: Tricycle Press, 1995.

Amerigo Vespucci (Famous Explorers)
Jeff Donaldson-Forbes
New York: PowerKids Press, 2002.

Beyond the Sea of Ice: The Voyages of Henry Hudson
Joan Elizabeth Goodman and Fernando Rangel, illus.
New York: Mikaya Press, 1999.

Buried in Ice: Unlocking the Secrets of an Arctic Voyage
Owen Beattie and John Geiger
New York: Scholastic/Madison Press, 1992.

Captain James Cook: Three Times around the World
Milton Meltzer
New York: Benchmark Books, 2002.

Captain John Smith (Discover the Life of an Explorer)
Trish Kline
Vero Beach, FL: Rourke Pub., 2002.

Daniel Boone: Beyond the Mountains
Patricia Calvert
New York: Benchmark Books, 2002.

Despite All Obstacles: La Salle and the Conquest of the Mississippi
Joan Elizabeth Goodman and Tom McNeely, illus.
New York: Mikaya Press, 2001.

Diary of John Wesley Powell: Conquering the Grand Canyon
Connie and Peter Roop, eds., and Laszlo Kubinyi, illus.
New York: Benchmark Books, 2001.

Eric the Red: The Vikings Sail the Atlantic
Anne Millard, Brian and Linda Watson, illus.
Austin, TX: Raintree Steck-Vaughn, 1994.

Exploration of Africa
Colin Hynson
Hauppauge, NY: Barron's Educational Series, Inc., 1998.

Ferdinand Magellan
Struan Reid
Chicago: Heinemann Library, 2001.

Ferdinand Magellan: First to Sail around the World
Milton Meltzer
New York: Benchmark Books, 2002.

Francisco Coronado: In Search of the Seven Cities of Gold
Steven Otfinoski
New York: Benchmark Books, 2002.

Francisco Pizarro: The Conquest of Peru
Milton Meltzer
New York: Benchmark Books, 2005.

Frozen in Time: The Fate of the Franklin Expedition
Owen Beattie and John Geiger
Vancouver: Greystone Books, 1998.

The Great Expedition of Lewis and Clark: By Private Reubin Field, Member of the Corps of Discovery
Judith Edwards and Sally Wern Comport, illus.
New York: Farrar Strauss Giroux, 2003.

Henry Hudson and His Voyages of Exploration in World History
Judith Edwards
Berkeley Heights, NJ: Enslow Publishers, 2002.

Hernando Cortés: Fortune Favored the Bold
Patricia Calvert
New York: Benchmark Books, 2002.

Hubble Vision: Further Adventures with the Hubble Space Telescope
Carolyn Collins Petersen and John C. Brandt
New York: Cambridge University Press, 1998.

Jacques Marquette and Louis Jolliet
Zachary Kent
Chicago: Childrens Press, 1994.

John Charles Frémont: Pathfinder to the West
Harold Faber
New York: Benchmark Books, 2002.

Juan Ponce de León: Discoverer of Florida
Steven Otfinoski
New York: Benchmark Books, 2005.

La Salle: A Life of Boundless Adventure
William J. Jacobs
New York: Franklin Watts, 1994.

La Salle: Down the Mississippi
Harold Faber
New York: Benchmark Books, 2002.

Letters from Mir: An Astronaut's Letters to His Son
Jerry M. Linenger
New York: McGraw-Hill 2003.

Lewis and Clark: From Ocean to Ocean
Harold Faber
New York: Benchmark Books, 2002.

Magellan
Tim Joyner
Camden, ME: International Marine, 1994.

Magellan: A Voyage around the World
Fiona Macdonald and Mark Bergin, illus.
New York: Franklin Watts, 1998.

Marco Polo (Historical Biographies)
Robert Strathloch
Chicago: Heinemann Library, 2002.

Marco Polo: A Journey through China
Fiona Macdonald and Mark Bergin, illus.
New York: Franklin Watts, 1998.

Men with Sand: Great Explorers of the North American West
John Moring
Helena, MO: TwoDot, 1998.

The Mississippi River
Maria Mudd-Ruth
New York: Benchmark Books, 2001.

The Mountain Men
James L. Collins
New York: Franklin Watts, 1996.

Mountain Men of the Frontier
Charles W. Sundling
Edina, MN: Abdo and Daughters, 2000.

Neil Armstrong (History Maker Bios)
Shannon Zemlicka
Minneapolis, MN: Lerner, 2003.

Neil Armstrong (Rookie Biographies)
Dana Meachen Rau
New York: Children's Press, 2003.

Neil Armstrong (Trailblazers of the Modern World)
Tim Goss
Milwaukee, WI: World Almanac Library, 2002.

Neil Armstrong: Young Flyer (Childhood of Famous Americans Series)
Montrew Dunham and Meryl Henderson, illus.
New York: Aladdin Paperbacks, 1996.

One Giant Leap: The Story of Neil Armstrong
Don Brown
Boston: Houghton Mifflin Co., 1998.

The Oregon Trail
Elizabeth D. Jaffe
Mankato, MN: Bridgestone Books, 2002.

Peary and Amundsen Race to the Poles
Antony Mason
Austin, TX: Raintree Steck-Vaughn, 1995.

Robert E. Peary: To the Top of the World
Patricia Calvert
New York: Benchmark Books, 2002.

The Rocky Mountains
Larry Bograd
New York: Benchmark Books, 2001.

Sailing Ships in Words and Pictures from Papyrus Boats to Full-riggers
Bjorn Landstrom
Garden City, NY: Doubleday & Co., 1978.

Samuel de Champlain: Explorer of Canada
Harold Faber
New York: Benchmark Books, 2005.

The Search for a Northern Route
Peter Chrisp
New York: Thomson Learning, 1993.

The Search for the East
Peter Chrisp
New York: Thomson Learning, 1993.

The Shoshone
Raymond Bial
New York: Benchmark Books, 2002.

The Silk Route: 7000 Miles of History
John S. Major and Stephen Fieser
New York: Harper Trophy, 1996.

Sir Ernest Shackleton: By Endurance We Conquer
Patricia Calvert
New York: Benchmark Books, 2002.

Sir Walter Raleigh and the Search for El Dorado (Explorers of the New Worlds)
Neil Chippendale
Philadelphia: Chelsea House Publishers, 2002.

The Spanish Exploration of South America: How the Discoveries of Christopher Columbus and Amerigo Vespucci and the Conquests of Vasco Núñez de Balboa, Francisco Pizarro, and Pedro de Valdivia Created an Empire for Spain
Mark McKain
Philadelphia: Mason Crest Publishers, 2003.

The Story of Sacajawea, Guide to Lewis and Clark
Della Rowland and Richard Leonard, illus.
New York: Dell Pub., 1989.

Thor Heyerdahl and the Kon-Tiki Voyage
Philip Steele
New York: Dillon, 1993.

The Travels of Ferdinand Magellan
Joanne Mattern and Patrick O'Brien, illus.
Austin, TX: Steadwell Books, 2000.

Uncommon Traveler: Mary Kingsley in Africa
Don Brown
Boston: Houghton Mifflin, 2000.

Vasco da Gama: So Strong a Spirit
Patricia Calvert
New York: Benchmark Books, 2005.

Vasco Núñez de Balboa: Explorer of the Pacific
Steven Otfinoski
New York: Benchmark Books, 2005.

Who's Who of NASA Astronauts
Lee Ellis
River Falls, WI: Americana Group, 2001.

Zebulon Pike
Susan Sinnott
Chicago: Children's Press, 1990.

Zebulon Pike: Lost in the Rockies
Patricia Calvert
New York: Benchmark Books, 2005.

INTERNET RESOURCES

BBC Science and Nature: Space
Take a 3-D tour of the solar system, play games and take quizzes, and find out everything there is to know about space and space exploration. Part of the British Broadcasting Corporation's extensive online educational material.
www.bbc.co.uk/science/space

BBC Vikings Homepage
This entertaining and informative site features a time line, glossary, and resources page. Students can experience a day in the life of a Viking, write a message in runes, and enjoy other Viking-themed activities.
www. bbc.co.uk/schools/vikings

Humanities Interactive—The New World
A series of interactive exhibits, with titles such as "Gold of El Dorado" and "Christopher Columbus and the Genoese," organize information about the Age of Discovery around visual elements (paintings, maps, and facsimiles of letters, for example). Each exhibit is backed up by games and lessons. Click on "The New World" at
http://www.humanities-interactive.org/a_base.html

Kids' Online Resources—Explorers: Vikings, English, Conquistadors
A page of links to a variety of relevant sites .
www.kidsolr.com/history/page2.html

Lewis and Clark the Trailblazers
Enlivened by a map, photographs, and graphics, this site places the Lewis and Clark Expedition in a historical context, and compares the achievements of Lewis and Clark with those of Alexander Mackenzie, John Frémont, Jedediah Strong Smith, and other contemporary explorers of the West.
www.trailblazers101.com

NASA—Kids Home
The gateway to NASA's online educational material aimed especially at a younger audience. Whether users want to search for and design a habitable planet, find out more about the *Cassini* probe's Saturn mission, or watch a meteor storm, this is the place to begin.
http://www.nasa.gov/audience/forkids/home/index.html

Passageways: True Tales of Adventure for Young Explorers
The Library and Archives of Canada presents a version of its history of the exploration of Canada, from prehistoric times to the twentieth century. Especially tailored for the younger student, the site includes a glossary, index, and links page.
www.collectionscanada.ca/explorers/kids/index-e.html

PBS: Conquistadors
A colorful online learning adventure that teaches students about the Spanish conquistadores in the New World and the legacy of their contact with Native Americans. Content is available in Spanish as well as English.
www.pbs.org/opb/conquistadors/home.htm

Who Goes There: European Exploration of the New World
A colorful and engaging site that examines why Portuguese, Spanish, English, and French explorers ventured forth in search of new lands. Explorers tell their own story through interviews, biographies, autobiographies, and journals.
http://library.thinkquest.org/J002678F/

Zoom Explorers
A collection of short and straightforward biographies of a large number of explorers, arranged alphabetically, chronologically, and according to where in the world (or space) they traveled.
www.enchantedlearning.com/explorers

INTERNET RESOURCES

ABC: The Navigators
In its examination of the search for Terra Australis and the early European exploration of Australia, this page, from the Australian Broadcasting Corporation, focuses particularly on maritime navigation during the eighteenth and nineteenth centuries.
http://www.abc.net.au/navigators/

Archiving Early America
This array of primary-source material, which includes newspaper cuttings, portraits, letters, and journals, documents life in the United States in the eighteenth century.
www.earlyamerica.com

B@tavia
This site, a virtual Dutch East India Company (VOC) factory, "trades" in historical information about the VOC; visitors are invited to take a tour and sample its wares, which include essays, contemporary illustrations and maps, and numerous links to other sites.
http://batavia.ugent.be/B@taviaE.htm

BBC History—Exploration
The British Broadcasting Corporation's comprehensive and interactive guide to the history of exploration focuses on the discovery and conquest of the Americas, the race to the South Pole, the voyages of James Cook, and the charting of the oceans in the eighteenth century by the British Royal Navy.
www.bbc.co.uk/history/discovery/exploration/

Burke and Wills—Terra Incognita
Provided by the State Library of Victoria, this site examines all aspects of the Burke and Wills Expedition.
www.burkeandwills.net

Captain Cook Society
Contains a wealth of information and links related to James Cook, his voyages, and his ships.
www.captaincooksociety.com

Columbus and the Age of Discovery
Around 1,100 scholarly articles about every aspect of Christopher Columbus's life and journeys, as well as a wealth of background topics.
http://muweb.millersv.edu

Discoverers Web
This extensive collection of short biographical essays on a wide range of explorers is organized alphabetically and according to category; each short essay is accompanied by links to other relevant sites. There is also an extremely useful page of links to primary sources.
www.win.tue.nl/~engels/discovery

Epic Voyages: Uncovering the World
On this site created by Indian students, the voyages of fourteen exemplary explorers, including Roald Amundsen, Ferdinand Magellan, and Amerigo Vespucci, are treated in short essays with maps.
http://library.thinkquest.org/C004237/english/nond/list.html

The European Voyages of Exploration
Tutorials on this site, put together by the Applied History Research Group at th University of Calgary, focus on the role of Spain and Portugal in the Age of Exploration.
www.ucalgary.ca/applied_history/tutor/eurvoya

Famous Ships
This Web page contains links to over 150 sites that have information and pictures or photographs of ships that have made their mark on the history of exploration.
http://www.42explore2.com/ships2.htm

Female Explorers
Essays on Isabella Bishop, Gertrude Bell, Amelia Earhart, and many other women who have excelled in the field of exploration.
http://femexplorers.com

The Gertrude Bell Project
A unique online archive, created by Newcastle University in northern England, of Gertrude Bell's letters, diaries, and photographs.
www.gerty.ncl.ac.uk

Hanno
The full text of the *Periplus* of Hanno of Carthage is accompanied by an illuminating commentary, maps, and a short essay.
www.livius.org/ha-hd/hanno/hanno01.html

Internet Modern History Sourcebook: The Early Modern World
This page provides an index to an exceptional collection of primary source material relating to the European Age of Exploration. Includes many fascinating accounts of historic journeys by the explorers who made them and a selection of documents relating to mercantilism.
http://www.fordham.edu/halsall/mod/modsbook03.html

The James Fairfax Matthew Flinders Electronic Archive
This site, provided by the State Library of New South Wales, presents all the personal papers (journals, letter books, charts, and memorabilia) of Matthew Flinders, whose circumnavigation of Australia (1801–1803) defined the shape of the Australian continent.
www.sl.nsw.gov.au/flinders/

Mariners' Museum Age of Exploration On-line Curriculum Guide
A range of very short essays, some accompanied by maps, that address maritime discovery from ancient times to James Cook's 1768 voyage to the South Pacific. Includes a time line of exploration.
www.mariner.org/age/

The Mountain Men: Pathfinders of the West 1810–1860
This site, part of the University of Virginia's American Studies online resource, examines the role played in the opening up of the West by the intrepid fur trappers who ventured into the Rockies in search of beaver.
http://xroads.virginia.edu/~HYPER/HNS/Mtmen/home.html

NASA: Spacelink
NASA's educational resource provides a fully searchable archive that contains huge amount of information on all subjects related to the exploration of space. A useful starting point from which to navigate through the entire body NASA's online material.
http://spacelink.nasa.gov

National Maritime Museum, London: Fact Files
Britain's National Maritime Museum in Greenwich has an extensive collection of on-line fact files that provide short introductions to themes ranging from ancient astronomers to space exploration.
www.nmm.ac.uk/site/navId/00500300f

The Northern Lights Route

Visit the Travels section of this Web site dedicated to Arctic northern Europe and North America for a number of illustrated articles about journeys in the northern polar regions, from Pytheas of Massalia (c. 350 BCE) to the searches for the Northeast and Northwest Passages.

http://www.ub.uit.no/northernlights/eng/travels.htm

Pathfinders and Passageways: The Exploration of Canada

This site, provided by the Library and Archives of Canada, gives a comprehensive overview of the discovery and settlement of Canada by Europeans and discusses the role that native peoples played in the European exploration and mapping of this vast country.

www.collectionscanada.ca/explorers

PBS: Into the Abyss

In part a companion site to the PBS NOVA documentary *Volcanoes of the Deep,* which followed the attempt to retrieve life-forms from the depths of the Pacific Ocean, this site also contains information on the history of underwater exploration.

http://www.pbs.org/wgbh/nova/abyss/

PBS: Lewis and Clark: The Journey of the Corps of Discovery

This companion Web site to the PBS documentary tells the story of the Lewis and Clark expedition and the Native Americans whose lands they crossed with the help of journals written by corps members, interactive maps and time lines, and an engaging narrative.

www.pbs.org/lewisandclark

PBS: New Perspectives on the West

A companion Web site to the eight-part PBS documentary, first aired in 1996, that tells the remarkable story of the American West. Includes an interactive biographical dictionary.

www.pbs.org/weta/thewest

PBS: Shackleton's Voyage of Endurance

This companion site to a PBS NOVA documentary about Ernest Shackleton's 1914–1916 voyage (one of the greatest of all survival stories) charts the remarkable Antarctic journey made by Shackleton and includes a number of games and short animations.

www.pbs.org/wgbh/nova/shackleton/

The People and History of Mexico

This page gives a chronology of Mexican history with links to over three hundred articles, many of them dealing with the conquest and settlement of Mexico by Spanish conquistadores.

http://www.mexconnect.com/mex_/history.html

SETI@home

Download a free screen-saver program that engages a computer, during its idle moments, in the search for extraterrestrial intelligence.

http://setiathome.ssl.berkeley.edu/

SETI Institute

The institute's mission is to explore, understand, and explain the origin, nature, and prevalence of life in the universe. The site contains articles on the possible existence of extraterrestrial life.

www.seti.org

70South

The history section of this Web site contains a 20-chapter narrative history of Antarctic exploration, a guide to the particular role of Belgium in that history, and biographies of each of the key explorers.

www.70south.com/resources/history

The Silkroad Foundation

The Web site of the Silkroad Foundation posts articles on all the notable travelers of the Silk Road, from Zhang Qian to Marco Polo to Nikolay Przhevalsky and Marc Aurel Stein, and examines the cultural importance of the bridge between East and West.

www.silk-road.com

South-Pole.com

Though officially dedicated to the expedition mail sent and received by explorers of both polar regions, this site is in fact a resource for information on the history of polar exploration that is both comprehensive and extremely detailed.

www.south-pole.com/homepage.html

Spanish Exploration and Conquest of Native America

This discussion of the expeditions of Álvar Núñez Cabeza de Vaca and Hernando de Soto in the present-day southern United States also includes information on the fruitless search for Quivira led by Francisco Vásquez de Coronado.

www.floridahistory.com

To the Ends of the Earth: Death, Deceit, and the Nile

This companion Web site to a documentary series made by Britain's Channel 4 backs up its story of the search for the source of the Nile with interactive maps and illustrations.

http://www.channel4.com/history/microsites/E/ends/nile1.html

The Ultimate Space Place

Tells the story of humankind's quest to leave the earth, with a particular emphasis on statistical information.

www.thespaceplace.com

Vikings: The North Atlantic Saga

This Web site accompanies a major new exhibition, at the Smithsonian's National Museum of Natural History, that documents the history of the westward expansion of the Vikings and explores the impact of Leif Eriksson's momentous voyage to the Americas.

www.mnh.si.edu/vikings

The Virtual Library: United States History: Discovery and Exploration 1492–1650

A page of links to primary and secondary sources (maps, journals, biographies, essays, and bibliographies) relating to the history of the exploration of the United States.

http://vlib.iue.it/history/USA/ERAS/discovery.html

Virtual Museum of New France

The Canadian Museum of Civilization presents a history of the exploration and discovery of New France from the sixteenth to the eighteenth century. Essays on key explorers are accompanied by maps of their routes.

www.civilization.ca/vmnf/vmnfe.asp

Voyage of Exploration: Discovering New Horizons

Designed by students for students, this Web site uses interactive features to enliven accounts about a number of key explorers, from Queen Hatshepsut to Neil Armstrong, and examines the historical background to their journeys.

http://library.thinkquest.org/C001692/

LIST OF MAPS

Boldface numbers preceding a colon indicate the volume number.

Alexander the Great
Conquest of an area extending from Greece to India, 334–323 BCE **1:**16

Baffin, William
Voyages in search of the Northwest Passage, 1615 and 1616 **1:**66

Belalcázar, Sebastián de
Conquest of Quito and expedition across the Andes in search of El Dorado, 1531–1538 **1:**74

Bellingshausen, Fabian Gottlieb von
Circumnavigation of Antarctica, 1819–1821 **2:**85

Bering, Vitus Jonassen
Great Northern Expedition across northern and eastern Russia, 1733–1742 **2:**88

Burke, Robert O'Hara
Ultimately fatal coast-to-coast crossing of Australia with John Wills, 1860–1861 **2:**111

Burton, Richard Francis
Exploration of the East African Great Lakes region with John Hanning Speke, 1857–1858 **2:**115

Cabot, John
Voyage across the Atlantic from England to North America, 1497 **2:**128

Cabral, Pedro Álvares
Voyage to India via Brazil and southern Africa, 1500–1501 **2:**134

Cabrillo, Juan Rodríguez
Exploration of the Pacific coast of North America (1542–1543) **2:**137

Carteret, Philip
Crossing of the South Pacific during second circumnavigation, 1766–1768 **2:**149

Cheng Ho
Seventh voyage across the Indian Ocean from China, 1431–1433 **3:**165

Columbus, Christopher
Four voyages west across the Atlantic from Spain to the Americas, 1492–1503 **3:**188

Cook, James
Three Pacific voyages, 1768–1779 **3:**197

Coronado, Francisco Vásquez de
Journey from New Spain (Mexico) into the southern United States and across the Great Plains, 1539–1543 **3:**202

Cortés, Hernán
Conquest of the empire of the Aztecs, 1519–1520 **3:**205

Dias, Bartolomeu
Pioneering voyage from Lisbon around the Cape of Good Hope, 1487–1488 **3:**224

Eratosthenes of Cyrene
Map of the world, third century BCE (reconstructed) **4:**246

Erik the Red
Colonization of Greenland, c. 982–c. 1000 **4:**249

Faxian
Journey in search of Buddhist texts across China and India and via Sumatra and Ceylon back to China, 399–414 **4:**258

Flinders, Matthew
Circumnavigation of Tasmania, 1798–1799, and Australia, 1801–1803 **4:**269

Franklin, John
Explorations of the Canadian Arctic (1819–1847) **4:**277

Frémont, John
Explorations of the American West, 1842–1846 **4:**282

Frobisher, Martin
First voyage to North American Arctic, 1576 **4:**285

Gama, Vasco da
Historic voyage around the Cape of Good Hope (the southern tip of Africa) to India, 1497–1498 **4:**292

Garnier, Francis
Mekong River Expedition (Southeast Asia), 1866–1868 **4:**296

Hanno of Carthage
Voyage from North Africa through the Straits of Gibraltar and along the African coast, c. 500 BCE **5:**328

Hudson, Henry
Fatal voyage in search of a northwest passage through the Canadian Arctic, 1610–1611 **5:**352

Ibn Battutah
Journeys through Africa and Asia that took in almost every Muslim country in the world, 1325–1354 **5:**358

Leif Erikkson
Landing on Newfoundland, in North America, c. 1000 **6:**405

Lewis and Clark Expedition
Journey from Saint Louis to the Pacific Ocean. **6:**410

Livingstone, David
Coast-to-coast crossing of Africa; discovery and naming of the Victoria Falls, 1853–1856 **6:**415

Mackenzie, Alexander
Journeys from the Canadian interior to the Arctic Ocean, 1789, and the Pacific Ocean, 1792–1793 **6:**420

Magellan, Ferdinand
First circumnavigation of the world, 1519–1522 **6:**424

Marquette, Jacques
Voyage with Louis Jolliet south along the Mississippi River, 1673 **6:**437

Nansen, Fridtjof
Attempt on the North Pole, 1893–1896 **6:**460

Narváez, Pánfilo de
Disastrous attempt to conquer Florida; subsequent journey of Cabeza de Vaca overland to Mexico City, 1528–1536 **6:**464

Northeast Passage
Voyages in search of a route to the Pacific across the northern coast of Russia, 1553–1932 **7:**512

Northwest Passage
Search for a route to the Pacific through the Canadian Arctic, 1576–1906 **7:**516

Núñez de Balboa, Vasco
First European sighting of the Pacific Ocean, 1513 **7:**521

Oñate, Juan de
Journey along the Camino Real north from New Spain (Mexico) through present-day Texas, New Mexico, and Arizona, 1598–1605 **7:**523

Park, Mungo
Explorations of the Niger River, in West Africa, 1795–1796 and 1805–1806 **7:**534

Pike, Zebulon Montgomery
Exploration of the American Southwest, 1806–1807 **7:**546

Polo, Marco
Journey from Europe to China and back, 1271–1295 **8:**567

Ponce de León, Juan
Discovery of the Gulf Stream while exploring the Florida coast, 1513 **8:**571

Przhevalsky, Nikolay
Explorations of central Asia, 1879–1885 **8:**586

Quirós, Pedro Fernández de
Voyage west from South America across the Pacific, 1595–1606 **8:**596

Shackleton, Ernest Henry
Attempts on the South Pole, 1902 and 1908–1909, and heroic rescue of his men when all seemed doomed, 1915–1916 **8:**637

Smith, Jedediah Strong
Pioneering journeys throughout the American West, 1826–1829 **9:**667

Smith, John
Detailed surveys of the Chesapeake Bay region (present-day Delaware, Maryland, and Virginia), 1607–1608 **9:**670

Soto, Hernando de
First major European expedition to penetrate the interior of the United States (the area of present-day Florida, Georgia, Alabama, and Mississippi), 1539–1543 **9:**684

Speke, John Hanning
Discovery of the source of the Nile River (Lake Victoria in East Africa), 1857–1862 **9:**708

Stanley, Henry Morton
Epic east-west crossing of Africa, 1874–1877 **9:**714

Tasman, Abel
South Pacific voyage touching land at Tasmania, New Zealand, Tonga, and Fiji, 1642–1643 **10:**734

Verrazzano, Giovanni da
Exploration of the eastern coast of North America, 1524 **10:**768

Vespucci, Amerigo
Exploration of the eastern coast of South America, 1499 **10:**771

Zhang Qian
Journey west from China, along what would become the Silk Road, to Bactria, 138–125 BCE **10:**797

INDEX OF MAPS

This index includes place-names appearing in the maps. For place-names mentioned in the articles and captions, see the Geographical Index.

Boldface numbers preceding a colon indicate the volume number.

Acapulco **8:**596
Adriatic Sea **1:**16
Afghanistan **5:**358, **8:**586
Africa **2:**134, **3:**165, **3:**188, **3:**224, **4:**292, **5:**328, **5:**358, **6:**415, **6:**424, **8:**567
Alabama River **6:**464, **9:**684
A-la Shan **8:**586
Alaska **3:**197, **4:**277, **6:**460, **7:**516
Albert Nile **9:**708, **9:**714
Albuquerque **3:**202
Aleutian Islands **2:**88
Alexander Bay **4:**292
Alexander Island **2:**85
Alexandria **1:**16, **4:**246
Alexandria Arachoton **1:**16
Al Hasa **5:**358
Altai Mountains **8:**586
Altun Shan **8:**586, **10:**797
Amazon River **1:**74, **10:**771
Amecameca **3:**205
Amundsen Gulf **4:**277, **6:**420, **7:**516
Amundsen Sea **2:**85, **8:**637
Andes Mountains **1:**74, **10:**771
Angkor **4:**296
Angra dos Vaqueiros **3:**224
Angra dos Voltas **3:**224
Annam **4:**296
Antarctica **2:**85
Antarctic Circle **2:**85, **8:**637
Antarctic Peninsula **2:**85, **8:**637
Antigua **3:**205
Antilles Current **8:**571
Antioch **8:**567
Apalachee Bay **6:**464
Appalachian Mountains **6:**437, **9:**684, **10:**768
Arabia **3:**165, **4:**246, **5:**358, **8:**567
Arabian Peninsula **1:**16
Arabian Sea **1:**16, **3:**165, **4:**258, **5:**358, **8:**567
Arachiosia **4:**246
Aral Sea **5:**358, **8:**567, **8:**586
Archangel **2:**88, **7:**512
Arctic Circle **1:**66, **4:**249, **5:**352, **6:**405, **6:**460
Arctic Ocean **2:**88, **6:**420, **6:**460, **7:**512

Arguin **3:**224
Ariana **4:**246
Arkansas River **4:**282, **6:**410, **6:**437, **7:**546, **9:**684
Armenia **5:**358
Asia **3:**197, **4:**246, **6:**424
Asia Minor **1:**16
Athabasca River **6:**420
Athens **1:**16, **4:**246
Athi River **2:**115
Atlantic Ocean **3:**188, **3:**224, **4:**246, **5:**358, **6:**415, **6:**437, **8:**571, **9:**670, **9:**714, **10:**768, **10:**771 *see also* North Atlantic Ocean; South Atlantic Ocean
Australia **2:**111, **2:**149, **4:**269, **6:**424, **8:**596 *see also* New Holland
Ayas **8:**567
Azores **3:**188, **6:**424

Babylon **1:**16
Back River **6:**420
Bactria **1:**16, **4:**246, **10:**797
Badakhshan **8:**567
Badlands **4:**282
Baffin Bay **1:**66, **4:**277, **4:**285, **5:**352, **6:**460, **7:**516
Baffin Island **1:**66, **4:**277, **4:**285, **5:**352, **6:**405, **6:**420, **6:**460, **7:**516
Bagamoyo **9:**714
Baghdad **5:**358, **8:**567
Bahamas **3:**188, **8:**571, **10:**768
Bahrain **5:**358
Baja California **2:**137
Bamako **7:**534
Banana **9:**714
Bangka Island **3:**165
Banks Island **4:**277, **7:**516
Baracoa **6:**464
Barents Sea **2:**88, **6:**460, **7:**512
Barkly Tableland **2:**111
Bassac **4:**296
Bass Strait **4:**269
Batavia *see* Jakarta
Bathurst Inlet **4:**277
Bathurst Island **4:**277
Bay of Bengal **3:**165, **4:**258, **5:**358, **8:**567
Bay of Campeche **3:**205
Beardmore Glacier **8:**637
Bear Island **7:**512
Bear Lake **6:**410, **9:**667
Beaufort Sea **4:**277, **6:**420, **6:**460,

7:516
Beechey Island **4:**277
Beijing **8:**567, **8:**586
Bella Coola **6:**420
Bellingshausen Sea **2:**85, **8:**637
Benares **4:**258
Benguela **6:**415
Benin **3:**224, **4:**292
Bent's Fort **4:**282
Bering Island **7:**512
Bering Sea **3:**197, **6:**424, **7:**512, **7:**516
Bering Strait **2:**88, **6:**460, **7:**512, **7:**516
Bermuda **10:**768
Bighorn Mountains **6:**410, **9:**667
Bitterroot Mountains **6:**410
Black Hills **6:**410, **9:**667
Black Sea **1:**16, **5:**358, **8:**567
Blue Ridge Mountains **9:**684
Bogotá **1:**74
Bol'sheretsk **2:**88
Bombay **3:**165
Borneo **2:**149, **3:**165, **3:**197, **4:**269, **6:**424, **8:**567
Botany Bay **3:**197, **4:**269
Botswana **6:**415
Brattahlid (Julianehåb) **4:**249, **6:**405
Brazil **1:**74, **10:**771
Brisbane **2:**111
Bristol **2:**128
Britain **4:**246
Broach **8:**567
Bucephala **1:**16
Buddh Gaya **4:**258
Buenos Aires **6:**424
Bukhara **8:**567
Burma **4:**296, **8:**567
Bussa **7:**534
Bylot Island **1:**66, **5:**352, **7:**516
Byzantium **1:**16, **4:**246

Cabo das Correntes **4:**292
Cabo Santo Agostinho **10:**771
Cabo São Roque **10:**771
Cabot Strait **2:**128, **10:**768
Cadiz **3:**188
Cagliari **5:**358
Cairo **5:**358
Cajamarca **1:**74
Cajon Pass **9:**667
Calicut **2:**134, **3:**165, **4:**292, **5:**358
California **9:**667

Callao **8:**596
Cambodia **3:**165, **4:**296
Camino Real de Tierra Adentro **7:**523
Canadian River **9:**684
Canary Islands **3:**188, **3:**224, **5:**328
Cantor **3:**224
Cape Adare **8:**637
Cape Agostinho **3:**224
Cape Ann **10:**768
Cape Bathurst **4:**277, **6:**420
Cape Bauld **2:**128
Cape Bojador **3:**224, **4:**292
Cape Breton **2:**128
Cape Breton Island **2:**128, **10:**768
Cape Chaplíno **2:**88
Cape Charles **9:**670
Cape Chelyuskin **2:**88, **7:**512
Cape Cod **10:**768
Cape Cross **3:**224
Cape Dezhnev **2:**88
Cape Fear **10:**768
Cape Henry **9:**670
Cape Horn **3:**197, **6:**424
Cape Lookout **10:**768
Cape of Good Hope **2:**134, **3:**224, **4:**292, **6:**415
Cape Palmas **3:**224
Cape Saint Catherine **3:**224
Cape Sierra Leone **4:**292
Cape Verde **3:**224
Cape Verde Islands **2:**134, **3:**188, **4:**292, **6:**424
Cappadocia **1:**16
Careta **7:**521
Caria **1:**16
Caribbean Sea **3:**188, **6:**424, **6:**464, **7:**521, **8:**571, **8:**596, **9:**684
Carmania **4:**246
Carolina **10:**768
Carolina Outer Banks **10:**768
Cartagena **1:**74
Carthage **4:**246, **5:**328
Caspian Gates **1:**16
Caspian Sea **1:**16, **4:**246, **5:**358, **8:**567
Celebes **2:**149, **3:**197, **4:**269, **8:**596
Cempoala **3:**205
Central America **8:**571
Central Siberian Plateau **2:**88, **7:**512
Ceylon **3:**165, **4:**246, **4:**258, **5:**358, **8:**567

Chalco **3**:205
Chang'an **4**:258, **10**:797
Channel Country **2**:111
Channel Islands **2**:137
Chao Phraya (Menan) River **4**:296
Charlton Island **5**:352
Chen-Lai *see* Cambodia
Chesapeake Bay **9**:670, **10**:768
Chester River **9**:670
Chiaha **9**:684
Chiang Khan **4**:296
Chicasa **9**:684
Chichilticale **3**:202
Chickahominy River **9**:670
Chien shui **4**:296
Chihuahua **7**:523, **7**:546
China **3**:165, **3**:197, **4**:258, **4**:296,
    6:424, **8**:567, **8**:586, **10**:797
Chittagong **5**:358
Cholula **3**:205
Chukchi Peninsula **2**:88
Chukotka **2**:88, **7**:512
Churchill **6**:420
Churchill River **6**:420
Cinnamon Land **4**:246
Citaltépetl **3**:205
Coats Island **1**:66, **5**:352
Cochin **2**:134, **3**:165, **4**:292, **8**:567
Cochin China **4**:296, **8**:567
Colombia **1**:74, **7**:521
Colombo **3**:165
Colorado River **3**:202, **4**:282, **6**:410,
    6:464, **7**:523, **7**:546, **9**:667
Columbia River **4**:282, **6**:410, **9**:667
Compostela **3**:202, **6**:464
Congo River **3**:224, **4**:292, **5**:328,
    9:714
Connecticut River **10**:768
Cook Islands **3**:197
Cooper's Creek **2**:111
Coppermine **4**:277
Coppermine River **4**:277, **6**:420
Coral Sea **2**:111, **2**:149, **3**:197,
    8:596, **10**:734
Cornwallis Island **4**:277
Coronation Gulf **4**:277
Corsica **4**:246
Crete **1**:16, **4**:246
Crimea **1**:16, **5**:358
Cuando River **6**:415
Cuanza River **6**:415
Cuba **3**:188, **6**:464, **7**:521, **8**:571,
    9:684
Culiacán **3**:202, **6**:464
Cumberland Sound **1**:66, **4**:285,
    5:352
Cuzco **1**:74
Cyprus **1**:16, **5**:358

Cyrene **5**:246

Damascus **5**:358
Danube River **1**:16, **4**:246
Dardanelles **1**:16
Dar es Salaam **2**:115
Darién **1**:74
Darling River **2**:111
Darur **5**:358
Davis Strait **1**:66, **4**:285, **5**:352,
    6:460, **7**:516
Daybul **5**:358
Delaware **9**:670
Delaware Bay **9**:670, **10**:768
Delaware River **9**:670
Delhi **5**:358
Denmark Strait **4**:249, **6**:405
Des Moines River **4**:282, **6**:410
Devon Island **1**:66, **4**:277
Diamantina River **2**:111
Dionysia **4**:246
Dominica **3**:188, **8**:571
Don (Tanais) River **1**:16
Duke of Gloucester Islands **2**:149
Dunhuang **8**:586
Dvina River **2**:88, **7**:512

East Africa **2**:115, **5**:358, **9**:708
East China Sea **8**:567
Easter Island **2**:149, **3**:197
East Indies **2**:149, **3**:197, **6**:424,
    10:734
East Siberian Sea **2**:88, **6**:460, **7**:512
Ecbatana **1**:16
Ecuador **1**:74
Egypt **1**:16
Elephant Island **2**:85, **8**:637
Ellesmere Island **6**:460, **7**:516
Ellsworth Land **8**:637
Elmina **3**:224
El Paso **7**:523
El Paso del Norte **6**:464
Encounter Bay **4**:269
Endeavour River **3**:197
Enderby Land **2**:85, **8**:637
England **2**:128, **4**:249, **6**:405
Epirus **1**:16
Equator **6**:424
Espiritu Santo **8**:596
Estero Bay **8**:571
Euphrates River **1**:16, **4**:246, **5**:358,
    8:567
Europe **2**:134, **3**:188, **4**:246, **4**:292,
    5:328, **6**:424

Faeroe Islands **4**:249, **6**:405
Falkland Islands **3**:197
Fang-pan *see* Bombay

Fez **5**:358
Fiji **3**:197, **8**:596, **10**:734
Fisheaters **4**:246
Flinders River **2**:111
Flint River **9**:684
Florida **6**:464, **8**:571, **9**:684, **10**:768
Florida Current **8**:571
Florida Keys **8**:571
Formosa **8**:567
Fort Boise **4**:282
Fort Bridger **4**:282
Fort Chipewyan **6**:420
Fort Clatsop **6**:410
Fort Colville **9**:667
Fort Franklin **4**:277
Fort Hall **4**:282
Fort Laramie **4**:282
Fort Mandan **6**:410
Fort Resolution **4**:277
Fort Smith **4**:282
Fort Vancouver **4**:282, **9**:667
Foxe Basin **1**:66, **4**:277, **4**:285, **5**:352,
    7:516
Foxe Channel **1**:66, **4**:285, **5**:352
Fox River **6**:437
France **2**:128
Franz Josef Land **6**:460, **7**:512
Fraser River **6**:420, **9**:667
Frederick Jackson Island **6**:460
Frederikshåb **4**:249, **6**:405
Frobisher Bay **1**:66, **4**:285, **5**:352,
    7:516
Fury and Hecla Strait **7**:516

Galápagos Islands **8**:596
Galveston Bay **6**:464
Gambia River **7**:534
Gandhara **4**:258
Ganges River **3**:165, **4**:246, **4**:258,
    5:358, **8**:567, **8**:586
Gaugamela **1**:16
Gedrosia **4**:246
Genoa **3**:188
George V Land **2**:85, **8**:637
Goa **2**:134
Gobi Desert **4**:258, **8**:567, **8**:586,
    10:797
Godthåb **4**:249, **6**:405
Gold Coast **7**:534
Golden Bay **10**:734
Golfo de Baleina **3**:224
Golfo dos Vaqueiros (Mossel Bay)
    4:292
Gordium **1**:16
Granada **5**:358
Grand Banks **2**:128
Grand Canyon **3**:202, **4**:282, **7**:523,
    9:667

Granicus **1**:16
Great American Desert **6**:410,
    9:667
Great Barrier Reef **3**:197, **4**:269
Great Basin **3**:202, **4**:282, **6**:410,
    9:667
Great Bear Lake **4**:277, **6**:420, **7**:516
Great Dividing Range **2**:111
Greater Armenia **8**:567
Great Falls **6**:410
Great Fish River **3**:224, **4**:277
Great Plains **3**:202, **4**:282, **6**:464,
    7:523
Great Rift Valley **2**:115, **9**:708
Great Salt Lake **4**:282, **6**:410, **9**:667
Great Salt Lake Desert **4**:282
Great Slave Lake **4**:277, **6**:420,
    7:516
Green Bay **6**:437
Greenland **1**:66, **2**:128, **4**:249, **4**:277,
    4:285, **5**:352, **6**:405, **6**:460, **7**:516
  Eastern settlement **4**:249, **6**:405
  Middle settlement **4**:249, **6**:405
  Western settlement **4**:249, **6**:405
Greenland Sea **6**:460
Green River **6**:410, **7**:546, **9**:667
Guam **6**:424, **8**:596
Guanabara Bay **10**:771
Guayaquil **1**:74
Gulf of Alaska **3**:197
Gulf of Boothia **4**:277, **6**:420, **7**:516
Gulf of California **2**:137, **3**:202,
    4:282, **6**:464, **7**:523, **7**:546, **9**:667
Gulf of Carpentaria **2**:111, **4**:269,
    10:734
Gulf of Chihli **10**:797
Gulf of Darién **1**:74, **7**:521
Gulf of Guayaquil **1**:74
Gulf of Guinea **3**:224, **5**:328, **7**:534
Gulf of Mexico **3**:202, **6**:437, **6**:464,
    7:523, **7**:546, **8**:571, **9**:667, **9**:684,
    10:768
Gulf of Panama **7**:521
Gulf of Saint Lawrence **2**:128,
    6:405, **6**:437, **10**:768
Gulf of Siam **4**:296
Gulf of Tonkin **4**:296
Gulf of Urabá **7**:521
Gulf Stream **8**:571

Hangchow **8**:567
Hanoi **4**:296
Havana **6**:464, **8**:571, **9**:684
Hawaiian Islands **3**:197, **6**:424,
    8:596
Hebrides **6**:405
Hellespont **1**:16
Helluland (Baffin Island) **6**:405

Himalayas **1:**16, **3:**165, **4:**258, **5:**358, **8:**567, **8:**586, **10:**797

Hindu Kush **1:**16, **4:**258, **5:**358, **8:**567, **10:**797

Hispaniola **3:**188, **7:**521, **8:**571

Hormuz **3:**165, **8:**567

Hsien-Lo *see* Siam

Huancabamba **1:**74

Hudson Bay **1:**66, **4:**277, **4:**285, **5:**352, **6:**405, **6:**420, **6:**460, **7:**516

Hudson River **6:**437, **10:**768

Hudson Strait **1:**66, **4:**285, **5:**352, **6:**405, **7:**516

Hueyotlipan **3:**205

Hui-tse **4:**296

Hydaspes River **1:**16

Hyrcanian Sea (Caspian Sea) **1:**16

Iceland **2:**128, **4:**249, **6:**405

Icy Cape **7:**516

Illinois River **6:**437

India **1:**16, **2:**134, **3:**165, **4:**246, **4:**258, **4:**292, **5:**358, **6:**424, **8:**567, **8:**586

Indian Ocean **2:**85, **2:**115, **2:**134, **2:**149, **3:**165, **3:**197, **4:**258, **4:**269, **4:**292, **5:**358, **6:**415, **6:**424, **8:**567, **8:**637, **9:**708, **9:**714, **10:**734

Indigirka River **2:**88, **7:**512

Indus River **1:**16, **3:**165, **4:**258, **5:**358, **8:**567, **8:**586

Ireland **2:**128, **4:**249, **6:**405

Irkutsk **8:**586

Irrawaddy River **8:**567

Issus **1:**16, **4:**246

Issyk-Kul **8:**586

Isthmus of Panama **7:**521

Ivory Coast **7:**534

Ixhuácan **3:**205

Iznil **5:**358

Iztacamaxtitlan **5:**205

Iztapalapa **3:**205

Jakarta (Batavia) **2:**149, **3:**197, **10:**734

Jalapa **3:**205

Jamaica **3:**188, **6:**464, **7:**521, **8:**571

James Bay **4:**285, **5:**352, **6:**437, **7:**516

James River **9:**670

James Ross Island **2:**85

Jamestown **9:**670

Japan **8:**596

Java **2:**149, **3:**165, **3:**197, **4:**258, **4:**269

Jaxartes River **1:**16, **4:**246, **5:**358, **8:**567, **8:**586

Jedda **5:**358

Jerusalem **1:**16, **5:**358, **8:**567

Juan Fernández Islands **2:**149

Julianehåb (Brattahlid) **4:**249, **6:**405

Kagera River **9:**708

Kalahari Desert **6:**415

Kamchatka **2:**88, **7:**512

Kan-chou **8:**567

Kandahar **1:**16

Kansas River **4:**282, **7:**546

Kapilavastu **4:**258

Karakol **8:**586

Karakorum Mountains **4:**258

Kara Sea **2:**88, **6:**460, **7:**512

Kashgar **8:**567, **10:**797

Kashmir **4:**258, **10:**797

Kawlam **5:**358

Kazembe **2:**115

Kemp Land **2:**85

Khemmarat **4:**296

Kheta River **2:**88

Khotan **4:**258, **8:**567, **10:**797

Kilwa **2:**134, **4:**292

King William Island **4:**277

Kirman **8:**567

Ko-chih *see* Cochin

Koko Nor **8:**586

Ko-lan *see* Quilan

Kola Peninsula **7:**512

Kolobeng **6:**415

Kolyma River **2:**88, **7:**512

Kongtung **4:**296

Korea **8:**567

Kuala Pasal **3:**165

Ku-li-ko *see* Calicut

Kunlun Mountains **4:**258, **8:**586, **10:**797

Kunming **4:**296

Kuruman **6:**415

Kusingara **4:**258

Kyakhta **8:**586

Labrador **1:**66, **2:**128, **4:**285, **5:**352, **6:**405, **7:**516

Labrador Sea **1:**66, **4:**285, **5:**352, **6:**405, **7:**516

Lachlan River **2:**111

La Florida **9:**684, **10:**768

Lake Albert **2:**115, **9:**708, **9:**714

Lake Athabasca **6:**420

Lake Baikal **8:**586

Lake Balkhash **8:**586

Lake Bangweulu **2:**115, **6:**415, **9:**708

Lake Champlain **6:**437

Lake Edward **2:**115, **9:**708, **9:**714

Lake Erie **6:**437

Lake Eyre **2:**111

Lake Huron **6:**437

Lake Kivu **2:**115, **9:**708, **9:**714

Lake Kyoga **2:**115, **9:**708, **9:**714

Lake Michigan **6:**437

Lake Mweru **2:**115, **6:**415, **9:**708

Lake Ngami **6:**415

Lake Nyasa **2:**115, **6:**415, **9:**708, **9:**714

Lake of the Woods **6:**437

Lake Ontario **6:**405, **6:**437

Lake Reindeer **6:**420

Lake Rukwa **2:**115, **9:**708

Lake Superior **6:**437

Lake Tanganyika **2:**115, **5:**358, **6:**415, **9:**708, **9:**714

Lake Victoria **2:**115, **5:**358, **9:**708, **9:**714

Lake Winnipeg **6:**420

Lake Winnepegosis **6:**410

Lancaster Sound **1:**66, **4:**277, **5:**352, **7:**516

L'Anse aux Meadows **6:**405

Laos **4:**296

La Pointe du Saint-Esprit **6:**437

Laptev Sea **2:**88, **6:**460, **7:**512

Lemhi Pass **9:**667

Lena River **2:**88, **7:**512

Lesser Antilles **7:**521, **8:**571

Lhasa **8:**586

Libya **1:**16

Limpopo River **6:**415

Linyanti **6:**415

Lisbon **2:**134, **3:**188, **3:**224, **4:**292

Little Armenia **8:**567

Long Island **10:**768

Lop Nur **8:**586

Loş Angeles **2:**137, **4:**282

Lower California **3:**202, **4:**282, **6:**410, **6:**464, **7:**523

Lualaba River **6:**415, **9:**708, **9:**714

Luanda **6:**415

Luang Prabang **4:**296

Luitpold Coast **2:**85, **8:**637

Lukuga River **9:**708

Lunda **2:**115

Luvua River **9:**708

Lycia **1:**16

Lydia **1:**16

McClintock Channel **4:**277, **6:**420

Macedonia **1:**16

Mackenzie Bay **4:**277, **7:**516

Mackenzie Mountains **6:**420

Mackenzie River **4:**277, **6:**420

Macquarie Island **2:**85

MacRobertson Land **2:**85

Mactan Island **6:**424

Madagascar **2:**134, **4:**292

Madeira **3:**188, **3:**224

Madeira River **10:**771

Madura **5:**358

Magdalena River **1:**74

Magellan Strait **6:**424

Maghrib **5:**358

Ma-i-mai *see* Philippine Islands

Makran Desert **1:**16

Malacca **3:**165

Malaya **2:**149, **4:**269, **8:**567, **10:**734

Malay Peninsula **3:**165

Maldives **3:**165, **5:**358

Mali **5:**358

Malindi **2:**134, **3:**165, **4:**292

Mangazeva Sea **2:**88

Manila **8:**596

Maracanda **1:**16

Marias River **6:**410

Marie Byrd Land **2:**85, **8:**637

Markland (Labrador) **6:**405

Marquesas Islands **8:**596

Martinique **3:**188

Maryland **9:**670

Masai **2:**115

Matagorda Bay **6:**464

Mattaponi River **9:**670

Mauvila **9:**684

Mecca **5:**358

Medellin **3:**205

Mediterranean Sea **1:**16, **3:**188, **5:**328, **5:**358, **6:**424, **8:**567

Mekong River **3:**165, **4:**296, **8:**567

Melanesia **2:**149, **3:**197, **8:**596

Melbourne **2:**111

Melville Island **4:**277, **7:**516

Melville Peninsula **1:**66, **4:**285, **5:**352

Memphis **1:**16

Menan (Chao Phraya) River **4:**296

Menindee **2:**111

Meroe **4:**246

Mesopotamia **1:**16

Mexico (New Spain) **3:**202, **4:**282, **6:**410, **6:**424, **6:**464, **7:**523, **7:**546, **8:**596, **9:**667

Mexico City *see* Tenochtitlán

Micronesia **2:**149, **3:**197, **8:**596

Milk River **6:**410

Mindanao **2:**149

Mississippi River **4:**282, **6:**410, **6:**437, **6:**464, **7:**546, **9:**684

Missouri River **3:**202, **6:**410, **6:**437, **9:**667

  Great Falls **6:**410

Mogadishu **3:**165, **4:**292, **5:**358

Mojave Desert **4:**282, **6:**410, **7:**546, **9:**667

Mojave villages **9**:667

Moluccas (Spice Islands) **2**:149, **6**:424, **10**:734

Mombasa **2**:115, **4**:292, **9**:708

Mongolia **8**:567, **8**:586, **10**:797

Montana **6**:410

Monterey **2**:137

Morocco **5**:328

Moscow **7**:512

Mossel Bay (Golfo dos Vaqueíros) **4**:292

Mosul **8**:567

Mount Cameroon **5**:328

Mount Kakulima **5**:328

Mount Kenya **2**:115

Mount Kilimanjaro **2**:115

Mozambique **2**:115, **2**:134, **4**:292, **9**:708

Muisca **1**:74

Mu-ku-tu-shu *see* Mogadishu

Murray River **2**:111

Mysia **1**:16

Nacogdoches **7**:546

Nagchu **8**:586

Nanking **3**:165, **4**:258

Nanticoke River **9**:670

Natchitoches **7**:546

Nazwa **5**:358

Nepal **4**:258

New Britain **2**:149, **3**:197, **4**:269, **10**:734

New Caledonia **3**:197, **10**:734

Newfoundland **1**:66, **2**:128, **4**:285, **5**:352, **7**:516, **10**:768 *see also* Vinland

New France **6**:437

New Guinea **2**:149, **3**:197, **4**:269, **8**:596, **10**:734

New Hebrides (Vanuatu) **3**:197, **10**:734

New Holland (Australia) **3**:197, **4**:269, **10**:734

New Ireland **2**:149, **10**:734

New Jerusalem **8**:596

New Mexico **7**:523

New Siberian Islands **2**:88, **6**:460, **7**:512

New South Wales **2**:111, **3**:197

New Spain (Mexico) **3**:202, **6**:424, **6**:464, **7**:523, **8**:596

New York **10**:768

New Zealand **2**:149, **3**:197, **4**:269, **6**:424, **8**:596, **10**:734

Nicobar Islands **3**:165, **8**:567

Niger River **3**:224, **4**:292, **5**:328, **5**:358, **7**:534

Nile River **1**:16, **4**:246, **5**:328, **5**:358,

8:567, **9**:708, **9**:714

Nineveh **1**:16

Nizline-Kamchatsk **2**:88

Nootka Sound **3**:197

Norfolk Island **3**:197

North America **2**:128, **2**:137, **3**:188, **3**:197, **4**:277, **6**:405, **6**:424, **7**:516, **8**:571, **8**:596

British **4**:282

North Atlantic Ocean **2**:128, **2**:134, **4**:249, **4**:292, **5**:328, **6**:405, **6**:424, **6**:460

North Dakota **6**:410

Northeast Passage **7**:512

Northern Ocean **4**:246

Northern Territory **2**:111

North Pacific Ocean **2**:88, **2**:149, **3**:197, **6**:424, **7**:512

North Platte River **4**:282

North Pole **6**:460

North Sea **4**:249, **6**:405

Northwest Passage **7**:516

Norway **6**:460, **7**:512

Norwegian Sea **4**:249, **6**:405, **6**:460

Nova Scotia **6**:437, **10**:768

Novaya Zemlya **6**:460, **7**:512

Nubia **4**:246

Nuuk **6**:460

Nyamwezi **2**:115

Nyangwe **9**:714

Ob River **2**:88

Ocala **9**:684

Ochus **4**:246

Ohio River **6**:437

Okhotsk **2**:88, **7**:512

Orange River **3**:224, **4**:292, **6**:415

Ordos Desert **8**:586, **10**:797

Oregon Country **4**:282, **9**:667

Orinoco River **7**:521, **10**:771

Orizaba **3**:205

Osage villages **7**:546

Ottawa River **6**:437

Oxus River **1**:16, **4**:246, **5**:358, **8**:567, **8**:586, **10**:797

Pacific Ocean **1**:74, **2**:137, **3**:165, **3**:202, **4**:282, **6**:410, **6**:464, **7**:523, **7**:546, **8**:571, **9**:667, **10**:734 *see also* North Pacific Ocean; South Pacific Ocean

Pagan **8**:567

Paita **8**:596

Palestine **1**:16

Pamlico Sound **10**:768

Pamunkey River **9**:670

Panama **1**:74, **7**:521

Panama City **1**:74

Paphlagonia **1**:16

Paroo River **2**:111

Parthia **1**:16

Pasargadae **1**:16

Pataliputra **4**:258

Patapsco River **9**:670

Pattala **1**:16

Patuxent River **9**:670

Pawnee villages **7**:546

Peace River **6**:420

Pecos River **7**:523

Pella **1**:16

Pemba **2**:115

Persepolis **1**:16

Persia **1**:16, **3**:165, **5**:358, **8**:567

Persian Gulf **1**:16, **3**:165, **5**:358, **8**:567

Persis **4**:246

Peru **1**:74, **8**:596

Peshawar **4**:258

Peter I Island **2**:85

Petropavlovsk **2**:88

Philippine Islands **2**:149, **3**:165, **3**:197, **4**:258, **6**:424, **8**:567, **8**:596

Phoenicia **5**:328

Phrygia **1**:16

Pike's Peak **7**:546

Pisania **7**:534

Pisidia **1**:16

Pitcairn Island **2**:149

Piura **1**:74

Platte River **4**:282

Pnom Penh **4**:296

Pocomoke River **9**:670

Polynesia **3**:197, **8**:596

Popayán **1**:74

Popocatepetl **3**:205

Port Jackson (Sydney) **4**:269

Portugal **2**:128, **3**:188

Potomac River **9**:670

Prince Charles Island **1**:66, **4**:285, **5**:352

Prince of Wales Island **4**:277

Princess Elizabeth Land **2**:85, **8**:637

Princess Martha Coast **2**:85, **8**:637

Prudhoe Bay **4**:277

Puerto Rico **3**:188, **8**:571

Pyrenees Mountains **4**:246

Qalhat **5**:358

Quecholac **3**:205

Queen Mary Land **2**:85, **8**:637

Queen Maud Land **2**:85, **8**:637

Queensland **2**:111

Quelimane **6**:415

Quiguate **9**:684

Quilan **3**:165

Quito **1**:74

Quivira **3**:202, **7**:523

Quizquiz **9**:684

Rappahannock River **9**:670

Red Deer River **6**:420

Red River **3**:202, **4**:296, **6**:437, **7**:523, **7**:546, **9**:684

Red Sea **1**:16, **3**:165, **4**:246, **8**:567

Republican River **4**:282, **7**:546

Republic of Texas **4**:282

Repulse Bay **7**:516

Rio de Janeiro **10**:771

Rio Grande **2**:137, **3**:202, **4**:282, **6**:464, **7**:523, **7**:546, **9**:667

Rio Negro **10**:771

Ripon Falls **9**:708

Roanoke River **10**:768

Rocky Mountains **3**:202, **4**:282, **6**:410, **6**:420, **9**:667

Ross Ice Shelf **8**:637

Ross Sea **2**:85, **8**:637

Rufiji River **2**:115

Russia **6**:460

Ruwenzori Mountains **9**:714

Sacramento **4**:282, **9**:667

Sacramento River **4**:282

Sahara Desert **3**:224, **5**:358, **7**:534

Saigon **4**:296

Saint Augustine **8**:571

Saint George's Channel **2**:149

Saint Lawrence River **6**:405, **6**:437

Saint Louis **4**:282, **6**:410, **7**:546, **9**:667

Saint Vrain **4**:282

Salween River **4**:296

Samarkand **1**:16, **5**:358, **8**:567, **10**:797

Samoa **2**:149

San Antonio **2**:137

San Diego **2**:137, **4**:282

San Fernando de Velicata **2**:137

San Francisco **2**:137, **4**:282, **6**:410

San Gabriel **2**:137, **4**:282, **7**:523

San Geronimo **3**:202, **6**:464

San Juan **8**:571

San Juan de los Caballeros **7**:523

San Juan Mountains **7**:523

San Julián **6**:424

San Luis Obispo **2**:137

San Miguel **1**:74

San Salvador (Watling Island) **3**:188

Santa Barbara **2**:137

Santa Bárbara **7**:523

Santa Catalina **2**:137

Santa Cruz Islands **8**:596

Santa Fe **3:**202, **4:**282, **7:**546, **9:**667
Santa María la Antigua del Darién
 7:521
Santiago **6:**464
São Francisco River **10:**771
Sardinia **4:**246, **5:**358
Sargasso Sea **3:**188
Sault Sainte Marie **6:**437
Savannah River **6:**464, **6:**684,
 10:768
Scandinavia **4:**249, **6:**405
Scotia Sea **2:**85
Scythia **1:**16, **4:**246
Sea of Okhotsk **2:**88, **7:**512
Sea of Verrazzano **10:**768
Ségou **7:**534
Semliki River **9:**714
Sena **6:**415
Senegal River **3:**224, **5:**328, **5:**358,
 7:534
Senegambia **7:**534
Seringapatam **3:**165
Sesheke **6:**415
Severnaya Zemlya **2:**88, **7:**512
Seville **3:**188, **6:**424
Sha-chou (Tunhwang) **4:**258
Shanghai **8:**567
Shang-tu **8:**567
Shantung **4:**258
Shetland Islands **4:**249, **6:**405
Shiraz **8:**567
Shire River **6:**415
Siam **2:**149, **3:**165, **4:**296, **8:**567
Siberia **2:**88, **6:**460, **7:**512, **7:**516
Sicily **4:**246
Sidonia **1:**16
Siem Reap **4:**296
Sierra Leone **5:**328
Sierra Madre **7:**523
Sierra Madre Occidental **2:**137,
 3:202, **6:**464, **7:**523
Sierra Madre Oriental **3:**205
Sierra Nevada **3:**202, **4:**282, **6:**410,
 7:546, **9:**667
Silk Road **10:**797
Singapore **8:**567
Siraf **5:**358
Slave Coast **7:**534
Smith Island **9:**670
Smith's Falls **9:**670
Smith Sound **1:**66, **5:**352, **7:**516
Snake River **4:**282, **6:**410, **9:**667
Society Islands **3:**197, **8:**596
Sofala **2:**134, **4:**292
Sogdiana **4:**246, **10:**797
Solomon Islands **2:**149, **8:**596,
 10:734
Sonora **2:**137

Sonora River **2:**137
Soudiana **1:**16
South America **2:**85, **2:**134, **2:**149,
 3:188, **3:**197, **6:**424, **8:**571
Southampton Island **1:**66, **4:**285,
 5:352
South Atlantic Ocean **2:**85, **2:**134,
 4:292, **6:**424, **8:**637
South China Sea **3:**165, **4:**258,
 4:296, **8:**567
South Dakota **6:**410
Southern Indian Lake **6:**420
South Georgia **2:**85, **3:**197, **8:**637
South Orkney Islands **2:**85
South Pacific Ocean **2:**85, **2:**111,
 2:149, **3:**197, **4:**269, **8:**596
South Pass **9:**667
South Platte **7:**546
South Polar Plateau **8:**637
South Pole **2:**85, **8:**637
South Sandwich Islands **2:**85, **8:**637
South Shetland Islands **2:**85
Spain **2:**128, **3:**188, **3:**224, **5:**328,
 5:358
Sparta **1:**16
Speke Gulf **9:**708
Spice Islands (Moluccas) **2:**149,
 6:424
Spitsbergen **6:**460, **7:**512
Stanley Falls **9:**714
Strait of Magellan **2:**149
Straits of Mackinac **6:**437
Suakin **5:**358
Sumatra **2:**149, **3:**165, **3:**197, **4:**269,
 5:358, **8:**567
Sunda Strait **4:**258
Surin **4:**296
Susa **1:**16
Susia **1:**16
Susquehanna River **9:**670
Svalbard **7:**512
Sydney (Port Jackson) **2:**111, **4:**269
Syene **4:**246
Sylhet **5:**358
Syria **1:**16, **5:**358

Tabora **2:**115, **9:**708, **9:**714
Tagadda **5:**358
Taghaza **5:**358
Tahiti **2:**149, **3:**197, **8:**596
Taimy Peninsula **2:**88
Taiwan **3:**165, **4:**258, **8:**567
Takla Makan Desert **8:**567, **8:**586,
 10:797
Tampa Bay **6:**464, **9:**684
Tana River **2:**115
Tangier **5:**358
Tapajós River **10:**771

Tashkent **1:**16
Tasmania (Van Diemen's Land)
 3:197, **4:**269, **10:**734
Tasman Sea **3:**197, **4:**269, **8:**596,
 10:734
Taxila **1:**16, **4:**258
Tecoac **3:**205
Tenerife **4:**292, **6:**424
Tenochtitlán (Mexico City) **3:**202,
 3:205, **6:**464
Tepeaca **3:**205
Tete **6:**415
Texas **3:**202, **4:**282 **6:**464, **7:**523,
 7:546, **9:**667, **9:**684
Thebes **1:**16, **4:**246
Thule **4:**246
Tibet **3:**165, **4:**258, **4:**296, **8:**567,
 8:586, **10:**797
Tien-kan *see* Maldives
Tien Shan Mountains **4:**258, **8:**586,
 10:797
Tierra del Fuego **3:**197
Tierra de San Buenaventura **8:**596
Tigris River **1:**16, **4:**246, **5:**358, **8:**567
Timbuktu **7:**534
Timor Sea **10:**734
Tlaxcala **3:**205
Tocantins River **10:**771
Tokelau Islands **2:**149
Tombouctou **5:**358
Tonga **8:**596, **10:**734
Tongo **3:**197
Torres Strait **8:**596, **10:**734
Trebizond **8:**567
Trinidad **3:**188, **10:**771
Tristan da Cunha **2:**134
Tropic of Cancer **6:**424
Tropic of Capricorn **6:**415, **6:**424
Troy **1:**16
Tsung-chou **4:**258
Tuametu Archipelago **8:**596
Tuban **3:**165
Tunhwang (Sha-chou) **4:**258
Tunis **5:**358
Turkistan **8:**586
Tyre **1:**16
Tzompantzinco **3:**205

Ujiji **2:**115, **6:**415, **9:**708, **9:**714
Ungava Bay **4:**285, **5:**352, **7:**516
Union Pass **9:**667
United States of America **4:**282,
 6:410, **7:**546, **9:**667
Upper California **3:**202
Upper Zambezi River **6:**415
Ural Mountains **2:**88
Urga **8:**586
Usambara **2:**115

Vancouver Island **3:**197, **6:**410
Van Diemen's Land (Tasmania)
 3:197, **4:**269, **10:**734
Vanuatu (New Hebrides) **3:**197,
 10:734
Venezuela **1:**74
Veracruz **2:**134, **3:**205
Victoria **2:**111
Victoria Falls **6:**415
Victoria Island **4:**277, **6:**420, **7:**516
Victoria Nile **2:**115, **9:**708
Vinland (Newfoundland) **6:**405
Volga River **5:**358
Volta River **7:**534

Wallaston Lake **6:**420
Washington **9:**670
Watling Island (San Salvador)
 3:188
Weddell Sea **2:**85
Werowocomoco **9:**670
Westport **4:**282
White Sea **2:**88, **7:**512
Whitman Mission **4:**282
Wilhelm II Land **2:**85, **8:**637
Wilkes Land **2:**85, **8:**637
Wisconsin River **6:**437
Wrangel Island **2:**88

Xingu River **10:**771
Xuala **9:**684

Yakutsk **2:**88, **7:**512
Yang-chou **8:**567
Yangtze River **3:**165, **4:**258, **8:**567,
 8:586
Yellow River **4:**258, **8:**567, **8:**586,
 10:797
Yellow Sea **4:**258, **8:**567
Yellowstone River **6:**410, **9:**667
Yenisei River **2:**88, **7:**512
York Fort **6:**420
York River **9:**670
Yucatán **6:**464
Yunnan **8:**567

Zacatecas **7:**523
Zagros Mountains **5:**358
Zaisan **8:**586
Zambezi River **4:**292, **6:**415
Zanzibar **2:**115, **3:**165, **6:**415, **9:**708,
 9:714
Zautla **3:**205
Zuñi **3:**202

BIOGRAPHICAL INDEX

Page numbers in *italic type* refer to illustrations. **Boldface** numbers preceding a colon indicate the volume number. Page numbers entirely in **boldface** type refer to main articles.

Abu Inan, Sultan **5**:358, **5**:361
Adams, George **10**:737
Adams, John Couch **9**:681
Adams, John Quincy **9**:673
Afonso V, king of Portugal **5**:331, **8**:574
Afonso the Great *see* Albuquerque, Afonso de
Aláminos, Anton de **8**:569
Alarcón, Hernando de **3**:202
Albuquerque, Afonso de **8**:574, **8**:576
Aldrin, Buzz (Edwin Eugene, Jr.) **1**:28, **1**:29, **1**:38, **1**:39, **6**:466, **7**:544, **9**:692, **9**:696
Alexander VI, Pope **3**:175, **4**:271, **6**:423, **6**:448
Alexander I, Czar **2**:84
Alexander II, Czar **9**:675
Alexander III of Macedonia *see* Alexander the Great
Alexander the Great **1**:14–17, **4**:246, **4**:300, **5**:377, **6**:455, **6**:474, **8**:589, **9**:659, **9**:660, **9**:661, **10**:797
Alexander, William **4**:313
Allouez, Claude **6**:450, **6**:451
Almagro, Diego de **1**:73
Almeida, Charles de **2**:138
Almeida, Francisco de **6**:422, **8**:574
Alvarado, Luis de Moscoso **9**:684, **9**:685
Amundsen, Roald **1**:18–21, **1**:60, **1**:62, **2**:101, **2**:119, **3**:171, **3**:231, **3**:235, **3**:236, **3**:238, **4**:315, **4**:339, **5**:340, **5**:381, **7**:*502*, **7**:515, **7**:518, **7**:519, **7**:539, **7**:543, **7**:555, **7**:558, **8**:625, **8**:627, **8**:628, **8**:629, **8**:636, **8**:655
Anaximander of Miletus **4**:*298*, **4**:299, **9**:686
Andrée, Salomon August **1**:61, **1**:62, **8**:627
Andronicus of Cyrrhus **10**:783
Anna, empress of Russia **2**:88
Anne, queen of Britain **1**:51

Anson, George **5**:366, **5**:*366*, **5**:367, **5**:367
Archer, Colin **6**:459
Archer, Frederick Scott **7**:541, **7**:542
Aristarchus of Samos **1**:50
Aristotle **1**:14, **4**:299, **6**:428, **6**:444, **7**:484, **7**:485, **9**:686, **10**:781
Armstrong, Neil **1**:27–29, **1**:38, **1**:39, **6**:466, **7**:544, **9**:692, **9**:696
Arrest, Heinrich Louis d' **9**:681
Arrian **1**:17
Arundel, Isabel **2**:*113*
Ashley, William Henry **1**:30–32, **2**:107, **9**:664, **9**:665, **9**:666
Ashmole, Elias **6**:457
Asimov, Isaac **7**:532
Astor, Caroline Schermerhorn **1**:36
Astor, George **1**:33
Astor, John Jacob **1**:33–36, **9**:664
Astor, John Jacob, II **1**:36
Astor, John Jacob, IV **1**:36
Astor, Nancy Witcher Langhorne **1**:36
Astor, William Backhouse **1**:36
Astor, William Waldorf **1**:36
Atahualpa **6**:478, **9**:682, **9**:683, **9**:705
Audubon, John James **1**:55–58
Augustus, emperor of Rome **4**:300
Avilés, Pedro Menéndez de **8**:572

Bachman, John **1**:57
Backhuysen, Ludolf **7**:503
Bacon, Francis **7**:485
Baffin, William **1**:66–68, **5**:325, **7**:516
Baines, Thomas **9**:652
Baird, Spencer Fullerton **9**:673, **9**:674, **9**:675
Baker, Florence **9**:710
Baker, Samuel **9**:710
Bakewell, Lucy **1**:55, **1**:56
Ballantyne, J. M. **7**:530
Ballard, Robert **4**:311, **7**:544, **10**:726–727
Bancroft, Ann **7**:555, **7**:558, **10**:792
Banks, Joseph **1**:69–71, **2**:85, **3**:197, **3**:198, **4**:251, **4**:270, **4**:314, **6**:454, **7**:486, **7**:533, **7**:534, **10**:764
Barents, Willem **7**:503, **7**:504, **7**:512, **7**:513, **7**:554, **7**:556

Barison, Giuseppe **6**:455
Barros, João de **3**:225, **4**:291
Barrow, John **4**:254, **4**:275
Barton, Otis **10**:724
Bass, George **4**:268
Bates, Henry Walter **7**:487, **10**:777, **10**:*778*, **10**:779
Baudin, Nicolas **4**:269
Beattie, Dr. Owen **4**:278
Beaufort, Francis **10**:783
Beaufoy, Henry **4**:251, **4**:252
Beauharnois, Charles de **5**:395, **5**:396
Becknell, William **2**:145
Bede, Venerable **10**:741
Bedford, Francis **7**:543
Beebe, William **10**:724, **10**:725, **10**:726
Behaim, Martin **4**:303, **6**:429
Belalcázar, Sebastián de **1**:72–75, **9**:704
Bell, Alexander Graham **3**:190, **3**:192
Bell, Gertrude **1**:76–78, **10**:788, **10**:790
Bell, Mark **10**:793
Bellingshausen, Fabian Gottlieb von **2**:84–86, **7**:554, **7**:556, **8**:613, **8**:614, **9**:656, **9**:689
Benalcázar *see* Belalcázar, Sebastián de
Bennett, Floyd **1**:60, **1**:62, **2**:103, **2**:119, **3**:237
Bennett, Gordon **9**:711
Bent, Charles **2**:145
Benton, Thomas Hart **4**:279, **4**:280
Berghaus, Heinrich **4**:252–253, **4**:254, **4**:255
Bering, Vitus Jonassen **2**:87–90, **7**:512, **7**:514, **8**:612, **8**:614, **8**:624, **8**:626–627
Bernoulli, Daniel **10**:742
Berrio, Antonio de **8**:600
Beuningen, Gerrit van **5**:348
Bierstadt, Albert **1**:*35*
Billings, Joseph **8**:613
Bingham, George Caleb **2**:95
Bingham, Hiram **4**:256
Bird, Isabella Lucy *see* Bishop, Isabella Lucy
Bishop, Isabella Lucy **2**:91–93, **10**:788, **10**:789
Bjaarland, Olav **1**:21
Bjarni Herjolfsson **6**:406

Bjorn, son of Gudrid **4**:318
Blaeu, Jan **9**:*687*, **10**:733
Blanchard, Jean-Pierre **1**:62
Blériot, Louis **1**:*59*
Blessing, Henrik **7**:554
Bligh, Captain William **4**:268, **9**:656
Boas, Franz **1**:23, **1**:24, **1**:25
Bobadilla, Francisco de **3**:185, **3**:189
Bonpland, Aimé **5**:355–356, **5**:357, **7**:486, **7**:487
Boone, Daniel **2**:94–96
Bougainville, Hyacinthe **2**:100
Bougainville, Louis-Antoine de **2**:97–100, **4**:273, **4**:274, **6**:471, **7**:486, **9**:655
Boullé, Hélène **2**:158
Bourdillon, Tom **5**:339
Bouvet de Lozier, Jean-Baptiste Charles **9**:688
Bowers, Henry **8**:629
Boxer, C. R. **10**:751
Boyd, Louise Arner **2**:101–103, **10**:788, **10**:790
Boyle, Robert **10**:756, **10**:760
Bradbury, Ray **7**:530, **7**:532
Braddock, General James **2**:94
Brahe, Tycho **1**:49
Brahe, William **2**:111, **2**:112
Bransfield, Edward **2**:85, **9**:689
Braun, Wernher von **9**:690
Brendan **2**:104–106
Bressant, Father **6**:451
Bridger, Jim **1**:31, **2**:107–109, **2**:145, **9**:667
Broughton, Lieutenant **10**:763
Brouwer, Hendrik **7**:504, **7**:505, **10**:734
Brulé, Étienne **2**:157
Bry, Theodore de **7**:505, **8**:570
Bryan, Rebecca **2**:94, **2**:96
Buade, Louis de, Comte de Frontenac **5**:384, **5**:386
Buchan, David **4**:313
Buchanan, James **3**:193
Buckingham, duke of **6**:455
Burke, Robert O'Hara **2**:110–112, **4**:299, **4**:314, **6**:470, **6**:473
Burr, Aaron **7**:547
Burton, Richard Francis **2**:113–117, **4**:253, **4**:255, **4**:314, **5**:366, **5**:368, **6**:417, **9**:707–708, **9**:709, **9**:710
Bush, George W. **9**:699

Button, Thomas **7**:516, **7**:518

Bykovsky, Valery **8**:*615*

Bylot, Robert **1**:67, **1**:68, **7**:516, **7**:518

Byrd, Richard E. **1**:60, **1**:62, **2**:103, **2**:118–121, **3**:237, **7**:555

Byron, Captain John **2**:148

Cabeza de Vaca, Alvar Núñez **2**:122–125, **3**:201, **6**:463, **6**:464, **6**:465

Cabot, John **2**:126–128, **2**:129, **2**:131, **3**:177, **3**:220, **5**:324, **6**:406, **6**:474, **9**:652, **9**:654, **10**:751, **10**:765

Cabot, Sebastian **2**:127, **2**:129–132, **3**:220, **5**:324, **6**:406, **7**:511

Cabral, Pedro Álvares **2**:133–135, **3**:223, **3**:225, **4**:293, **8**:574, **10**:743

Cabrillo, Juan Rodríguez **2**:136–138

Cadamosto, Alvise da **5**:332, **5**:335

Caillié, René-Auguste **4**:252, **4**:273, **4**:274, **7**:536

Callimachus of Cyrene **4**:244

Camões, Luis Vaz de **8**:575

Campbell, John **7**:495, **7**:502

Cão, Diogo **3**:223, **3**:224, **8**:574, **8**:575

Cárdenas, García López de **3**:202, **3**:203

Carpenter, M. Scott **9**:645

Carson, Kit (Christopher) **2**:144–147, **4**:280

Carteret, Philip **2**:148–150, **9**:655

Cartier, Jacques **2**:151–154, **2**:155, **3**:220, **4**:271, **4**:272, **4**:273, **10**:764

Cassini, Dian Domenico **9**:680

Catherine the Great (Catherine II) **8**:613

Champlain, Samuel de **2**:155–158, **3**:179, **4**:272, **5**:353, **5**:366, **9**::653, **9**:655

Chancellor, Richard **7**:511–512

Chang Chi'en (Zhang Qian) **4**:300, **9**:659, **9**:660, **10**:796–798

Chappe, Claude **3**:190, **3**:191

Charbonneau, Toussaint **6**:410, **8**:616–618

Charles I, king of England **3**:178

Charles II, king of England **4**:264, **5**:391

Charles I, king of Spain **1**:72, **6**:422, **6**:463, **6**:464, **9**:682, **9**:683 see also Charles V, Holy Roman emperor

Charles IV, king of Spain **5**:355

Charles V, Holy Roman Emperor **2**:131, **6**:463

Charles, Jacques **10**:784

Charner, Léonard **4**:295

Chaves, Jeronimo de **9**:685

Cheng Ho **3**:164–167, **3**:191, **6**:454, **6**:455

Chkalov, Valery **8**:615

Christy, Henry **10**:753, **10**:754

Chu Chan-chi **3**:167

Chu Kao-chih **3**:167

Chu Ti, Prince **3**:164, **3**:165, **3**:166, **3**:*167*

Clark, William **6**:408–412, **8**:616–618, **8**:625, **9**:654, **10**:783, **10**:787

Clarke, Arthur C. **3**:195, **7**:532

Claudius, Emperor **8**:589

Clement IV, Pope **8**:564

Clement VII, Pope **4**:271, **4**:272, **6**:448, **6**:450

Clement VIII, Pope **8**:595

Clerke, Charles **3**:200

Cockerell, C. R. **6**:457

Coen, Jan Pieterszoon **7**:504

Colbert, Jean-Baptiste **6**:440, **6**:442, **6**:443

Coleridge, Samuel Taylor **8**:567

Collins, Eileen 791, **10**:791

Collins, Michael **1**:28, **1**:29

Columbus, Bartolomeo **3**:188

Columbus, Christopher **2**:105, **2**:126, **2**:127, **3**:175, **3**:176, **3**:181, **3**:182, **3**:184–189, **3**:204, **3**:220, **3**:223, **3**:231, **3**:232, **4**:260–263, **4**:302, **4**:303, **5**:338, **5**:370, **6**:422, **6**:429, **6**:431, **6**:451, **6**:453, **6**:454, **6**:462, **6**:470, **6**:474, **7**:494

Columbus, Diego **3**:189, **6**:462

Columbus, Hernando **2**:127

Commerson, Philibert de **7**:486

Condoy, Julio Garcia **7**:551

Confucius **10**:796

Cook, Frederick Albert **4**:255, **7**:539–540

Cook, James **2**:84, **2**:85, **2**:86, **3**:169, **3**:180, **3**:196–200, **3**:212, **4**:252, **4**:269, **4**:270, **4**:299, **4**:303, **4**:314, **5**:368, **6**:430, **6**:470, **6**:471, **7**:486, **7**:502, **7**:554, **7**:556, **8**:626, **9**:651, **9**:655, **9**:656, **9**:688–689, **10**:733

Cooper, James Fenimore **2**:96

Cooper, L. Gordon, Jr. **9**:645

Copernicus, Nicolaus **1**:44, **1**:49, **3**:233, **7**:484, **7**:486, **8**:591, **9**:676, **9**:680

Coronado, Francisco Vásquez de **3**:201–203, **6**:477, **7**:525

Coronelli, Vincenzo **6**:*438*

Corry, Captain **6**:431

Cortés, Hernán **2**:136, **3**:182, **3**:204–208, **5**:376, **6**:439, **6**:455, **6**:462–464, **6**:478, **7**:522, **7**:523, **9**:*704*, **9**:705, **9**:706

Cortés, Martín **3**:206

Cortés, Tolosa **7**:523

Cotton, Robert **6**:456

Courten, William **6**:456

Cousin, Jean **7**:549

Cousteau, Jacques-Yves **3**:209–211, **4**:274, **10**:758, **10**:760, **10**:761

Crean, Thomas **8**:638

Cromwell, Oliver **6**:440

Cronin, Vincent **8**:611

Crosby, Alfred **3**:181

Crozier, Francis **4**:276, **4**:277, **4**:278

Cunningham, Alan **1**:70, **4**:314

Curzon, George **10**:794

Dablon, Claude **6**:438, **6**:450, **6**:451

Daguerre, Louis-Jacques-Mandé **7**:541, **7**:542

Dalrymple, Alexander **9**:689

Dampier, William **2**:149, **3**:212–215, **4**:313, **9**:651, **9**:655

Dance, Lieutenant **1**:*19*

Dandonneau du Sablé, Marie-Anne **5**:394, **5**:396

Dannett, Captain **4**:276

Dare, Virginia **8**:603

Darius III, king of the Persians **1**:15, **1**:16

Darwin, Charles **3**:212, **3**:216–219, **4**:264, **4**:265, **4**:266, **4**:267, **5**:357, **7**:486, **7**:487–488, **7**:494, **10**:777, **10**:780

Darwin, Emma **3**:219

Darwin, Erasmus **3**:216

David, Jacques-Louis **1**:55, **2**:100

Dávila, Pedro Arias **1**:72, **7**:521, **7**:522, **9**:683

Davis, John **1**:67, **1**:68, **7**:494, **7**:500, **7**:516, **7**:518

Daza, Louis de **1**:74

Dease, Peter **7**:519

Defoe, Daniel **3**:213, **3**:214, **3**:*215*, **4**:268, **7**:530

Delaporte, Louis **4**:295

de la Roche, Antoine **9**:688

de las Casas, Bartolomé **6**:472

del Conte, Jacopino **8**:609

de le Torre, Bernard **10**:743

Dellenbaugh, Frederick **8**:579

de Monts, Sieur see Gua, Pierre du

de Moucheron, **5**:349

Desceliers, Pierre **2**:*154*, **6**:431

de Solís, Juan Díaz **7**:551, **7**:552

Dezhnyov, Semyon **8**:612, **8**:614

Dias, Bartolomeu **2**:133, **3**:222–225, **4**:291, **4**:293, **4**:299, **6**:474, **7**:500, **8**:574, **8**:575, **8**:593, **10**:743, **10**:749

Dias, Dinis **5**:332, **5**:335

Dicaearchus of Messina **5**:388

Din, Rashid al- **9**:662

Dodge, Grenville **2**:109

Dollier, François **5**:38

Drake, Francis **3**:226–228, **4**:285, **4**:287, **4**:312, **5**:326, **5**:366, **6**:440, **8**:598, **8**:599, **9**:651, **9**:654, **9**:687, **9**:706

Drake, Frank **8**:632

Dudley, Ambrose, earl of Warwick **4**:285

Dupré, Marie-Jules **4**:296–297

Dupuis, Jean **4**:296, **4**:297

Durrance, Samuel **1**:*40*

Eannes, Gil **5**:332, **5**:335

Earhart, Amelia **10**:788, **10**:789

Earle, Sylvia **10**:759

Eastman, George **7**:541, **7**:542

Edwards, William Henry **10**:777

Eilson, Carl Ben **1**:61, **1**:62

Einstein, Albert **1**:50–51, **9**:677

Elcano, Sebastián de **6**:426

Elizabeth I **3**:226, **3**:228, **4**:285, **4**:312, **5**:325, **5**:326, **6**:*440*, **6**:441, **8**:598, **8**:600, **9**:669

Elizabeth II **5**:340

Ellsworth, Lincoln **1**:18, **1**:21, **1**:60, **1**:62, **2**:119, **3**:235–238

Emery, Josiah **7**:495

Eratosthenes of Cyrene **1**:50, **4**:244–247, **4**:298, **4**:299, **5**:345, **5**:390

Erik the Red **4**:248–250, **4**:316, **6**:404, **10**:774, **10**:775

Estrada, Beatriz **3**:201

Euler, Leonhard **10**:742

Evans, Charles **5**:339

Evans, Edgar **8**:629, **8**:630

Everest, George **5**:341, **10**:731

Eyre, Edward John **6**:473

Fa-hsien see Faxian

Faisal I, king of Iraq **1**:78

Faxian **4**:257–259, **4**:*299*, **4**:300, **9**:660

Fedorov, Eugeny **8**:614

Ferdinand, king of Spain **3**:184, **3**:185, **3**:186, **3**:187, **3**:188, **4**:260–263, **4**:303, **6**:463, **8**:569, **8**:571, **9**:703, **9**:704

Ferrelo, Bartolomé **2**:138

Fiennes, Ranulph **4**:255, **4**:315

Filson, John **2**:95

Findlay, John **2**:94–95

Fisher, George **3**:214

Fitzroy, Robert **3**:216–217, **3**:218, **4**:264–267, **7**:486, **7**:487

Flamsteed, John **5**:393

Flinders, Matthew **1**:71, **4**:268–270, **4**:275, **4**:314

Ford, Edsel **2**:118

Forest, Lee de **3**:193

Forster, Johann Georg Adam **7**:486

Forster, Johann Reinhold **7**:486

Foxe, Luke **4**:287, **7**:516, **7**:518

Fox Talbot, W. H. **7**:541, **7**:542

Francis I, Holy Roman emperor **10**:753

Francis I, king of France **2**:151, **2**:152, **2**:153, **2**:154, **4**:271, **6**:448, **10**:765, **10**:766, **10**:767, **10**:768

Franklin, John **4**:252, **4**:275–278, **4**:313, **7**:517, **7**:518, **7**:519

Fraser, Simon **4**:313

Fray Marcos de Niza **3**:201, **3**:202

Frémont, Charles **4**:279

Frémont, Jessie Benton **4**:279, **4**:280, **4**:281, **10**:788

Frémont, John Charles **2**:145–146, **2**:147, **4**:279–283

Freuchen, Peter **8**:627

Freydis Eriksdottir **4**:248, **4**:316, **6**:407

Frisius, Gemma **6**:444, **6**:445, **7**:495

Frith, Francis **7**:542, **7**:543

Frobisher, Martin **3**:172, **4**:284–287, **4**:313, **6**:470, **6**:473, **7**:515, **7**:518, **8**:603

Frontenac, Louis de Buade, Comte de **5**:384, **5**:386

Fuchs, Vivian **5**:340

Fulton, Robert **9**:648

Furneaux, Tobias **3**:199

Gaffarel, Jacques **10**:752–753, **10**:754

Gagarin, Yury **1**:37, **1**:38, **1**:40, **4**:288–290, **4**:306, **8**:615, **9**:644, **9**:692, **9**:695, **9**:696, **10**:791

Gagnan, Émile **3**:209, **3**:210, **10**:758, **10**:760

Galilei, Galileo **1**:44, **1**:49, **1**:50, **3**:233, **7**:484, **7**:532, **9**:680, **10**:782

Galinée, René de **5**:384

Galle, Johann Gottfried **9**:681

Galton, Francis **4**:256

Gama, Paolo da **4**:291

Gama, Vasco da **2**:133, **2**:135,

2:143, **3**:222, **3**:223, **3**:224, **3**:231, **4**:291–294, **4**:298, **4**:302–303, **5**:366, **6**:476, **8**:574, **8**:575, **9**:650, **9**:651, **9**:654, **9**:660, **9**:686–687, **10**:749, **10**:751

Ganswindt, Hermann **9**:690

Garcia, Stephanus, **3**:230

Garnier, Francis **4**:274, **4**:295–297

Gaspar à Myrica **6**:444, **6**:447

Gates, Horatio **6**:409

Gautama Siddhartha, Prince **4**:259

Genghis Khan **3**:190, **3**:191, **9**:661

Gentz, Wilhelm **10**:744

George III **1**:52, **1**:71, **6**:420, **6**:421

Gilbert, Humphrey, **7**:515

Glaisher, James **10**:784

Glenn, John **1**:37, **1**:38, **4**:306–308, **9**:645

Goddard, Robert **1**:37, **1**:38, **9**:690

Goldin, Dan **4**:308

Golding, William **7**:530

Gomes, Fernão **8**:574

Goodacre, Glenna **8**:618

Goode, J. Paul **6**:435

Gosnold, Bartholomew **3**:182

Gosse, Philip Henry **7**:488

Grant, James Augustus **9**:707, **9**:709

Gray, Charles **2**:111

Greene, Henry **5**:353

Gregory X, Pope **8**:565

Grenville, Richard **8**:598, **8**:599

Grinnell, George Bird **1**:58

Grissom, Virgil "Gus" **4**:306, **9**:645

Gromov, Mikhail **8**:615

Gua, Pierre du (Sieur de Monts) **2**:156

Gudrid (Gudridur Thorbjarnarsdottir) **4**:316–318, **10**:787, **10**:788

Gulliver, Lemuel **7**:529

Gunnbjörn Ulf-Krakason **4**:249

Gunter, Edmund **10**:729, **10**:730

Haakon VII, king of Norway **2**:101

Hadley, John **1**:46, **7**:495, **7**:501

Haggard, H. Rider **6**:477

Hakluyt, Richard **5**:324–327

Hall, Charles **9**:674

Hall, James **1**:66

Halley, Edmond **1**:53, **4**:252, **9**:688

Hallveig Einarsdottir **4**:316

Hancock, Thomas **3**:172

Hanno of Carthage **5**:328–330, **8**:602

Hanssen, Helmer **1**:21

Harbaugh, Gregory **1**:47

Harley, Robert **6**:456

Harold, king of England **1**:53

Harriot, Thomas **8**:598, **8**:603

Harrison, John **1**:43, **3**:168–169, **3**:232, **5**:388, **5**:391, **5**:393, **7**:495

Harun al-Rashid, caliph **2**:140

Hasselborough, Frederick **9**:689

Hassel, Sverre **1**:21

Hatshepsut **6**:474, **6**:477

Hawkins, John **3**:182, **3**:226, **4**:312

Hearne, Samuel **10**:735, **10**:736

Hecataeus **4**:298, **4**:299

Heinlein, Robert **7**:532

Hennepin, Father Louis **5**:384, **5**:385, **5**:387

Henry VII, king of England **2**:126

Henry VIII, king of England **2**:130, **7**:511

Henry IV, king of France **2**:155, **3**:178, **4**:272

Henry the Navigator **3**:175, **4**:298, **4**:302, **5**:331–335, **8**:573, **8**:574, **9**:650, **9**:651, **9**:654

Henry, Andrew **1**:30, **9**:665

Henry, Joseph **3**:190, **3**:192, **9**:673, **9**:675, **10**:783

Henslow, John **3**:216

Henson, Matthew **5**:370, **7**:538, **7**:539

Heracles (Hercules) **9**:718

Herbert, Wally **4**:255

Herodotus **4**:299, **4**:300, **5**:330, **6**:428, **7**:494, **7**:497, **9**:718

Herschel, William **1**:50, **1**:52, **9**:680

Heuglin, Theodor von **10**:745

Hevelius, Johannes **1**:43, **7**:532

Heyerdahl, Thor **5**:336–338, **9**:658

Hillary, Edmund **3**:192, **4**:253, **4**:315, **5**:339–341, **7**:543

Himilco **6**:474, **6**:477

Hipparchus **1**:50, **5**:342–345, **8**:590

Hippocrates **10**:781

Hoffman, Jeffrey **1**:40

Holbein, Ambrosius **7**:531

Hollick-Kenyon, Herbert **1**:62, **3**:236, **3**:238

Homer **7**:489, **7**:527, **7**:528

Hondius, Jodocus **7**:506

Hood, Robert **4**:275

Houtman, Cornelis **5**:346–349, **7**:504, **9**:654

Houtman, Frederik **5**:346–347, **5**:349, **9**:654

Howard, Lord Charles **9**:706

Howard, Luke **10**:785

Hsüan-tsang **4**:300, **9**:660, **9**:661, **9**:663

Hubble, Edwin **1**:47, **1**:51, **9**:677

Hudson, Henry **1**:66–67, **4**:313,

5:325, **5**:350–353, **7**:504, **7**:506, **7**:512, **7**:513, **7**:516, **7**:518, **7**:553, **7**:554

Hudson, John **5**:351

Humboldt, Alexander von **3**:233, **4**:252–253, **4**:254, **4**:255, **4**:305, **5**:354–357, **6**:452, **6**:454, **7**:486–487, **10**:745

Hungerford, Henry **9**:672

Hunt, John **4**:315, **5**:339

Hurd, Thomas **4**:265

Hurley, Frank **7**:542, **7**:543, **8**:604, **8**:636

Hutchins, Thomas **10**:730

Huxley, Aldous **7**:528, **7**:530

Huxley, Thomas Henry **4**:267, **7**:488

Hythloday, Raphael **7**:531

Ibn Battutah **5**:358–361

Ibn Juzay **5**:361

Ibn Khalaf, Ahmad **7**:500

Ibn Khordadhbeh **5**:363

Idrisi, al-Sharif al- **5**:362–365, **6**:428

Innocent IV, Pope **9**:662

Irvine, Andrew **4**:315, **5**:341, **10**:795

Irving, Washington **1**:32, **1**:35

Isabella, queen of Spain **3**:175, **3**:184, **3**:185, **3**:186, **3**:187, **3**:188, **4**:260–263, **4**:303, **9**:703, **9**:704

Istakhri, al- **6**:429

Ita (abbess) **2**:105

Ivan IV, Czar (Ivan the Terrible) **2**:132, **7**:512

Ivanov, Kurbat **8**:613

Jackson, Frederick **6**:458, **6**:461

Jackson, William H. **7**:543

James I (James VI), king of England **3**:177, **8**:600, **9**:669, **9**:670

James IV, king of Scotland **4**:312

James, duke of York **7**:506

James, Thomas **4**:287, **7**:516, **7**:518

Jane, John **5**:327

Jansky, Karl **1**:46, **1**:51

Jansz, Willem **3**:198, **7**:504

Jaramillo, Maria Josefa **2**:144, **2**:145, **2**:146, **2**:147

Jefferson, Thomas **6**:408, **6**:409, **6**:411, **6**:412

Jeffries, John **1**:62

Jenkins, Robert **6**:439

Johansen, Hjalmar **6**:458, **6**:460, **6**:461, **8**:627

John II, king of Castile **9**:703

John I, king of Portugal **5**:331, **8**:573, **8**:574

John II, king of Portugal **3**:184, **3**:185, **3**:222, **3**:223, **4**:261, **8**:575
John of Piano Carpini **9**:660, **9**:662
Johnson, Donald **5**:351
Jolliet, Louis **4**:272, **4**:273, **5**:371–372, **6**:436–438
Juana La Loca, queen of Castile **4**:*260*
Juet, Robert **5**:353
Justinian, Emperor **9**:*659*

Kagge, Erling **7**:555, **7**:558
Karlsefni, Thorfinn **4**:316, **4**:317, **4**:318, **6**:405, **6**:407, **10**:787
Keats, John **7**:522
Kelsey, Henry **10**:751
Kelvin, Baron see Thompson, William
Kendall, Larcum **3**:169
Kennedy, John F. **1**:28, **6**:466, **6**:467, **8**:621
Kennicott, Robert **9**:675
Kepler, Johannes **1**:49, **1**:50, **3**:233, **7**:485, **9**:676
Kerguélen-Trémarec, Yves-Joseph de **9**:688
King, Clarence **8**:580
King, John **2**:111, **6**:470, **6**:473
King, Philip Parker **4**:264
Kingsley, Mary Henrietta **4**:315, **10**:788, **10**:790
Kino, Eusebio Francisco **5**:373–375
Knutson, Paul **8**:624, **8**:625
Kotzebue, Otto von **8**:612
Kremer, Gerhard see Mercator, Gerardus
Krenitsyn, Petr **8**:613
Krenkel, Ernest **8**:614
Kublai Khan **8**:564, **8**:566–568, **9**:660, **9**:662, **9**:663

Lagrée, Ernest Doudart de **4**:295, **4**:296
Lane, Ralph **8**:598, **8**:599
Laplace, Simon de **10**:742
Lartet, Édouard-Armand-Isidore-Hippolyte **10**:753, **10**:754
La Salle, René-Robert Cavelier de **5**:383–387, **6**:438
La Vérendrye, François **5**:398
La Vérendrye, Jacques-René **5**:396
La Vérendrye, Jean-Baptiste **5**:395, **5**:397
La Vérendrye, Louis **5**:398
La Vérendrye, Pierre **5**:395, **5**:398
La Vérendrye, Pierre Gaultier de Varennes de **5**:394–398, **8**:625
Lawrence, Thomas **6**:418

Lawson, John **8**:599
Lazarev, Mikhail **2**:84
Leif Eriksson **2**:105, **3**:231, **4**:248, **4**:301, **4**:316, **4**:317, **4**:318, **6**:404–407, **7**:550, **8**:624, **10**:743, **10**:775, **10**:776
Le Maire, Jakob **7**:504, **7**:505, **10**:734
Lemoine, Auguste **2**:152
Le Moyne, Jacques **6**:470
Leonov, Alexei **1**:38
Lescarbot, Marc **6**:470
le Tetsu, Guillaume **6**:*475*
Levashov, Mikhail **8**:613
Leverrier, Urbain-Jean-Joseph **9**:681
Lewis, Meriwether **6**:408–412, **8**:616–618, **8**:625, **9**:654, **10**:783, **10**:787
Li Madou see Ricci, Matteo
Lind, James **8**:584
Linnaeus, Carolus (Carl von Linné) **1**:71, **7**:486, **7**:487, **8**:624, **8**:626
Lippershey, Hans **1**:44, **1**:46
Liu Ch'e see Wu Ti
Livingstone, David **2**:143, **4**:253, **4**:255, **4**:299, **4**:314, **5**:366, **5**:369, **6**:413–417, **6**:452, **6**:472, **7**:501, **9**:*652*, **9**:710, **9**:711–712
Lopes, Tomé **4**:294
Louis IX, king of France **9**:663
Louis XIV, king of France **4**:272, **5**:*383*, **5**:386, **6**:442, **6**:*443*
Louis XV, king of France **2**:99, **2**:100
Lounge, John **1**:*40*
Loyola, Ignatius **8**:609
Lucian of Samosata **7**:528, **7**:532
Lucretia, Caroline **1**:52
Lysanias of Cyrene **4**:244
Lysippos **1**:14

McArthur, Ellen **10**:789, **10**:792
McCandless, Bruce **1**:*38*
McClintock, Francis **4**:277
McClure, Robert **7**:518, **7**:519
MacGillivray, William **1**:58
Macguire, Thomas **4**:276
Macie, James see Smithson, James Lewis
Macintosh, Charles **3**:172
Mackenzie, Alexander **4**:313, **6**:408, **6**:418–421, **9**:654, **10**:751
McNeish, Harry "Chips" **8**:636
Maetsuyker, Joan **7**:504
Magellan, Ferdinand **2**:130–131, **3**:231, **4**:299, **4**:302, **5**:366, **6**:422–426, **8**:574, **9**:650, **9**:651,

9:653, **9**:654, **9**:687, **9**:688, **9**:704–705, **10**:749, **10**:751
Makarov, S. O. **8**:612, **8**:614
Mallory, George **4**:315, **5**:341, **10**:795
Malthus, Thomas Robert **10**:779
Mandeville, John **5**:333, **7**:527, **7**:528
Mansa Musa **2**:143, **6**:*471*
Manuel I, king of Portugal **2**:133, **2**:135, **4**:291, **6**:422
Marconi, Guglielmo **3**:190, **3**:193
Marinus of Tyre **8**:591
Markham, Clement **4**:255
Marquette, Jacques **4**:272, **4**:273, **5**:371, **6**:436–438
Marsili, Luigi Ferdinando **10**:756, **10**:760
Martel, Édouard-Alfred **10**:754, **10**:755
Martellus, Henricus **5**:*332*
Ma San-pao (Ma Ho) see Cheng Ho
Matoaka see Pocahontas
Matta, Jeronymo de **6**:452
Mauro, Fra **5**:333
Maury, Matthew Fontaine **10**:757
Mead, Margaret **1**:23, **1**:25, **1**:26
Medici, Ferdinand II de' **10**:782
Medici, Lorenzo de **6**:453, **6**:*454*
Megasthenes **4**:246
Méliès, Georges **7**:528, **7**:532
Mendaña de Neira, Alvaro **8**:594–595, **8**:596
Mendoza, Antonio de **2**:137, **3**:201, **3**:202–203
Mendoza, Luis de **6**:424
Menzies, Archibald **10**:764
Mercator, Gerardus **6**:429, **6**:434–435, **6**:444–447
Michael, Czar **7**:512, **7**:513
Michiel, Giovanni **2**:132
Miller, Alfred Jacob **10**:750
Minuit, Peter **7**:506
Mirza Abdullah see Burton, Richard Francis
Mitchell, Edgar D. **9**:*646*
Mitchell, Samuel **1**:58
Moffat, Mary **6**:414, **6**:452
Moffat, Robert **6**:414, **6**:452
Mollard, Jean **3**:210
Montaigne, Michel Eyquem de **6**:471
Montezuma **3**:206
Montezuma II **3**:206, **3**:207
Montgolfier, Jacques Étienne **1**:59, **1**:*61*, **1**:62, **10**:784
Montgolfier, Joseph-Michel **1**:59,

1:*61*, **1**:62, **10**:784
More, Thomas **7**:528, **7**:530, **7**:*531*
Morse, Samuel **3**:190, **3**:191, **3**:192
Moskvitin, Ivan **8**:612, **8**:614
Mounteney-Jephson, A. J. **9**:*715*
Moyano, Sebastián see Belalcázar, Sebastián de
Muhammad **6**:431
Muhammad ibn Tughluq, Sultan **5**:360
Munster, Sebastian **10**:*766*
Muybridge, Eadweard **7**:543

Nagel, J. A. **10**:753, **10**:754
Nagursky, Jan **1**:60, **1**:62
Nansen, Fridtjof **1**:19, **6**:458–461, **7**:510, **7**:537, **7**:554, **7**:555, **8**:624, **8**:627
Napoleon Bonaparte **2**:100, **6**:408, **6**:409
Narváez, Pánfilo de **2**:122, **2**:136, **3**:207, **6**:462–465, **6**:477, **9**:684
Nattier, Marc **6**:443
Nearchus **1**:17, **4**:246
Neck, Jacob van **7**:504
Nelson, Horatio **8**:*601*
Nelson, R. H. **9**:*715*
Newport, Christopher **4**:313
Newton, Isaac **1**:45, **1**:46, **1**:49, **1**:50, **1**:51, **1**:53, **3**:233, **5**:393, **8**:620, **9**:677
Nicholas of Cusa **10**:782
Nicolet, Jean **2**:158
Niepce, Joseph-Nicéfore **7**:541, **7**:542
Nobile, Umberto **1**:18, **1**:21, **2**:101, **3**:236, **3**:237, **3**:238
Noonan, Fred **10**:789
Nordenskiöld, Nils Adolf Erik **7**:507–510, **7**:511, **7**:512, **7**:514, **8**:624, **8**:627, **9**:655
Northrop, W. B. **10**:780
Norton, Edward **5**:341
Nugent, Jim (Rocky Mountain Jim) **2**:93
Núñez de Balboa, Vasco **6**:422, **7**:520–522, **9**:704

Oates, Lawrence **5**:370, **8**:629, **8**:630, **8**:*631*
Oberth, Hermann **9**:690
Ojeda, Alonso de **2**:128, **6**:462, **10**:770, **10**:771
O'Keefe, Sean **1**:48
Olaf Tryggvason **6**:404
Oleson, Olaf **8**:625
Olmeda, Father **6**:465
Ommanney, Erasmus **4**:276

Oñate, Juan de **7:523–526**
Orellana, Francisco de **9:**652, **9:**654
Ortelius, Abraham **6:**425, **6:**429, **8:**610, **8:***611*
Ortiz, Juan **6:**464
Orwell, George **7:**530
Oscar II, king of Sweden and Norway **7:**509
Oswell, William **6:**414
Ousland, Borge **8:**625, **8:**627
Ovando, Nicolás de **8:**569, **8:**570
Owen, Robert **10:**780

Palmer, Nathaniel D. **2:**85, **7:**556, **9:**689
Papanin, Ivan **8:**614
Park, Mungo **1:**70, **4:**251, **7:533–536**
Parke, Thomas Heazle **9:***715*
Parkinson, Sydney **1:**69
Parkman, Francis **5:**372
Parma, duke of **9:**706
Parry, William **7:**517, **7:**518, **7:**554, **7:**555
Paul III, Pope **6:**470, **6:**472
Peary, Robert E. **1:**19, **1:**60, **3:**231, **3:**237, **4:**253, **4:**255, **5:**366, **5:**370, **5:**381, **7:**502, **7:537–540**, **7:**554
Pedrarias *see* Dávila, Pedro Arias
Penny, William **4:**276
Peralta, Don Pedro de **7:**524
Perestello e Moniz, Felipa **3:**184
Peters, Arno **6:**434
Peter the Great, Czar **2:**87, **2:**89, **7:**514, **8:**612
Philip II, king of Macedonia **1:**14
Philip II, king of Spain and Portugal **5:**388, **8:**594, **8:***597*, **9:**704
Philip III, king of Spain **8:**595
Philip of Bourbon **5:**394
Philip of Macedonia **10:**753
Philopater **4:**244
Piccard, Auguste **1:**61, **10:**725, **10:**726
Piccard, Jacques **10:**725
Piccard, Jean **1:**61
Pigafetta, Antonio **6:**425, **6:**426
Pike, Zebulon Montgomery **7:545–548**
Pinzón, Francisco **7:**550
Pinzón, Martín Alonso **7:549–550**, **7:**551
Pinzón, Vicente Yáñez **7:**550, **7:551–552**
Pitcairn, Robert **2:**150
Pitt Rivers, Augustus Henry Lane Fox **1:**24
Pizarro, Francisco **1:**72–73, **1:**74,

3:176–177, **5:**379, **6:**439, **6:**475, **6:**478, **7:**521, **9:**682, **9:**683, **9:**704, **9:**705
Pizarro, Gonzalo **9:**652
Plato **7:**529, **7:**530
Pliny the Elder **5:**329, **5:**330
Pocahontas **6:**464, **9:**668, **9:**669
Pocock, Frank **9:**714
Polk, James **4:**283
Polo, Maffeo **8:**564, **8:**565, **8:**566
Polo, Marco **1:**22, **2:**126, **4:**301, **5:**361, **6:**478, **8:564–568**, **8:**586, **9:**647, **9:**660, **9:**663, **10:**748, **10:**749, **10:**751, **10:**798
Polo, Niccolò **8:**564, **8:**565, **8:**566, **8:***568*
Polyakov, Valeri V. **8:**615, **9:***694*
Ponce de León, Juan **8:569–572**, **9:**704, **10:**765
Ponce de León, Luis **3:**204, **3:**208
Pond, Peter **6:**418
Ponting, Herbert **7:**558, **8:**604, **8:***630*
Powell, John Wesley **8:577–580**
Powhatan, Chief **9:**668, **9:**669
Prescott, William H. **6:**465
Prester John **5:**332, **5:**333, **7:**528
Provins, Guy de **7:**493
Przhevalsky, Nikolay **8:585–588**, **8:**613
Ptahhotep **9:**647
Ptolemy III **4:**244, **4:**245
Ptolemy, Claudius **4:**300, **4:**302, **5:**345, **5:**363, **7:**484, **8:589–593**, **9:**676, **9:**680, **9:**686, **9:**688, **9:**715, **9:**718
Purchas, Samuel **1:**68, **5:**327
Pythagoras **4:**246, **6:**428, **9:**686
Pytheas of Massalia **4:**246, **4:**247, **9:**717, **9:**718

Quast, Matthijs **10:**732
Quen, Jean de **6:**450, **6:**451
Querini, Pietro **1:**22, **1:**23
Quicheberg, Samuel van **6:**454
Quintilian **8:**608
Quirós, Pedro Fernández de **8:594–597, 9:**655, **9:**687, **9:**688

Rabin, Jean Fougère *see* Audubon, John James
Rae, John **4:**276, **4:**313
Raleigh, Walter **3:**228, **4:**285, **4:**287, **4:**313, **5:**324, **5:**325, **5:**326, **8:598–600, 8:**603
Rasmussen, Knud **8:**627
Real, Gaspar Corte **2:**128
Rebecca *see* Pocahontas

Reber, Grote **1:**46
Remington, Frederic **9:**666
Renwick, James, Jr. **9:**672
Ricci, Matteo **8:608–611**
Richards, Emma **8:***604*
Richardson, John **4:**275
Richelieu, Cardinal **2:**158, **6:**450
Ride, Sally **1:**42, **10:**789, **10:**791
Ritter, Carl **4:***252*, **4:**253, **4:**254, **4:**305
Roberval, Jean-François de la Roque, sieur de **2:**153, **2:**154
Robinson, Bradley **5:**370
Robledo, Jorge **1:**75
Rockefeller, John D. **2:**118
Rocky Mountain Jim *see* Nugent, Jim
Roger II, king of Sicily **4:**301, **5:**362, **5:**363–364
Rolfe, John **9:**669
Roosa, Stuart A. **9:***646*
Roosevelt, Theodore **9:**674
Ross, James Clark **7:**554, **7:**556–557
Ross, John **8:**583
Rosselli, Francesco **6:**428
Rotz, Jean **2:**154
Rousseau, Jean Jacques **2:**99
Rowlands, John *see* Stanley, Henry Morton
Rozier, Ferdinand **1:**56
Ruggieri, Michel **8:**609, **8:**610
Rumford, Count **1:**71
Rush, Richard **9:**672
Rusticello of Pisa **8:**568
Ruxton, George F. **1:**31

Sacagawea **6:**409, **6:**410, **8:616–618**, **10:**787, **10:**788
Sagan, Carl **1:**54, **8:**632
Saint-Lusson, Daumont de **5:**372
Salas, Juan de **3:**176
Salazar, Eugenio de **7:**500
Sanderson, William **1:**68
Sandwich, Lord **4:***314*
Sautuola, Marcellino de **10:**754
Schelleken, Barbara **6:**444
Schirra, Walter M., Jr. **9:**645
Schouten, Willem **7:**504, **7:**505, **10:**734
Scott, David R. **1:**27
Scott, Robert Falcon **1:**19, **1:**21, **1:**62, **3:**170, **3:**171, **3:**190, **4:**253, **4:**255, **4:**315, **5:**339, **5:**340, **5:**366, **5:**370, **5:**381, **7:**502, **7:**537, **7:**543, **7:**553, **7:**554, **7:**555, **7:**557, **7:**558, **8:***602*, **8:**604, **8:628–631**, **8:**635, **8:**636, **9:**657

Sehi *see* Faxian
Seleucus of Babylon **10:**740
Selkirk, Alexander **3:**213, **3:**214, **3:**215, **7:**530
Seneca **10:**753
Sennacherib, King **5:**329
Severin, Tim **2:**106, **9:**658
Shackleton, Ernest Henry **4:**315, **5:**381, **7:**542, **7:**543, **7:**554, **7:**555, **7:**557, **8:**604, **8:**628, **8:635–638**, **9:**656
Shepard, Alan B., Jr. **1:**37, **1:**38, **4:**306, **9:644–646**
Shepherd, Ollie **3:***190*
Shirshov, Peter **8:**614
Sikdhar, Radhanath **10:**731
Simpson, Thomas **7:**519
Sintra, Pedro de **5:**332
Slayton, Donald "Deke" **9:**645
Slessor, Mary **4:**314
Sloane, Sir Hans **6:**456
Small, Charlotte **10:**736, **10:**737
Smith, Adam **6:***442*, **6:**443
Smith, Annie Peck **10:**788, **10:**791
Smith, Jedediah Strong **1:**31, **1:**32, **1:**35, **9:664–667**
Smith, John **6:**432, **9:668–671**
Smith, Joseph **2:**109
Smith, Thomas **1:**66
Smithson, James Lewis **9:**672–673, **9:**675
Smith, William **9:**689
Snorri Thorfinnsson **4:**316, **4:**318, **10:**787
Soderini, Pier **10:**771
Solander, Daniel **1:**69, **7:**486, **8:**626
Somervell, Howard **5:**341
Soto, Hernando de **3:**182, **9:682–685**
Speke, John Hanning **2:**114–117, **4:**253, **4:**255, **4:**314, **5:**366, **5:**368, **6:**417, **9:707–710**, **9:**714, **10:**745, **10:**746
Sperry, Elmer **7:**502
Stafford, Edward **5:**324
Stairs, William G. **9:***715*
Stanhope, Lady Hester **10:***788*, **10:**789
Stanley, Henry Hope **9:**711
Stanley, Henry Morton **6:**414, **6:**417, **9:**708, **9:**710, **9:711–715**, **10:**746
Stark, Freya **10:**790–791
Steele, Richard **3:**214
Steengracht-Capellan, Baroness Henrietta van **10:**744
Stein, Marc Aurel **9:**660, **9:**663
Steudner, Hermann **10:**745, **10:**746

Stine Ingstad, Helge and Ann **4**:317

Stokes, Pringle **4**:264

Strabo **4**:247, **4**:298, **4**:300, **4**:301, **9**:716–718

Stradling, Captain **3**:214

Stuart, John McDouall **2**:110

Stuart, Robert **1**:35

Süleyman I, Sultan **4**:300

Sverdrup, Otto Neumann **8**:627

Swan, Captain **3**:213

Swift, Jonathan **6**:429

Talon, Jean-Baptiste **5**:371

Tamburlaine *see* Timur (Tamerlane)

Tanner, Joseph **1**:*47*

Tasman, Abel **3**:198, **4**:303, **7**:504, **9**:687, **9**:688, **10**:732–734

Taylor, Annie Royle **4**:314

Taylor, E. G. R. **7**:493

Tchou Yu **7**:498

Teixeira, Tristão Vaz **5**:332, **5**:333

Tenzing Norgay **4**:253, **4**:315, **5**:339, **5**:340

Tereshkova, Valentina **1**:37, **1**:38, **8**:615, **10**:789, **10**:791

Teroahauté, Michel **4**:275

Thales of Miletus **6**:434

Thomas, Pascoe **5**:367

Thompson, Almon **8**:579

Thompson, Benjamin **1**:71

Thompson, David **4**:313, **10**:735–738

Thomson, Charles Wyville **10**:758

Thomson, George Malcolm **1**:68

Thomson, William (Baron Kelvin) **10**:741, **10**:757

Thorbjarn Vifilsson **4**:316

Thorfinn Thordarsson *see* Karlsefni, Thorfinn

Thorne, Robert **7**:511

Thorstein Eriksson **4**:248, **4**:316

Thorvald Aswaldsson **4**:248

Thorvald Eriksson **4**:248, **4**:316, **6**:407

Thunberg, Carl Peter **8**:626

Tiberius, Emperor **10**:798

Timur (Tamerlane) **9**:661

Tinn, Philip F. **10**:744

Tinné, Alexandrine-Pieternella-Françoise **10**:744–746, **10**:786, **10**:788

Titian **6**:463

Todd, Sarah **1**:34

Tombaugh, Clyde W. **9**:680

Tonty, Henri de **5**:383, **5**:384, **5**:386, **5**:387

Torell, Otto **7**:507, **7**:508

Torricelli, Evangelista **10**:782

Tradescant, John **6**:455, **6**:457

Tradescant, John, Jr. **6**:454, **6**:456, **6**:457

Trana, Kristian **6**:458

Treschler, Christoph **7**:499

Tristão, Nuno **5**:332, **5**:335

Tsiolkovsky, Konstantin **1**:37, **9**:690

Tuckey, James **5**:366

Turnor, Philip **10**:735

Usodimare, Antonio di **5**:332, **5**:335

Valenzuela, Maria de **6**:462

Valignano, Alessandro **8**:609

Vallseca, Gabriel **6**:471

Vancouver, George **4**:313, **10**:762–764

van Diemen, Anthony **7**:504, **10**:733, **10**:734

Varenius **4**:*304*, **4**:305

Vasquez, Louis **2**:108

Vecelli, Tiziano *see* Titian

Veer, Gerrit de **7**:513, **7**:556

Velázquez, Diego **3**:204, **3**:205, **3**:207, **3**:208, **6**:462, **6**:464, **9**:*704*

Vergil, Polydore **2**:128

Vermeer, Jan **4**:*304*

Verne, Jules **7**:528, **7**:530

Verrazzano, Giovanni da **4**:271, **4**:272, **5**:324, **10**:765–768

Verrazzano, Girolamo da **10**:766, **10**:767

Vespucci, Amerigo **2**:129, **2**:135, **6**:431, **7**:*497*, **7**:530, **7**:531, **10**:769–1**10**:772

Victoria, Queen **2**:115, **2**:117, **3**:190, **3**:193, **9**:713, **9**:715

Vieira, Antonio **8**:576

Vignau, Nicolas de **5**:353

Vilgerdarsen, Floki **7**:491, **7**:494

Villagra, Gasper Perez de **7**:526

Vine, Allyn **10**:727

Visscher, Frans Jacobszoon **10**:733

Waldseemüller, Martin **4**:303, **6**:428, **6**:431, **10**:771, **10**:772

Walker, John **3**:196

Wallace, Alfred Russel **7**:486, **7**:487, **7**:488, **10**:777–780

Wallace, William **10**:777

Wallis, Samuel **2**:148, **2**:150

Walsh, Don **10**:725, **10**:726

Wang-P'an **8**:610

Warwick, Ambrose Dudley, earl of **4**:285

Warwijck, Wijbrandt van **7**:504

Washington, George **2**:94, **6**:430

Watson-Watt, Robert Alexander **7**:495

Webb, James **1**:48

Webber, John **9**:688

Wedgwood, Josiah **3**:216

Wells, H. G. **7**:528, **7**:530

Wen Wang **6**:455

White, Edward **1**:38, **6**:*468*

White, John **6**:473, **8**:598, **8**:599, **8**:603

Wilhelm, Duke **6**:447

Wilkes, Charles **6**:430, **7**:556

Wilkes, Hubert **1**:62

Wilkins, George Hubert **1**:61

Wilkinson, James **7**:545, **7**:546, **7**:547

William I, king of Sicily **5**:365

William of Rubruck **9**:662

Willoughby, Hugh **2**:132, **7**:511–512, **7**:553

Wills, William John **2**:111–112, **4**:299, **4**:314, **6**:470, **6**:473

Wilson, Edward **8**:628, **8**:629

Wilson, William **5**:353

Wisting, Oskar **1**:21

Woodman, David C. **4**:278

Worsley, Frank **8**:638

Wrangel, Ferdinand Petrovich von **8**:612

Wren, Christopher **5**:390

Wright, Orville and Wilbur **1**:59, **1**:62, **8**:606

Wu Ti, emperor of China **10**:796, **10**:797

Wu Tsu-Hsu **10**:741

Xeres, Francisco de **6**:478

Yanov, Colonel **10**:793

Young, Brigham **2**:109

Young, John W. **9**:*695*, **9**:697

Younghusband, Francis Edward **10**:793–795

Zarco, João Gonçalves **5**:332, **5**:333

Zhang Qian (Chang Chi'en) **4**:300, **9**:659, **9**:660, **10**:796–798

Zheng He *see* Cheng Ho

Zubayda **2**:140

Zurara, Gomes Eanes de **5**:335

GEOGRAPHICAL INDEX

Page numbers in *italic type* refer to illustrations. **Boldface** numbers preceding a colon indicate the volume number. Page numbers entirely in **boldface** type refer to main articles.

Abukir Bay **8**:601
Abyssinia **9**:711 *see also* Ethiopia
Acadia **4**:272, **6**:450
Acapulco **2**:137, **8**:594, **8**:597
Aceh **5**:346, **5**:349
Acoma, New Mexico **3**:*203*
Adelaide **2**:110, **3**:180, **4**:269
Adobe Walls **2**:144
Adriatic Sea **10**:753, **10**:754
Afghanistan **1**:16, **5**:358, **5**:359, **8**:566, **9**:*660*, **10**:793, **10**:794
Africa **2**:113, **2**:114–117, **2**:131, **2**:133, **2**:139, **2**:143, **3**:175, **3**:181, **3**:222, **3**:230, **4**:253, **4**:256, **4**:271, **4**:291, **4**:299, **4**:304, **4**:312, **5**:368, **5**:377, **5**:380, **6**:415–417, **6**:428, **6**:440–441, **6**:443, **6**:452, **6**:472–473, **6**:476, **6**:477, **6**:478, **7**:528, **8**:573–574, **8**:576, **8**:593, **9**:650, **9**:658, **9**:674, **9**:686, **9**:717, **10**:743, **10**:744–746, **10**:747, **10**:749, **10**:786 *see also* Central Africa; East Africa; South Africa; southern Africa; West Africa
Alabama **9**:685
A-la Shan **8**:585
Alaska **2**:87–90, **3**:196, **3**:200, **3**:237, **7**:538, **7**:539, **8**:607, **8**:612, **8**:613, **8**:614, **8**:624, **9**:675, **10**:763
Alborg **10**:*776*
Aleutian Islands **2**:87, **2**:90
Alexander Island **2**:84, **2**:86
Alexandria **1**:15, **1**:16, **1**:17, **4**:245, **4**:300, **5**:390, **8**:589, **8**:592, **9**:716
Alexandria, Minnesota **8**:625
Algarve **5**:331
Algiers **10**:746
Alps **1**:76, **1**:77, **10**:790
Altai Mountains **8**:587
Altamira **10**:754
Altun Shan range **8**:586
Amaseia (Amasya) **9**:716
Amazon Basin **1**:60, **1**:63, **1**:64–65, **10**:777, **10**:778–779
Amazon River **5**:355, **6**:455, **7**:486, **7**:487, **7**:551, **7**:552, **9**:652, **9**:654, **10**:770

Amboina **5**:349
Ambon **6**:*475*
America **2**:129–131, **3**:235–238, **4**:279–283, **6**:431, **7**:514, **7**:515, **7**:522, **7**:537–540, **8**:613, **10**:769, **10**:772, **10**:787–788
    southwestern United States **7**:545–548
    see also Central America; North America; South America
American River **9**:666
American West **1**:30–32, **4**:279–283, **8**:577–580
Americas **3**:176, **3**:181, **3**:184, **3**:226, **3**:230, **5**:380, **6**:448, **6**:470, **7**:528, **10**:749, **10**:752, **10**:772 *see also* New World
Amsterdam **5**:346, **5**:347, **5**:*348*, **5**:351, **7**:*503*, **10**:732
Amu Darya River **10**:794
Anastasia Island **3**:*179*
Anatolia **10**:752
Andes Mountains **1**:73, **1**:74, **1**:75, **3**:177, **3**:217, **3**:235, **4**:256, **5**:356, **7**:486, **7**:487, **9**:652, **9**:682, **9**:705
Angola **6**:415
Annaghdown **2**:105
Annapolis **10**:760
Antarctic **1**:60, **1**:61–62, **3**:238, **5**:339, **5**:340, **5**:368–370, **5**:377, **7**:506, **7**:543, **7**:557, **8**:581, **8**:602, **8**:613, **8**:614, **8**:628–631, **8**:635–638
Antarctica **1**:18, **1**:20–21, **1**:61–62, **1**:71, **2**:84–86, **2**:118–121, **3**:170, **3**:190, **3**:196, **3**:199, **3**:200, **3**:231, **3**:238, **4**:253, **4**:255, **4**:305, **4**:315, **6**:430, **6**:432, **6**:477, **7**:539, **7**:553, **7**:554, **7**:555, **7**:556–557, **7**:558, **8**:*581*, **8**:607, **8**:625, **8**:629–630, **9**:656, **9**:*658*, **9**:689, **10**:757, **10**:762, **10**:792
Antarctic Circle **2**:85, **3**:196, **3**:199, **9**:688
Antarctic Peninsula **9**:689
Anticosti Island **2**:151, **2**:152
Antioch **8**:565
Antwerp **6**:445
Apalachee Bay **2**:123
Appa Glacier, British Columbia **10**:753
Appalachian Mountains **2**:94, **9**:685
Apure River **5**:356

Arabia **1**:76, **2**:114, **2**:115, **5**:359, **5**:363, **6**:477, **10**:741
Arabian Desert **1**:76–77
Arabian Gulf **8**:576
Arabian Sea **1**:17, **10**:745
Aragon **4**:260–263, **8**:569, **8**:639
Arcadia **6**:471
Arcata, California **10**:*729*
Arctic **1**:18, **1**:19, **1**:60, **1**:66–68, **2**:101–103, **2**:118, **3**:171–172, **3**:231, **3**:235–238, **4**:275–278, **4**:286–287, **5**:367, **5**:368–370, **6**:458–461, **6**:473, **7**:503, **7**:504, **7**:507–510, **7**:512, **7**:513, **7**:537–540, **7**:553, **7**:554, **7**:556, **8**:583, **8**:614, **8**:627, **10**:749, **10**:757, **10**:790
    Canadian **7**:514, **7**:515–519
    Russian **7**:507–514, **8**:612, **8**:614, **9**:650, **9**:653
Arctic Circle **4**:247, **5**:381, **7**:507, **9**:717
Arctic Ocean **1**:60, **3**:237, **6**:418–419, **6**:458–461, **8**:625, **8**:627, **10**:736
Arctic Sea **8**:614
Argentina **1**:69, **2**:97, **2**:125, **2**:131, **4**:264, **6**:424, **7**:552, **10**:772
Arizona **2**:145, **3**:201, **5**:373, **5**:374, **5**:375
Arkansas **9**:684
Arkansas River **5**:371, **5**:386, **7**:546, **9**:684
Armenia **9**:716
Ascension Island **2**:98, **3**:214, **3**:218
Asia **1**:15, **1**:16, **1**:22, **2**:87, **2**:113, **2**:139, **2**:141, **2**:143, **3**:175, **3**:181, **3**:185, **4**:246, **4**:259, **4**:271, **4**:300, **5**:350, **5**:377, **5**:394, **6**:423, **6**:428, **6**:430, **6**:431, **6**:432, **6**:448, **6**:474, **6**:477, **7**:504, **7**:511, **7**:514, **7**:515, **8**:564, **8**:568, **9**:652–653, **9**:660, **9**:705, **9**:717, **10**:748, **10**:749, **10**:779
    central **8**:585–588, **8**:612, **10**:793
Asia Minor **1**:14, **1**:16, **1**:76, **1**:77, **5**:358 *see also* Turkey
Assiniboine River **5**:395, **5**:397
Asunción **2**:123, **2**:125
Aswan **4**:245, **9**:716
Atbara River **9**:709
Athabasca country **10**:736
Athens **4**:244, **10**:783
Atlantic Ocean **1**:59, **2**:104–106,

2:118, **2**:126–128, **2**:129, **2**:133–134, **2**:151, **2**:155, **3**:178, **3**:184, **3**:185, **3**:186, **3**:234, **4**:247, **4**:275, **4**:298, **4**:300, **4**:307, **5**:336, **5**:337, **5**:349, **5**:351, **7**:515, **7**:529, **7**:551, **8**:606, **8**:621, **9**:644, **9**:650, **9**:651, **9**:652, **9**:653, **9**:669, **9**:714, **10**:725, **10**:743, **10**:749, **10**:757, **10**:765, **10**:766–767, **10**:770, **10**:788, **10**:789 *see also* North Atlantic; South Atlantic
Auckland **5**:339
Australia **1**:70–71, **2**:92, **2**:110–112, **3**:180, **3**:196, **3**:198–200, **3**:212, **3**:214, **3**:218, **3**:231, **4**:268–270, **4**:*270*, **4**:275, **4**:299, **4**:303, **4**:314, **5**:349, **5**:380, **7**:504, **9**:655, **10**:732, **10**:733, **10**:734, **10**:763, **10**:779, **10**:789 *see also* New Holland; southern continent; *Terra Australis*
Austria **6**:463
Avon River, Bristol **6**:473
Ayas **8**:565
Azores **2**:105, **3**:175, **5**:332, **5**:333, **5**:335, **7**:549, **7**:550, **10**:747

Babylon **1**:16, **1**:17
Babylonia **6**:427
Back River **4**:276
Bactria **10**:796, **10**:797, **10**:798
Badajoz **7**:520, **9**:683
Badakhshan **8**:566
Baffin Bay **1**:66, **1**:67, **1**:68, **7**:516
Baffin Island **1**:67, **4**:286, **4**:317, **6**:406, **6**:470, **7**:515, **7**:516, **7**:518, **8**:603
Bafing River **7**:*535*
Bagamoyo **9**:712, **9**:714
Baghdad **1**:76, **1**:77, **1**:78, **2**:139, **2**:140, **5**:358, **5**:361, **5**:390, **10**:773, **10**:775, **10**:790
Bahamas **2**:105, **3**:186, **3**:189, **4**:307
Bahr al-Ghazal (Gazelle River) **10**:745
Baie de Chaleur **2**:151, **2**:154
Baja California **3**:205
Baja Peninsula **2**:137
Bali **5**:346, **5**:348, **10**:779
Balkans **6**:447
Baltic Sea **2**:84, **7**:514, **8**:624, **10**:775
Bamako **7**:535, **7**:536
Bamian, Afghanistan **9**:*660*
Banana **9**:714, **9**:715

Banda Islands **6**:475
Bangladesh **5**:341
Bantam **5**:348, **7**:504
Baracoa **6**:462
Barbados **5**:337
Barcelona **4**:262
Barents Sea **1**:60, **7**:512
Basra **7**:527
Batavia (Jakarta) **2**:150, **3**:214, **7**:504, **10**:732, **10**:733, **10**:734
Bavaria **1**:71, **5**:373, **5**:394, **8**:605, **8**:606
Bay of Bengal **5**:359
Bay of Cambay **10**:*748*
Bay of Fundy **10**:739
Bay of Whales **1**:20, **1**:62, **2**:120
Beardmore Glacier **7**:*553*, **7**:557, **8**:629
Bear Island **2**:103, **7**:513
Bechuanaland **6**:414
Beechey Island **4**:276, **4**:277, **4**:278
Beijing **8**:564, **8**:565, **8**:566, **8**:567, **8**:586, **8**:610, **8**:611, **9**:660, **10**:749
Belalcázar (town) **1**:72
Belém (Pará) **10**:779
Belgium **6**:444–445, **9**:711, **9**:714–715
Bella Coola River **6**:420, **6**:*421*
Bellingshausen Sea **2**:86, **9**:656
Benares **4**:259
Bent's Fort **2**:145
Bergen **6**:*459*, **6**:461
Bering Island **2**:88, **2**:89, **2**:90
Bering Sea **3**:200
Bering Strait **2**:90, **5**:389, **7**:512, **8**:612
Berkner Island **8**:627
Berlin **3**:223, **4**:252, **4**:254, **4**:305, **5**:354
Bermuda **2**:105, **6**:455, **10**:724
Bhutan **10**:731
Big Horn Mountains **5**:395, **5**:398
Bilma **2**:142
Bimini **8**:570, **8**:571
Bismarck, North Dakota **6**:410, **8**:617
Bitterroot Mountains **6**:410, **6**:411
Black Hills of South Dakota **9**:664
Black River **10**:736
Black Sea **3**:176, **5**:359, **7**:*527*, **9**:712, **9**:716, **10**:751
Blantyre **4**:314, **6**:413
Block Island **10**:767–768
Blue Nile **9**:709, **10**:745
Bodø **2**:103
Boise, Idaho **8**:616
Bolivia **9**:705
Bologna **5**:388, **10**:783

Boonesborough **2**:94, **2**:95, **2**:96
Boothia Peninsula **4**:313
Borinquen **8**:570
Borneo **10**:779
Bosporus **7**:*527*
Boston **5**:390
Botany Bay **1**:70, **3**:198, **4**:269
Botswana **6**:414, **6**:415
Bouvet Island **9**:688
Brahmaputra River **10**:794
Brattahlid **4**:250, **4**:316
Brazil **1**:69, **2**:115, **2**:117, **2**:123, **2**:125, **2**:133–134, **3**:182, **3**:214, **3**:217, **3**:225, **4**:252, **6**:471, **7**:*529*, **7**:549, **7**:551, **8**:574, **8**:576, **10**:743, **10**:767, **10**:768, **10**:770, **10**:771, **10**:779
Bremen **9**:*650*
Brest **2**:97, **4**:287, **4**:296
Bridger's Pass **2**:109
Bristol **2**:127, **2**:129
Britain *see* Great Britain
British Columbia **1**:24, **6**:421, **9**:674, **10**:737, **10**:753
British Isles *see* Great Britain
Brittany **2**:97, **2**:105, **4**:287, **4**:296
Brooklyn **7**:539
Brouage **2**:155, **2**:156
Brussels **10**:757
Bucephala (city) **1**:17
Buddh Gaya **4**:259
Bukhara **8**:564
Burma **5**:358, **6**:430, **8**:567, **8**:*574*, **10**:794
Buru, Indonesia **2**:98
Bussa **7**:536
Buzzards Bay, Massachusetts **3**:182

Cadiz **3**:184, **3**:185, **3**:228, **10**:770
Cairo **1**:76, **1**:77, **1**:78, **2**:139, **2**:141, **2**:143, **5**:338, **5**:358, **9**:709, **10**:744, **10**:745, **10**:746, **10**:748
Cajamarca **5**:379, **9**:682, **9**:683
Calabar coast **4**:314
Calicut **2**:135, **3**:167, **4**:292, **4**:293, **4**:294, **5**:358, **6**:476, **8**:*575*
California **2**:101, **2**:136–138, **2**:145, **2**:146–147, **3**:226, **3**:227, **3**:228, **4**:281, **4**:282, **4**:283, **5**:324, **5**:374, **5**:375, **6**:437, **7**:526, **8**:615, **9**:645, **9**:665, **9**:666, **9**:692, **9**:701, **10**:*729*, **10**:763, **10**:785, **10**:788
Callao **5**:337
Cambay **10**:*748*
Cambodia **4**:295
Cambridge, England **3**:216, **5**:391
Camp Fortunate **6**:411

Canada **2**:91, **2**:97, **2**:126–128, **2**:151–154, **2**:*154*, **2**:155–158, **3**:179, **3**:196, **4**:271–273, **4**:275, **4**:312, **4**:313, **5**:350, **5**:351–353, **5**:*352*, **5**:371–372, **5**:377, **5**:394–398, **6**:408, **:6**:418–421, **6**:443, **6**:450–451, **6**:473, **6**:478, **7**:548, **8**:627, **9**:653, **9**:675, **10**:735–738, **10**:739, **10**:751, **10**:771
Canary Islands **2**:105, **3**:187, **5**:390, **6**:464, **9**:703
Canberra **9**:701
Canton **6**:449, **8**:574
Caparra **8**:570
Cape Arctichesky **8**:627
Cape Bauld **2**:127
Cape Blanc **5**:332, **5**:335
Cape Bojador **5**:332, **5**:335
Cape Breton **2**:127
Cape Cabrillo **10**:763
Cape Canaveral, Florida **1**:27, **4**:307, **6**:468, **9**:*645*, **9**:*698*
Cape Chelyuskin **8**:612
Cape Cod **10**:726, **10**:768
Cape Colony **8**:626
Cape Cross **3**:*223*, **3**:224
Cape Fear **10**:767
Cape Henry **9**:670
Cape Horn **2**:137, **3**:197, **3**:213, **3**:214, **4**:264, **7**:504–505, **7**:511, **10**:764
Cape Non **5**:332
Cape of Good Hope **2**:134, **3**:214, **3**:218, **3**:222, **3**:223, **3**:224, **3**:225, **3**:228, **4**:291, **4**:292, **4**:293, **4**:299, **4**:302, **6**:474, **7**:500, **7**:504, **7**:511, **8**:573, **8**:575, **8**:593, **9**:654, **9**:687
Cape Town **2**:98, **7**:504, **7**:505
Cape Verde Islands **3**:184, **3**:217, **3**:224, **4**:291, **5**:332, **5**:390, **6**:423, **8**:606, **9**:704, **10**:770
Cape Vert **5**:332, **5**:335
Cape York Peninsula **3**:198
Carcassone **2**:154
Caribbean islands **3**:176, **3**:182
Caribbean Sea **2**:128, **3**:*205*, **3**:226, **5**:337, **6**:472, **7**:552, **8**:569, **8**:*570*, **8**:603, **9**:652, **9**:682, **9**:683, **9**:704, **10**:739, **10**:761, **10**:762, **10**:765, **10**:768, **10**:769
Carlsberg Ridge **10**:761
Carolina Outer Banks **10**:767
Carolinas **3**:228, **6**:441, **9**:684
Caroline County, Virginia **6**:410
Cartagena, Colombia **1**:74, **1**:75
Carthage **5**:328, **5**:329, **5**:330, **8**:602
Caspian Sea **9**:659, **9**:716

Castile **4**:260–263, **6**:462
Catalonia **8**:565
Cathay *see* China
Central Africa **4**:299, **9**:713
Central America **2**:137, **3**:176, **3**:204, **3**:226, **5**:354, **7**:520–522, **9**:703, **9**:706, **10**:765
Ceram **6**:475
Ceuta **3**:175, **5**:331, **5**:332, **5**:363, **8**:573, **8**:574
Ceylon (Sri Lanka) **3**:167, **4**:257, **4**:259, **5**:358, **5**:359
Chaeronea **1**:14
Champa **3**:166
Chang'an **4**:258, **10**:796, **10**:797, **10**:798
Channel Islands **2**:137, **2**:148, **2**:149
Charlesbourg-Royal **2**:153
Charleston **4**:279, **6**:432
Chesapeake Bay **9**:669, **9**:670, **9**:675
Cheyenne Peak **7**:548
Cheyenne River **5**:398
Chicago **1**:26, **3**:190, **3**:236, **6**:438
Chickahominy River **9**:669
Chi Hoa **4**:295, **4**:296
Chihuahua **7**:548
Chile **1**:73, **2**:117, **2**:132, **2**:149, **2**:150, **3**:177, **3**:214, **3**:217, **4**:264, **7**:530, **9**:705
Chimborazo **5**:356
China **1**:22, **1**:34, **1**:59, **2**:93, **2**:126, **2**:142, **3**:165–167, **3**:175, **3**:182, **3**:184, **4**:257, **4**:259, **4**:295–297, **4**:300, **4**:301, **5**:347, **5**:350, **5**:351, **5**:358, **5**:360, **5**:361, **5**:379, **5**:383, **6**:428, **6**:430, **6**:*449*, **6**:*452*, **6**:478, **7**:543, **8**:564–568, **8**:576, **8**:585, **8**:586, **8**:602, **8**:608–611, **9**:659–663, **9**:*663*, **10**:731, **10**:741, **10**:748, **10**:749, **10**:751, **10**:788, **10**:789, **10**:793, **10**:796–798
Cho Lon **4**:295, **4**:296
Chomolungma *see* Mount Everest
Christmas Harbour, Kerguelen's Land **9**:*688*
Chumi Shengo **10**:794
Church Hill, near Tralee **2**:104
Churchill River **10**:*735*, **10**:736
Cibola **3**:201, **7**:529
Cincinnati, Ohio **4**:279
Citlaltépetl volcano **10**:791
Clonfert **2**:105
Cochin **2**:135, **4**:293, **4**:294
Cochin China **4**:295, **4**:297, **8**:567
Colla Micchati **5**:336

Colombia **1**:72, **1**:74, **1**:75, **5**:355,
    5:356, **7**:520, **7**:526
Colorado **2**:92, **2**:93, **2**:144, **2**:145,
    4:283, **7**:547
Colorado River **3**:202, **4**:304, **5**:374,
    5:375, **7**:524, **7**:526, **8**:577–580,
    9:666
Columbia River **1**:34, **2**:146, **4**:280,
    6:408, **6**:410, **6**:412, **10**:737
Commander Islands **2**:89
Congo **2**:115
    Belgian **9**:711, **9**:713, **9**:714–715
    Democratic Republic of **9**:715
Congo River **4**:304, **6**:417, **9**:713,
    9:714, **10**:745, **10**:746
Constantinople (Istanbul) **3**:175,
    8:591, **10**:747, **10**:748, **10**:773,
    10:775
Continental Divide **6**:411
Cooper's Creek **2**:111, **2**:112, **6**:473
Cordoba **5**:*362*, **5**:363
Cornwall **10**:739
Cornwallis Island **4**:276
Corsica **2**:100
Costa Rica **3**:185, **3**:189
County Kildare, Ireland **8**:636
Crévecoeur **5**:386
Crimea **5**:358, **9**:712
Cuba **3**:176, **3**:185, **3**:186, **3**:188,
    3:205, **6**:440, **6**:462, **8**:569, **8**:570,
    8:571, **9**:682
Cuzco **1**:72, **9**:682, **9**:683
Cyrene **4**:244–247

Dakar **5**:392
Dakota **5**:397, **5**:398, **9**:664
Damascus **1**:76, **1**:77, **2**:115, **2**:117,
    5:360
Dampier Archipelago **3**:213
Dampier Strait **3**:213, **3**:214
Danskøya Island **1**:61, **1**:62
Darién **1**:72, **3**:226, **7**:520, **7**:521,
    7:522
Davis Strait **1**:67, **1**:68, **7**:516, **7**:518
Daxia *see* Bactria
Deception Island **1**:61
De Geer Glacier **2**:102
Delaware **8**:624, **8**:625
Delhi **5**:358, **5**:359
Delphi **4**:247
Denbigh **9**:711, **9**:712
Denmark **2**:87, **2**:88, **4**:250, **8**:624,
    10:773, **10**:*776*
Deptford **3**:228, **4**:285
Deseret *see* Utah
Desolation Islands **9**:688
Devon **3**:226
Devon Island **1**:63, **1**:65

Devonport, England **3**:216, **8**:630
Dieppe **7**:549, **10**:766, **10**:767,
    10:768
Djibouti **5**:338, **9**:707
Dolomites **10**:791
Dominica **3**:187, **8**:569
Dominican Republic **3**:186
Donington **4**:268
Dorset **10**:779
Down, Kent **3**:218
Dublin **10**:775
Duisburg **6**:444, **6**:446, **6**:447
Dundee **4**:314
Dunhuang **9**:663
Durham **1**:76, **1**:77, **4**:264, **4**:267
Dvina River **7**:512

East Africa **3**:166, **3**:167, **4**:292,
    5:358, **7**:528, **9**:707–715, **10**:744
East Asia **2**:143, **3**:167, **10**:748
East Derry, New Hampshire **9**:644
Easter Island **3**:199, **5**:336, **5**:338
Eastern Europe **10**:775
East Indies **2**:150, **3**:227, **4**:285,
    5:346–349, **6**:455, **7**:503, **7**:504,
    8:573, **8**:576, **9**:653, **9**:654–655,
    9:687, **10**:732–733, **10**:751
East Liverpool, Ohio **10**:730
East Pacific Rise **7**:*488*
Ecbatana **1**:16
Ecuador **1**:*64*, **1**:72–73, **5**:355, **9**:705
Edinburgh **1**:56, **1**:58, **2**:91, **2**:93
Egmont Island **2**:150
Egypt **1**:15, **1**:16, **1**:77, **2**:115, **2**:141,
    2:142, **4**:244–245, **5**:337, **5**:338,
    5:359, **5**:360, **5**:377, **5**:390, **7**:497,
    7:543, **8**:565, **8**:589, **8**:592, **9**:709,
    9:710, **9**:712, **9**:717, **10**:730,
    10:747, **10**:752
Elephant Island **4**:315, **8**:636, **8**:637,
    8:638
Ellesmere Island **2**:118, **5**:370,
    8:627
Elmina **3**:222, **3**:224
El Paso (del Rio del Norte) **7**:524
Encounter Bay **4**:269
England **2**:113, **2**:127, **2**:132, **2**:148,
    3:182, **3**:184, **3**:196, **4**:268, **5**:363,
    5:390, **6**:441, **6**:451, **6**:470, **6**:473,
    9:671, **9**:713, **9**:715, **10**:740–741,
    10:742, **10**:750, **10**:774, **10**:775,
    10:793
English Channel **1**:59, **1**:62, **3**:190
Erbil, Iraq **1**:16
Eriksey **4**:249
Eriksfjord **4**:248, **4**:249
Escalante River **8**:579
Espíritu Santo **8**:596, **8**:597

Estero Bay **8**:571
Ethiopia **9**:707, **9**:709
Euphrates River **1**:16, **1**:77, **6**:*429*
Europe **1**:24, **1**:34, **2**:113, **2**:143,
    3:179, **3**:181, **4**:251, **4**:283, **4**:291,
    4:300, **5**:377, **6**:428, **6**:430, **6**:441,
    6:453, **7**:511, **7**:515, **8**:564, **8**:591,
    9:659, **9**:660, **9**:662, **9**:717,
    10:748, **10**:749, **10**:776
    northern **9**:648–649
Évora, Portugal **8**:594, **8**:596

Faeroe Islands **2**:105, **4**:250, **7**:491,
    8:624, **10**:775
Fairness Point **1**:67
Falkland Islands **2**:97, **2**:98, **2**:148,
    3:217
Falmouth **3**:218, **10**:762
Far East **9**:718
Fatu Hiva **5**:336
Fertile Crescent **5**:377
Fez **5**:361
Fichtel Mountains **5**:354
Fiji **10**:732, **10**:734
Fimbul Ice Shelf **2**:85, **7**:556
Finisterre **4**:267
Finland **7**:507, **8**:624
Flanders **6**:444
Florence **6**:453, **8**:*591*, **10**:765,
    10:769, **10**:770, **10**:771, **10**:783
Florida **1**:27, **1**:56, **1**:57, **2**:94,
    2:122–125, **3**:*179*, **3**:182, **3**:211,
    3:234, **4**:307, **6**:462, **6**:463, **6**:464,
    6:468, **6**:470, **8**:569, **8**:570, **8**:572,
    9:*645*, **9**:682, **9**:683, **9**:684, **9**:*685*,
    9:692, **9**:696, **10**:767, **10**:768
Florida Keys **8**:571, **10**:761
Fogo **8**:*606*
Fort Astoria **1**:34, **1**:35
Fort Bourbon **5**:395, **5**:398
Fort Bridger **2**:108, **2**:109
Fort Chipewyan **6**:418, **6**:420
Fort Churchill **10**:735
Fort Crozon **4**:287
Fort Cumberland **10**:735
Fort Dauphin **5**:395, **5**:398
Fort Duquesne **2**:94
Fort Fork **6**:419
Fort Kaministikwia **5**:396
Fort Laramie **2**:146
Fort Mandan **6**:410, **6**:411, **8**:616
Fort Manuel **8**:618
Fort Maurepas **5**:394, **5**:397
Fort Resolution **6**:*419*
Fort Rouge **5**:395, **5**:397
Fort Saint-Charles **5**:*394*, **5**:396,
    5:397
Fort Saint-Pierre **5**:394, **5**:396

Fort William **5**:*398*
Foulshiels **7**:533
Foxe Basin **1**:67, **7**:518
Foxe Channel **7**:516
Fox River **5**:371, **6**:437
Framheim **1**:*21*
France **1**:55, **2**:97–100, **2**:114,
    2:151–154, **2**:155–158, **3**:196,
    3:209, **3**:231, **4**:246, **4**:265, **4**:269,
    4:271–274, **4**:287, **4**:313, **5**:363,
    5:394, **6**:436–438, **6**:441, **6**:442,
    6:443, **6**:447, **6**:448, **6**:450, **7**:543,
    8:624, **10**:750, **10**:753, **10**:756,
    10:761, **10**:765, **10**:775, **10**:776
Francisco River **3**:227
Franklin Strait **4**:276
Franz Josef Land **2**:101, **2**:102,
    3:238
Fraser River **6**:419, **6**:420
Frederick Jackson Island **6**:458,
    6:460
Frederikshåb **4**:250
Freiberg **5**:354
Fukien, China **2**:*92*
Fury and Hecla Strait **7**:517, **7**:518
Fury Beach **8**:583

Gabon **4**:315, **10**:788, **10**:790
Galápagos Islands **3**:216, **3**:217,
    3:*218*, **5**:336, **5**:338, **7**:487
Galveston Island, Texas **2**:123
Gambia River **5**:332, **5**:335, **7**:534,
    8:574
Gandhara **4**:259
Ganges River **1**:17, **4**:246
Gaspé Bay **4**:*271*
Gaspé Peninsula **2**:151
Gaugamela **1**:16
Gaul **3**:176
Gazelle River (Bahr al-Ghazal)
    10:745
Genoa **2**:126, **3**:184, **8**:566, **8**:568,
    10:748–749
Georgetown **9**:671
Georgia **2**:94, **4**:279, **4**:281, **6**:470,
    9:684
Germany **1**:24, **1**:33, **1**:34, **1**:71,
    3:191, **4**:252–253, **4**:255, **4**:299,
    5:354–357, **6**:447, **6**:463, **9**:*650*,
    9:690, **9**:702, **10**:743
Ghana **2**:115, **2**:143, **3**:222, **4**:284,
    5:365
Gibraltar **4**:247
Gila River **5**:374, **5**:375
Giza **7**:542
Glasgow **1**:23, **1**:26
Goa **8**:576, **8**:608, **8**:610
Gobi Desert **4**:258, **8**:565, **8**:566,

8:585, 8:586, 8:587, 9:659, 9:663,
10:793, 10:794, 10:796
Godthåb (Nuuk) 4:250
Gold Coast 3:222, 6:478
Golden Bay 10:733
Goldstone 9:701
Gondokoro 10:745
Gordium, Temple of Zeus 1:15
Gouda 5:346
Graham Land 1:61
Granada 4:260, 4:261, 4:263, 5:358,
5:359, 8:569, 8:570, 9:704
Grand Canyon 3:202, 3:203, 8:577,
8:578, 8:580
Grand Portage 10:737
Granicus River 1:15
Great Barrier Reef 3:198, 4:268,
4:269, 4:270, 9:656
Great Basin 2:107, 2:109, 2:146,
4:280, 4:281, 9:665, 9:666, 9:667
Great Britain 1:33, 1:56, 3:169,
3:176, 3:190, 4:246, 4:312–315,
6:446, 6:477, 8:624, 9:706, 9:717,
9:718, 10:739, 10:747 see also
England; Ireland; Scotland;
Wales
Great Fish River 3:224
Great Lakes
(East Africa) 9:708, 9:709
(U.S.) 2:155, 5:371, 5:384, 6:436,
6:450, 7:545
Great Plains 3:183, 3:203, 5:398,
8:616
Great Salt Desert 9:666, 9:667
Great Salt Lake 2:107, 2:109, 2:146,
9:665, 9:666, 9:667
Great Slave Lake 6:418, 6:419
Greece 1:14, 6:428, 6:447, 8:565,
9:659
Green Bay 2:158, 5:371, 6:437,
6:438
Greenland 1:66, 1:67, 2:101, 2:102,
2:118, 4:248–250, 4:276, 4:285,
4:300, 4:316–318, 5:353, 5:377,
6:404, 6:406–407, 6:458–461,
7:491, 7:507, 7:508, 7:509, 7:510,
7:516, 7:517, 7:537–538, 7:555,
7:558, 8:625, 8:627, 10:743,
10:747, 10:773, 10:774, 10:775,
10:781, 10:787, 10:788
Green River 1:30, 1:32, 2:145, 8:578
Greenwich 7:496
Greve 10:765, 10:767
Guadalupe, Texas 2:125
Guadeloupe Island 6:443
Guam 3:213, 6:426
Guatemala 2:137
Guayaquil 1:73, 1:74

Guayas River 5:355
Guinea 5:330, 6:455, 6:478, 8:574,
8:602
Gulf of Bengal 8:574
Gulf of Cadiz 10:770
Gulf of California 5:375, 7:524,
7:526
Gulf of Cambay 10:741
Gulf of Carpentaria 2:111, 4:269,
10:734
Gulf of Mexico 2:122, 3:189, 3:205,
3:213, 5:371, 5:372, 5:386, 6:437,
8:571, 10:739, 10:743, 10:771
Gulf of Panama 7:521
Gulf of Paria 3:188
Gulf of Saint Lawrence 2:151,
2:154, 10:771
Gulf of San Miguel 7:522
Gulf of the Ganges 10:770
Gulf of Urabá 7:520
Gunnbjörn's Skerries 4:249
Gunung Mulu National Park,
Sarawak 10:755

Hague, The 10:744
Haiti 1:55, 1:56, 3:186, 4:262, 6:440
Halicarnassus 1:22
Hanoi 4:296, 4:297
Harer 2:114–115
Harvey's Lake 3:209
Harwich 4:286
Hastings 1:53
Havana 6:462
Hawaii 1:45, 2:92, 3:196, 3:200,
10:759, 10:789
Hawaiian Islands 6:470, 6:471
Hayes Barton, England 8:599
Hayes River 10:736
Hebrides 1:70, 1:71, 6:404, 8:624
Hellespont 1:14, 1:16
Helluland 4:317, 6:407
Helsinki 7:507
Henry Mountains 8:579
Hierro, Canary Islands 3:187
Higueruela 9:703
Himalayas 1:60, 1:62, 4:247, 5:339,
5:382, 8:588, 9:707, 9:709,
10:731, 10:793, 10:794
Hindu Kush Mountains 1:16,
5:359, 8:566, 9:660, 10:794
Hispaniola 3:176, 3:184, 3:185,
3:186, 3:187, 3:188, 3:204, 4:262,
6:443, 7:520, 7:521, 7:550, 8:569,
8:570, 8:572, 9:653
Hochelaga 2:152
Ho Chi Minh City 4:295
Holland 734, 10:734
Hollandsche Kerckhoff 5:348

Holy Island (Lindisfarne) 10:740
Honduras 3:185, 3:189, 3:204,
3:208
Hong Kong 6:449
Hood Canal 10:763
Hoorn 7:505
Hop 4:318
Hopes Checked 7:516
Hormuz 8:576
Horn of Africa 5:338, 9:707, 10:745
Horsens 2:87, 2:88
Houston, Texas 9:693, 9:697
Houtman's Abrolhos 5:349
Howse Pass, Rocky Mountains
10:736, 10:737
Hudson Bay 1:66, 2:155, 4:273,
4:275, 5:350, 5:352–353, 5:372,
5:395, 7:516, 7:518, 7:553,
10:735, 10:736
Hudson River 5:350, 5:351
Hudson Strait 1:67, 2:130, 5:352,
7:518
Hwang Ho see Yellow River
Hydaspes River 1:16

Iberia see Spain
Iberian Peninsula 3:175, 9:704,
9:719 see also Portugal; Spain
Iceland 1:70, 1:71, 2:106, 3:184,
4:246, 4:247, 4:248–250,
4:316–318, 6:404, 7:491, 8:624,
8:625, 9:717, 10:743, 10:747,
10:773, 10:774, 10:775, 10:781,
10:785
Idaho 6:412, 8:616, 9:667, 10:737
Iguazú Falls 2:125
Île de France 4:270
Illinois 2:109, 8:577
Illinois River 5:372, 5:384, 5:386,
6:436, 6:438
Ilminster 9:707, 9:709
Independence, Missouri 10:787
India 1:16, 2:91, 2:113, 2:133, 2:134,
2:135, 2:143, 3:166, 3:167, 3:182,
3:184, 3:223, 3:224, 4:246, 4:247,
4:257, 4:258, 4:259, 4:291–293,
4:298, 4:300, 4:302, 4:313, 5:341,
5:359, 5:377, 6:422, 6:430, 6:443,
6:474, 7:543, 8:573, 8:574,
8:575–576, 9:651, 9:654, 9:659,
9:660, 9:689, 9:707, 9:709, 9:712,
10:731, 10:741, 10:748, 10:749,
10:751, 10:789, 10:793, 10:794
southern 8:567
Indian Ocean 1:17, 1:67, 1:68,
2:133, 3:164, 3:175, 3:218, 3:232,
4:292, 4:302, 5:336, 5:338, 6:416,
6:422, 6:428, 7:489, 7:491, 7:504,

7:505, 8:575, 8:593, 9:688,
10:732, 10:733, 10:743, 10:761
Indies 3:184, 3:185 see also East
Indies; West Indies
Indonesia 2:98, 3:184, 4:259, 5:347,
5:349, 6:475, 6:477, 7:503, 7:533,
8:573, 9:653, 10:732, 10:750,
10:779, 10:780
Indus River 1:16–17, 4:258
Indus valley 5:358, 10:741, 10:747,
10:797, 10:798
Innsbruck 10:783
Iowa 2:109
Iran 1:17, 1:68, 1:76, 9:712
Iraq 1:16, 1:76, 1:78, 5:338, 6:427,
7:500, 7:527, 10:728, 10:747,
10:752, 10:775, 10:790, 10:797
Ireland 2:104, 7:491, 8:599, 8:624,
8:636, 10:775
Irkutsk 8:585, 8:586, 8:588
Isla Fernandina 3:218
Islas de San Lucas (Channel
Islands) 2:137
Isleta Pueblo, New Mexico 3:176
Israel 6:476
Issus 1:15
Issyk-Kul 8:586, 8:588
Istanbul (Constantinople) 2:141,
4:300, 10:747, 10:775
Isthmus of Panama 7:521, 7:522
Italy 2:115, 2:117, 2:126–132, 3:177,
3:184, 3:238, 4:301, 5:363, 5:373,
5:388, 6:447, 6:448, 6:454–455,
8:564, 8:565, 8:566, 8:624,
10:765, 10:783
Ivory Coast 6:478
Iznik 5:342

Jaeder 4:248
Jakarta (Batavia) 3:214, 7:504,
10:732, 10:733
Jamaica 2:150, 3:169, 3:176, 3:184,
3:189, 3:213, 6:462
Jamestown 3:177, 3:182, 4:313,
9:668, 9:670–671
Jan Mayen Island 2:103
Japan 2:93, 3:175, 3:184, 3:185,
4:300, 4:303, 8:576, 8:626,
10:732, 10:743, 10:785, 10:789
Java 2:98, 4:259, 5:346, 5:348, 7:505
Jemmy Button Sound 4:265
Jerez 7:520
Jersey 2:148
Jerusalem 2:139, 4:300, 6:430,
8:565
Juan Fernández Islands 3:214
Julianehåb 4:250
Jungfrau 10:791

Kalahari Desert **6**:414–415
Kamchatka **2**:87, **2**:88, **2**:89, **2**:*90*, **7**:514, **8**:614
Kansas **3**:202, **3**:203, **7**:525, **7**:526, **7**:546
Kapilavastu **4**:259
Karakol **8**:586, **8**:588
Karakoram Mountains **4**:258, **10**:793, **10**:794
Karakorum **10**:*798*
Kara Sea **7**:513
Kashgar **9**:661
Kashmir **10**:793, **10**:794, **10**:795
Kasia **4**:259
Kazakhstan **1**:*37*
Kensington, West London **4**:*254*
Kentucky **1**:56, **2**:95, **2**:96, **2**:144, **5**:384, **6**:448, **7**:547
Kenya **4**:294
Kerguelen's Land **9**:688
Kezeh (Tabora) **2**:116, **9**:708
Khan-balik *see* Beijing
Khartoum **10**:744, **10**:745, **10**:746
Khotan **4**:258
Kikongo **5**:330
Kilkea, County Kildare, Ireland **8**:636
Killeedy, near Tralee **2**:105
King's Lynn, Norfolk **10**:742, **10**:762
King William Island **4**:276, **4**:277
Klushino **4**:288
Kodlurnan Island **4**:287
Kola Peninsula **7**:512
Kolobeng **6**:414
Korea **2**:93, **10**:788
Kosina, Alaska **7**:538
Krasnoyarsk **8**:612
Kristiania **6**:458, **6**:461
Kritøya Island **1**:61
Kronstadt, Saint Petersburg **2**:84, **2**:86
Kunlun Mountains **4**:258
Kuruman **6**:414, **6**:452
Kusinagara **4**:259
Kyrgyzstan **2**:*140*, **8**:588

La Australia del Espíritu Santo *see* Vanuatu
Labrador **1**:56, **1**:57, **1**:69, **1**:71, **2**:151, **3**:236, **3**:238, **4**:318, **5**:372, **6**:407
Lachine Rapids, Saint Lawrence River **4**:271
Lac Saint-Jean **6**:450, **6**:451
Lagos **5**:335
La Isabella **3**:188, **3**:189, **4**:262
Lake Athabasca **6**:418
Lake Baikal **8**:613

Lake Bangweulu **6**:414, **6**:417
Lake Chad **9**:658, **10**:746
Lake Champlain **2**:*158*
Lake Erie **5**:384, **5**:*385*, **9**:664, **9**:665
Lake Huron **4**:272, **6**:436
Lake Koko Nor (Tsing Hai) **8**:586
Lake Leopold II **9**:713
Lake Malawi **6**:417
Lake Manitoba **5**:395, **5**:398
Lake Michigan **2**:158, **5**:371, **6**:436, **6**:437, **6**:438
Lake Mistassini **5**:372
Lake Mweru **6**:414, **6**:417
Lake Ngami **6**:414
Lake Nyasa **6**:417
Lake of the Woods **5**:*394*, **5**:396, **5**:398
Lake Ontario **5**:384
Lake Piekouagami **6**:450
Lake Shirwa **6**:*414*
Lake Siecha **7**:526
Lake Superior **5**:394, **5**:396, **5**:*398*, **6**:436, **6**:*450*, **6**:451, **10**:737
Lake Tanganyika **2**:113, **2**:116–117, **4**:314, **6**:414, **6**:417, **9**:708, **9**:*709*, **9**:712, **9**:713, **9**:714
Lake Tumba **9**:713
Lake Ukerewe **2**:116
Lake Victoria **2**:117, **9**:707, **9**:*708*–710, **9**:713, **9**:714, **10**:746
Lake Winnipeg **5**:394, **5**:395, **5**:398
Lancaster Sound **1**:*66*, **1**:68, **4**:276, **7**:516, **7**:517, **7**:518
L'Anse aux Meadows, Newfoundland **4**:317, **6**:407, **10**:776
Laos **4**:*295*, **8**:567
Lapland **2**:132, **4**:254, **7**:487, **7**:512, **7**:553
La Pointe du Saint-Esprit **6**:436
Larvik, Norway **5**:336
Lascaux **5**:*379*, **10**:754
La Trinidad **3**:188
Lebanon **1**:15, **1**:*77*, **6**:476, **9**:647, **10**:747, **10**:752, **10**:789
Leeward Islands **3**:187
Leicester **10**:777
Lemhi, Idaho **8**:616
Lemnos **6**:431
Lesser Antilles **8**:569, **10**:767, **10**:768
Lewis, Island of **6**:418
Lhasa **4**:314, **8**:586, **8**:588, **10**:793, **10**:794–795
Libya **4**:244, **10**:746, **10**:788
Lima **9**:683, **9**:704
Lincolnshire **1**:69, **4**:275, **9**:668
Lindisfarne (Holy Island) **10**:740

Linyanti **6**:415, **6**:416
Lisbon **3**:184, **5**:346, **8**:*573*, **10**:770
Little Falls **7**:545
Little Loretto, Kentucky **6**:448
Lofoten Islands **1**:22, **1**:23
Lombok **10**:779
London **1**:33, **1**:34, **1**:69, **3**:214, **4**:252, **4**:254, **4**:264, **4**:267, **4**:276, **4**:*278*, **4**:285, **4**:287, **4**:299, **4**:314, **5**:324, **5**:350, **5**:351, **5**:390, **5**:391, **6**:454, **6**:455, **6**:461, **7**:486, **7**:488, **8**:599, **8**:600, **9**:669, **9**:670, **10**:735, **10**:736, **10**:742, **10**:762
Long Beach, California **5**:324
Long Island Sound **10**:767
Lop Nur **8**:586, **9**:661
Lothal **10**:741
Louisiana **4**:273, **5**:*383*, **5**:386, **6**:443, **7**:548
Louisiana Territory **1**:34, **1**:79, **7**:545, **7**:547, **7**:559, **8**:616, **8**:639, **10**:787, **10**:788
Louisville **1**:56, **5**:384
Louvain (Leuven) **6**:444, **6**:445
Lualaba River **6**:414, **6**:417, **9**:713, **9**:714
Luanda **6**:415
Lyons **10**:765

Maas River **7**:503
Mabotsa **6**:414
Macao **3**:175, **6**:*452*, **8**:576, **8**:608, **8**:609, **8**:610, **10**:751
Macedonia **1**:14, **1**:16
Macerata **8**:608, **8**:610
Machu Picchu **4**:*256*
Mackenzie River **4**:275, **6**:420, **6**:421, **9**:654
Macquarie Island **2**:84, **2**:86, **9**:689
Mactan **6**:424, **6**:426
Madagascar **5**:346, **5**:347
Madeira **1**:69, **2**:105, **3**:175, **5**:332, **5**:333, **5**:335, **10**:766
Madras **9**:689
Madrid **6**:456, **9**:701
Magdalena Sonora **5**:375
Maine **2**:155, **2**:156, **8**:578, **10**:768
Makran **1**:17
Malabar coast **8**:574, **8**:576
Malacca **3**:166, **4**:303, **8**:574, **8**:576, **10**:751
Malawi **6**:*414*
Malaya **10**:750
Malay Archipelago **7**:486, **10**:779
Malaysia **3**:166, **3**:175, **4**:303, **8**:*574*, **8**:576, **10**:755
Maldive Islands **5**:336, **5**:358, **5**:359
Mali **2**:143, **5**:358, **5**:359, **6**:471,

6:472, **7**:534, **8**:602
Mali Empire **4**:274
Malindi **4**:292, **4**:293, **4**:*294*
Manchuria **10**:793, **10**:794
Mandlakazi **1**:23
Manhattan Island **7**:506
Manila **8**:595
Manitoba **5**:394, **5**:*395*, **10**:738
Mannheim **1**:71
Mar del Sur *see* Pacific Ocean
Marianas Trench **10**:725, **10**:726
Markland **4**:318, **6**:407
Marquesas Islands **5**:336
Marseilles **4**:247, **5**:355, **9**:717
Martinique **6**:443
Marton, England **3**:196
Maryland **7**:547, **10**:760
Mas-a-Tierra **3**:214
Maslennikovo **10**:791
Massachusetts **1**:71, **3**:*178*, **3**:182, **10**:726, **10**:758
Massachusetts Bay **3**:178
Massalia **4**:246, **4**:247, **9**:717
Matagorda Bay **5**:386
Mauna Kea, Hawaii **1**:45
Mauritania **2**:*139*
Mauritius **2**:98, **3**:218, **4**:270, **7**:504, **10**:733
Mauvila **9**:683, **9**:685
Mazocha Chasm **10**:753
Mecca **2**:114, **2**:126, **2**:139, **2**:140, **2**:143, **3**:166, **4**:294, **4**:314, **5**:358, **5**:359, **5**:361, **5**:363, **5**:365, **6**:431, **8**:602
Medina **2**:114, **5**:365
Mediterranean Sea **1**:17, **2**:126, **2**:142, **3**:176, **3**:210, **3**:211, **4**:299, **4**:300, **5**:363, **5**:377, **6**:428, **7**:492, **7**:498, **7**:527, **8**:571, **8**:624, **9**:647, **9**:648, **9**:649, **9**:659, **9**:709, **9**:716, **10**:739, **10**:747, **10**:750, **10**:753, **10**:756, **10**:757, **10**:761, **10**:765, **10**:775
Mekong River **4**:274, **4**:295, **4**:296, **10**:794
Melanesia **1**:26
Melbourne **2**:110
Melville Bay **4**:276
Melville Island **7**:517
Mesopotamia **1**:16, **1**:76, **1**:77, **5**:338, **10**:747, **10**:752, **10**:797
Meta River **5**:356
Mexico **1**:54, **2**:123, **2**:125, **2**:136, **2**:137, **2**:145, **2**:155, **3**:176, **3**:181, **3**:182, **3**:201, **3**:204, **3**:205, **5**:355, **5**:373, **5**:374, **5**:375, **5**:386, **6**:455, **6**:462–465, **7**:523, **7**:547–548, **7**:551, **7**:552, **8**:597, **10**:752,

10:791 *see also* New Spain

Mexico City **3**:203, **3**:208, **6**:463, **6**:464, **6**:465

Miami **3**:211

Mid-Atlantic Ridge **7**:486, **7**:488, **10**:727

Middle East **1**:76, **1**:78, **2**:113, **2**:139, **2**:141, **4**:298, **4**:301, **4**:312, **6**:475, **8**:565, **9**:662, **10**:765, **10**:790, **10**:791

Milan **10**:783

Mille Lacs **5**:385

Mill Grove **1**:55, **1**:57

Milwaukee, Wisconsin **6**:*436*

Mina **4**:284

Minden, Germany **1**:24

Minneapolis **7**:546

Minnesota **5**:385, **7**:545, **8**:625, **10**:737

Miquelon **4**:273

Mississippi River **1**:56, **2**:123, **4**:272, **4**:273, **4**:279, **5**:371–372, **5**:383–387, **6**:408, **6**:436–438, **6**:465, **7**:545, **7**:547, **8**:577, **8**:578, **9**:683, **9**:684, **9**:685, **10**:736

Mississippi River valley **2**:158, **4**:273

Missouri **1**:30, **1**:32, **2**:94, **2**:95, **2**:96, **2**:107, **2**:109, **2**:145, **2**:146, **4**:279, **6**:411, **8**:616, **8**:618, **9**:665, **9**:667, **10**:787

Missouri River **1**:31, **1**:56, **1**:57, **4**:279, **4**:304, **5**:371, **5**:397, **6**:408, **6**:410–412, **6**:437, **9**:664, **10**:736

  Great Bend **8**:617

  Great Falls **6**:410, **6**:411

Mobile, Alabama **9**:685

Mohenjo Daro **5**:377

Mojave Desert **8**:632, **9**:666, **9**:701

Moluccas *see* Spice Islands

Mombasa **4**:292

Mongolia **8**:585–588, **8**:613, **10**:794

Montana **2**:109, **6**:410, **6**:411, **10**:737

Monte Cristallo **10**:791

Monterey, California **9**:645

Monterey Bay **2**:137

Montreal **1**:35, **2**:152, **3**:194, **5**:372, **5**:383–384, **5**:385, **5**:394, **5**:395, **5**:397, **5**:398, **6**:418, **10**:736, **10**:738

Morocco **2**:93, **3**:175, **5**:328, **5**:331, **5**:337, **5**:338, **5**:358, **5**:361, **5**:362, **5**:363, **6**:422, **10**:789

Moscow **2**:90, **2**:132, **4**:288, **4**:290, **7**:512, **8**:615, **10**:791

Mount Baker **10**:763

Mount Cameroon **5**:330

Mount Cook **5**:339

Mount Erebus **7**:557

Mount Everest **1**:62–63, **3**:192, **4**:253, **4**:312, **4**:315, **5**:339–340, **5**:341, **7**:541, **7**:543, **10**:731, **10**:794, **10**:795

Mount Huascarán, Peru **10**:788, **10**:791

Mount Kakulima **5**:330, **8**:602

Mount McKinley **7**:539

Mount Meru **6**:431

Mount Saint Elias **2**:88, **2**:89

Mount Wutai **4**:*257*

Mozambique **1**:23, **4**:292, **4**:293

Mozambique Channel **3**:167

Murree, Pakistan **10**:793

Muztagh Pass **10**:793, **10**:794

Namibia **3**:223, **3**:224, **8**:574

Nan-ch'ang **8**:610

Nanking **8**:610

Nantes **1**:55

Nantucket Sound **2**:156, **10**:768

Naples **6**:463

Napo River **9**:652

Navidad **2**:137, **2**:138

Near East **9**:663

Nebraska **1**:32, **1**:56, **2**:96

Nelson River **8**:625, **10**:736

Nepal **5**:339, **5**:341, **10**:731

Netherlands **1**:44, **5**:346–349, **5**:390, **6**:429, **6**:447, **7**:503–506, **7**:512–513, **9**:668, **9**:706, **10**:732–734, **10**:744–746, **10**:750

New Amsterdam **7**:504, **7**:506

New Britain **2**:149, **3**:213, **3**:214, **3**:228

New Brunswick **2**:156

New Caledonia **4**:313

New Concord, Ohio **4**:306

New England **5**:394, **6**:432, **6**:441, **7**:526, **9**:669, **9**:670

Newfoundland **1**:69, **1**:71, **2**:105, **2**:106, **2**:127, **2**:128, **2**:151, **2**:154, **3**:177, **3**:184, **3**:196, **3**:213, **3**:231, **4**:271, **4**:317, **4**:318, **5**:394, **6**:407, **6**:455, **6**:474, **7**:549, **9**:652, **9**:654, **10**:739, **10**:749, **10**:751, **10**:765, **10**:768, **10**:776

New France **2**:156–157, **2**:158, **4**:271–273, **5**:371, **5**:383–384, **5**:394, **6**:436–438, **6**:450–451

New Galicia **3**:201, **3**:203

New Guinea **1**:25, **2**:98, **3**:214, **10**:732, **10**:733, **10**:734

New Hampshire **9**:644, **9**:645

New Hebrides **2**:98

New Holland **1**:71, **3**:198, **3**:213–214, **4**:268–270, **7**:504, **9**:687, **10**:734 *see also* Australia

New Ireland **2**:98

New Jersey **2**:148, **7**:545, **7**:547

New Jerusalem **8**:596, **8**:597

New Mexico **1**:46, **2**:144, **2**:145, **2**:147, **3**:*176*, **3**:201, **3**:202, **3**:*203*, **7**:523–526, **9**:667

New Orleans **9**:711, **9**:712

New Scotland **4**:313

New Siberian Islands **6**:460

New South France **9**:688

New South Wales **3**:198, **4**:269, **8**:634

New Spain **2**:155, **3**:201, **3**:203, **3**:204, **3**:208, **3**:213, **5**:374, **5**:375, **7**:523, **7**:525, **8**:594, **9**:684, **9**:685, **9**:704, **9**:705–706 *see also* Mexico

New World **1**:72, **3**:175–177, **3**:179, **3**:181, **3**:186, **3**:205, **3**:230, **4**:260, **4**:263 **4**:271–272, **4**:303, **4**:313, **6**:406–407, **6**:428, **6**:431, **6**:440–441, **6**:448, **6**:462–465, **6**:471–472, **7**:520, **7**:552, **8**:569–572, **8**:594, **9**:668, **9**:682, **9**:703, **9**:704, **10**:752, **10**:765–767, **10**:769, **10**:770–771

New York **1**:22, **1**:34, **1**:36, **1**:57, **1**:58, **2**:*158*, **3**:236, **4**:252, **4**:271, **4**:279, **5**:351, **7**:504, **7**:506, **8**:578, **9**:664, **9**:665, **9**:672, **9**:673, **10**:767

New York Bay **10**:765, **10**:767

New Zealand **2**:92, **3**:196, **3**:197, **3**:198, **3**:199, **3**:200, **3**:218, **4**:252, **4**:264, **4**:267, **4**:303, **5**:339, **9**:687, **9**:688, **10**:732, **10**:733, **10**:734, **10**:789

Niagara Falls **5**:384

Niagara River **5**:384

Nicaea **5**:342

Nicaragua **1**:72, **1**:74, **3**:185, **3**:189, **7**:521, **9**:683, **9**:704

Nigeria **2**:117, **2**:142, **7**:536

Niger River **4**:251, **4**:304, **4**:312, **7**:533, **7**:*534*, **7**:535, **7**:536, **9**:652

Nile River **1**:15, **1**:17, **2**:113, **2**:115–117, **4**:246, **4**:251, **4**:253, **4**:299, **4**:304, **4**:305, **4**:312, **4**:314, **5**:366, **5**:368, **6**:414, **6**:417, **6**:428, **7**:497, **9**:647, **9**:648, **9**:707–710, **9**:711, **9**:714, **9**:716, **10**:744, **10**:746, **10**:788

Nombre de Dios **3**:227

Nootka Sound **10**:762, **10**:763, **10**:*764*

Norfolk **10**:742, **10**:762

North Africa **4**:244, **4**:292, **5**:331, **5**:359, **6**:432, **8**:573, **9**:668

North America **1**:24, **2**:87, **2**:126–128, **2**:129–130, **2**:137–138, **2**:151–154, **3**:177–178, **3**:182, **3**:196, **3**:228, **4**:248, **4**:271, **4**:272, **4**:284, **4**:303, **4**:304, **4**:313, **4**:316, **4**:317, **5**:324–327, **5**:371–372, **5**:377, **5**:383–387, **5**:394–398, **6**:404–407, **6**:419–421, **6**:430, **6**:446, **6**:448, **6**:450–451, **6**:478, **7**:491, **8**:598–600, **8**:612, **8**:625, **9**:652, **9**:658, **9**:668–671, **9**:682–685, **10**:743, **10**:747, **10**:749, **10**:750, **10**:751, **10**:762, **10**:763, **10**:765–768, **10**:773, **10**:781, **10**:787, **10**:789

North Atlantic **7**:491, **8**:624–625, **9**:648, **9**:658, **10**:739, **10**:743, **10**:747, **10**:775, **10**:781

North Battleford **10**:735

North Carolina **2**:94, **8**:598, **8**:599, **8**:603, **10**:765, **10**:767

North Dakota **5**:395, **6**:410, **8**:617

North Pole **1**:18, **1**:19, **1**:21, **1**:62, **2**:101, **2**:103, **2**:118–120, **3**:*171*, **3**:*190*, **3**:231, **3**:235–237, **4**:253, **4**:255, **4**:313, **5**:351, **5**:381, **6**:458, **6**:459, **7**:491, **7**:492, **7**:498, **7**:508, **7**:517, **7**:538–540, **7**:553, **7**:554–556, **8**:614, **8**:615, **8**:624, **8**:625, **8**:627, **9**:648, **9**:655, **9**:674, **10**:790, **10**:792

North Saskatchewan River **10**:735, **10**:736

North Sea **3**:196, **4**:250, **7**:491, **10**:747

Northumberland **10**:740–741

Northwest Territories **6**:421, **10**:736, **10**:738

Norway **1**:23, **2**:101, **2**:103, **4**:247, **4**:248, **4**:250, **4**:316, **4**:318, **5**:336, **6**:404–407, **6**:458–461, **7**:492, **7**:509, **8**:624, **9**:717, **10**:739, **10**:773

Nouakchott, Mauritania **2**:*139*

Nova Albion **3**:227, **3**:228

Nova Scotia **2**:156, **4**:272, **4**:313, **5**:351

Novaya Zemlya **1**:60, **3**:238, **5**:350, **5**:351, **7**:512, **7**:513, **8**:612, **8**:614, **10**:745

Nubia **10**:*747*

Nuestra Señora de los Dolores **5**:374, **5**:375

Nuptse Mountain **5**:*341*

Nuremberg **4**:303

Nuuk (Godthåb) **4**:250, **6**:459

Ogooué River **4**:315
Ohio **1**:27, **4**:279, **4**:306, **6**:411,
    10:730
Ohio River **1**:56, **5**:371, **5**:384, **6**:437
Ohio River valley **4**:273
Okhotsk **2**:88
Okmok volcano **8**:607
Oman **5**:358
Ontario **4**:272, **10**:738
Orange River **3**:224
Ordos Desert **8**:586
Oregon **1**:34, **1**:35, **2**:137, **2**:138,
    4:280, **8**:618, **9**:665, **9**:666,
    10:737, **10**:787, **10**:788
Oregon City **10**:787
Orinoco River **5**:355, **5**:356, **8**:599,
    8:600
Orkney Islands **4**:250, **4**:313, **7**:491,
    8:624
Oslo **1**:18, **3**:*236*, **5**:337, **6**:458,
    6:459, **6**:461
Oxford, England **1**:23, **1**:24, **4**:264,
    4:267, **9**:669
Oxfordshire **10**:785

Paamiut **4**:250
Pacific Islands **3**:212, **6**:471, **9**:658
Pacific Northwest **1**:33–36, **1**:79
Pacific Ocean **1**:27, **1**:28, **1**:29, **1**:41,
    1:69, **2**:88, **2**:97, **2**:98, **2**:130,
    2:149, **3**:212, **3**:213–214,
    3:216–219, **3**:226, **3**:234, **4**:266,
    4:271, **4**:275, **4**:280, **4**:303, **4**:313,
    5:336, **5**:394, **6**:408, **6**:410, **6**:412,
    6:418, **6**:419–421, **6**:422,
    6:425–426, **7**:486, **7**:510, **7**:515,
    7:520, **7**:521–522, **7**:530,
    8:596–597, **8**:612, **8**:615, **8**:616,
    9:654, **9**:655, **9**:664, **9**:674, **9**:687,
    9:*692*, **9**:704–705, **10**:725,
    10:727, **10**:732, **10**:733, **10**:737,
    10:743, **10**:749, **10**:751, **10**:763,
    10:765, **10**:789 see also South
    Pacific
Pakistan **4**:258, **10**:793
Palestine **1**:15, **5**:358, **6**:444, **7**:543
Palmyra **10**:789
Palos **3**:184, **3**:186, **7**:549, **7**:551
Pamir Mountains **8**:566, **9**:663,
    10:793, **10**:794
Pamlico Sound **10**:767
Panama **1**:72, **1**:73, **3**:185, **3**:189,
    3:213, **3**:226, **3**:227, **3**:228, **4**:287,
    6:422, **7**:520, **7**:521, **8**:597, **9**:704,
    9:705
Panama City **7**:521
Papua New Guinea **1**:*25*
Pará (Belém) **10**:779

Paraguay **2**:117, **2**:123, **2**:125
Paraguay River **2**:125
Paris **1**:55, **2**:97, **3**:211, **5**:324, **5**:354,
    5:390, **7**:541, **10**:783
Patagonia **4**:264, **4**:266
Peace River **6**:419
Peebles **7**:536
Peel Sound **4**:276
Peking **5**:361
Pella, Macedonia **1**:16
Pennsylvania **1**:57, **2**:94, **7**:538,
    9:664, **10**:782
Pensacola, Florida **2**:94
Père Marquette River **6**:436
Perkiomen River **1**:57
Persepolis **1**:16
Persia **1**:14, **1**:68, **1**:76, **1**:77, **5**:358,
    5:359, **8**:565, **9**:659, **9**:712, **10**:798
Persian Gulf **1**:17, **1**:67, **1**:68, **3**:166,
    3:167, **5**:338
Perthshire **6**:420, **6**:421
Peru **1**:72–73, **3**:177, **3**:213, **4**:256,
    5:336, **5**:337, **5**:355, **5**:356, **5**:357,
    5:379, **6**:475, **6**:478, **7**:521, **8**:595,
    8:596, **8**:597, **9**:658, **9**:682, **9**:683,
    9:687, **9**:704, **9**:705, **10**:752,
    10:788, **10**:791
Peshawar **4**:259
Peter I Island **2**:84, **2**:86
Petropavlovsk **2**:88, **2**:89, **2**:90
Petropavlovsk Kamchatsky **2**:90
Philadelphia **1**:55, **4**:253, **5**:390
Philippines **1**:26, **3**:213, **3**:227,
    6:424, **6**:426, **8**:594, **8**:595, **8**:596
Phoenicia **10**:752
Pike's Peak **7**:547, **7**:*548*
Pillars of Hercules **5**:328
Pimeria Alta **5**:374, **5**:375
Pisa **1**:44, **10**:783
Pisania **7**:534, **7**:536
Pitcairn Island **2**:149, **2**:150
Piura **1**:73
Plate River (Río de la Plata) **2**:125,
    2:131, **3**:217, **7**:552, **10**:772
Platte River **2**:146
Plymouth, England **3**:197, **3**:199,
    4:285, **8**:598
Plymouth, Massachusetts **3**:*178*
Poland **7**:514
Polynesia **1**:69, **3**:198, **9**:658
Pompeii **1**:17
Popayán, Colombia **1**:74
Port Adelaide **3**:*180*
Port Conclusion **10**:763, **10**:764
Port Discovery **10**:763
Port Jackson **4**:268, **4**:269
Port Royal, Nova Scotia **2**:156
Portsmouth **2**:85, **4**:264, **7**:534

Portugal **2**:133–135, **2**:143,
    3:175–176, **3**:184, **4**:261, **4**:263,
    4:271, **4**:272, **4**:291–294, **4**:302,
    5:390, **6**:422–426, **6**:429, **6**:448,
    6:452, **6**:471, **7**:503, **7**:510,
    8:573–576, **8**:594, **9**:652–653,
    9:686, **9**:703, **9**:704, **10**:750,
    10:770
Portus Novae Albionis (Drake's
    Harbour) **3**:228
Potomac River **9**:670, **9**:671
Prince of Wales Island **4**:277
Prince William Sound **3**:200
Promontory, Utah **5**:380
Przhevalsk **8**:588
Puerto Rico **1**:46, **1**:*54*, **3**:176, **3**:187,
    6:440, **7**:551, **7**:552, **8**:569, **8**:570,
    8:571, **8**:572, **8**:632, **8**:*633*, **8**:634,
    9:704
Puget Sound **10**:763
Punt **6**:477
Punxsutawney, Pennsylvania
    10:782

Qassiarsuk **4**:250
Qeshm **1**:68
Qubbet ed Duris, Lebanon **1**:*77*
Quebec **2**:151, **2**:152, **2**:156, **2**:*157*,
    2:158, **3**:179, **3**:196, **4**:271, **4**:272,
    5:372, **5**:394, **6**:419, **6**:451, **9**:655
Queen Charlotte Islands **2**:149,
    9:674
Quelimane **6**:416
Quito **1**:73, **1**:74, **9**:652
Quivira **3**:202, **3**:203, **7**:524, **7**:525,
    7:529

Rae Strait **4**:313
Rainy Lake **5**:396
Rapa Nui see Easter Island
Raroia **5**:337
Recife **7**:551
Red River **4**:296–297, **5**:394, **7**:546,
    10:736
Red Sea **3**:210, **5**:*365*, **6**:474, **6**:477,
    10:757, **10**:761
Reindeer Lake **10**:736
Reindeer River **10**:736
Reykjavik **2**:106
Rhine **7**:503
Rhode Island **3**:178, **10**:767
Rhodes **5**:342, **5**:343, **10**:767
Rica de Oro **10**:732
Rica de Plata **10**:732
Richelieu River **2**:155
Rio Charna **7**:525
Rio de Janeiro **1**:69, **3**:197, **4**:252
Río de la Plata see Plate River

Río de Oro **3**:175
Rio Grande **5**:375, **6**:464,
    7:524–526, **7**:547
Río Negro **7**:552
Ripon Falls, **9**:709, **10**:746
Roanoke **3**:226, **3**:228
Roanoke Island **5**:326, **5**:*327*,
    8:598–599, **8**:603
Rochefort **1**:55
Rocky Mountains **1**:30–32,
    1:34–36, **2**:92, **2**:93, **2**:107–109,
    2:144–147, **4**:280, **4**:313, **6**:410,
    6:412, **6**:421, **7**:543, **8**:577, **8**:616,
    8:618, **9**:664–667, **10**:736,
    10:737, **10**:750
    South Pass **1**:35, **2**:146, **9**:664,
    9:665
Roebuck Bay **3**:214
Rome **3**:176, **4**:316, **4**:318, **5**:390,
    8:608, **9**:716, **9**:717, **10**:797
Ross Ice Shelf **2**:120, **5**:340, **7**:554,
    7:557, **8**:628, **9**:658
Ross Sea **8**:627
Rouen **5**:384
Russia **2**:84–86, **2**:87–90, **2**:100,
    2:115, **2**:132, **4**:288, **5**:359, **5**:377,
    6:455, **6**:476, **6**:478, **7**:507, **7**:508,
    7:512, **8**:612–615, **9**:668, **10**:747,
    10:774, **10**:775, **10**:794
Ruwenzori Mountains **9**:713, **9**:715

Saaremaa Island **2**:84
Sabarmati River **10**:741
Sacramento **2**:147
Sagres **4**:302, **5**:331, **8**:574
Saguenay (Ottawa) River **2**:152,
    2:153, **2**:155
Sahara Desert **2**:142, **2**:143, **4**:273,
    5:332, **5**:358, **5**:359, **5**:361, **7**:536,
    8:573, **10**:746
Saigon **4**:295, **4**:296
Saint-André-de-Cubzac **3**:209
Saint Augustine, Florida **3**:*179*,
    8:571, **8**:*572*
Saint Croix River **2**:156
Saint-Etienne **4**:295
Saint Helena **1**:53, **2**:100
Saint Lawrence colony **6**:419
Saint Lawrence Island **8**:612
Saint Lawrence River **2**:155, **2**:156,
    2:158, **3**:178, **3**:196, **4**:271, **5**:372,
    6:475
    Lachine Rapids **2**:152, **2**:153
Saint Lawrence valley **3**:178, **4**:273
Saint Louis **1**:30, **1**:36, **1**:56, **1**:57,
    4:280, **4**:281, **6**:408, **6**:409, **6**:410,
    6:412, **7**:545, **7**:547, **8**:616, **9**:664,
    9:665, **9**:667

Saint Malo **2:**99, **2:**151
Saint Paul and Minneapolis **7:**546
Saint Petersburg **2:**84, **2:**86, **2:**87, **2:**88, **2:**89, **4:**252, **5:**390, **7:**493
Saint Pierre **4:**273
Salamanca **3:**204
Salinas **1:**73
Salt Lake City **2:***109,* **2:**115
Salt River **5:**374
Samarkand **8:**565, **9:**660, **9:**661
Samoa **1:**25, **2:**98
Sanderson's Hope **1:***68*
San Diego Bay **2:**137, **2:**138, **10:**763
Sandwich Islands *see* Hawaii
San Francisco **2:**102, **2:**103, **4:**281, **10:**764
San Francisco Bay **3:**228
San Gabriel **7:**524, **7:**525
San Jacinto, California **8:**615
San Joaquin valley **9:**666
San Juan **8:**570
San Juan de los Caballeros **7:**524, **7:**525
San Juan Mountain **4:**283
San Julián **6:**424
Sanlucar **3:**185
San Miguel (San Diego) **2:**137
San Salvador Island (Santa Catalina Island) **2:**137, **3:**186
Sansandig **7:**536
San Sebastián de la Gomera **3:**186
San Servas, Campos **8:**570
Santa Barbara **7:**524
Santa Catalina Island **2:**136
Santa Cruz Islands **2:**150, **8:**595, **8:**596
Santa Fe **7:**548, **9:**665, **9:**667
Santa Hermandad **4:**262
Santa Lucie River, Uruguay **2:***99*
Santa Maria **10:**770
Santa María la Antigua del Darién **7:**520
Santiago **6:**462
Santiago River **9:**683
Santo Domingo **1:**55, **3:**205
Saqqara **6:**455
Sarawak **10:**755
Saskatchewan River **5:**397, **5:**398, **10:**736
Saudi Arabia **2:**114, **5:**358, **8:**602
Sault Sainte Marie **5:**372, **10:**737
Savannah **4:**281
Savannah River **9:**684
Scandinavia **8:624–627,** **10:**747, **10:**773–776 *see also* Denmark; Faeroe Islands; Finland; Iceland; Norway; Sweden

Schelde River **7:**503
Scilly Isles **3:**168, **5:**393
Scotland **1:**23, **1:**26, **2:**91, **2:**105, **4:**314, **6:**413, **6:**418, **6:**421, **6:**452, **7:**533, **8:**624, **10:**739, **10:**775, **10:**781
Scott-Amundsen Base, South Pole **1:**62
Scythia **6:**471
Sea of Okhotsk **8:**612, **8:**614
Sea of Ujiji *see* Lake Tanganyika
Segno **5:**373
Ségou **7:**535
Semliki River **9:**713, **9:**715
Senegal River **5:**329, **5:**332, **5:**335, **7:**535, **8:**574
Seville **2:**125, **2:**130, **3:**189, **3:**205, **3:**208, **6:**424, **6:**441, **9:**653, **10:**769, **10:**771, **10:**772
Shahhat **4:**244
Shantung **4:**259
Shanxi Province **4:**257
Shendu (Sind) **2:**113, **10:**798
Shetland Islands **4:**249, **4:**250, **4:**285, **7:**491, **8:**624
Shrewsbury **3:**216, **3:**218
Siam **3:**166
Sian (Chang'an) **4:**258
Siberia **2:**87–90, **6:**459, **7:**508, **7:**514, **7:**555, **8:**585, **8:**586, **8:**612, **8:**614, **8:**624, **8:**627
Sicily **5:**362, **10:**775
Sierra Leone **3:**184, **5:**327, **5:**328, **5:**332, **8:**574, **8:**602
Sierra Madre **2:***146*
Sierra Nevada **2:**146, **2:***147,* **4:**280, **9:**666, **9:**667
Sikkim **10:**731
Sinai Mountains **6:**427
Sind (Shendu) **2:**113, **10:**798
Sines **4:**291
Smolensk **8:**586
Snake River **6:**412
Sobat River **10:**744, **10:**745
Socotra **10:**745
Solomon Islands **2:**98, **8:**594
Somalia **6:**477, **9:**707
Somaliland **2:**114–115, **9:**707, **9:**709
Sonora Desert **5:**375
Sorocco, New Mexico **1:**46, **1:**47
South Africa **3:**214, **3:**224, **4:**291, **6:**452, **6:**477, **6:**478, **8:**626
South America **1:**60, **1:**70, **1:**72–75, **2:**98, **2:**113, **2:**115, **2:**117, **2:**130–132, **2:**137, **2:**155, **3:**176, **3:**182, **3:**188, **3:**204, **3:**212, **3:**213, **3:**216, **4:**253, **4:**264–265, **4:**303,

5:336, **5:**355–356, **5:**377, **5:**378, **6:**430, **6:**446, **6:**462, **6:**476, **6:**477, **6:**478, **7:**487, **7:**488, **7:**505, **7:**528, **7:**552, **7:***552,* **8:**574, **8:**600, **9:**652, **9:**653, **9:**658, **9:**682–685, **9:**687, **9:**703, **9:**704, **9:**705–706, **10:**734, **10:**769–772, **10:**777, **10:**778
Southampton, England **2:**149, **2:**150
South Asia **4:***258,* **9:**647
South Atlantic **1:**53, **2:**84–86, **2:**97, **2:**100, **2:**134, **9:**689
South Australia **2:**110
South Carolina **1:**57, **4:**279, **6:**432
South Dakota **1:**26, **5:**398, **6:**411
Southeast Asia **3:**166, **3:**184, **4:***258,* **6:**474, **7:**487, **8:**576, **10:**732, **10:**748, **10:**777
Southern Africa **4:**299, **7:**504, **9:**650, **10:**763
southern continent **3:**197, **4:**303, **7:**529, **9:**654, **9:**656, **9:686–689,** **10:**733, **10:**734 *see also* Terra Australis
Southern Ocean **7:**504
South Georgia **2:**85, **4:**315, **8:**636, **8:**637–638, **9:**688, **9:**689
South Orkney Islands **9:**689
South Pacific **1:**25, **1:**70–71, **2:**84, **2:**85, **2:**148–150, **3:**196–200, **7:**529, **8:***596,* **8:**613, **8:**626, **9:**687, **10:**762
South Pass, Rocky Mountains **1:**35, **2:**146, **9:**664, **9:**665
South Pole **1:**18, **1:**19, **1:**20–21, **1:**62, **2:**84, **2:***118,* **2:**120, **3:**171, **3:**231, **4:**255, **4:**315, **5:**339, **5:**381, **7:**502, **7:**553, **7:**554, **7:**557–558, **8:**595, **8:**602, **8:**625, **8:**627, **8:**629–630, **10:**762, **10:**792
South Sandwich Islands **2:**85, **2:**86, **9:**689
South Shetland Islands **1:**61, **8:**637, **9:**689
Soviet Union **1:**37–42, **4:**288–290, **4:**306, **4:**310, **5:**382, **6:**466, **6:**468, **8:**620, **8:**632, **9:**690–694, **9:**695–702 *see also* Russia
Spain **2:**97, **2:**122–125, **2:**130, **2:**131, **3:**175–177, **3:**186, **3:**205, **4:**247, **4:**261, **4:**263, **4:**271, **4:**272, **5:**363, **5:**373, **5:**390, **5:**394, **6:**423, **6:**426, **6:**442, **6:**448, **6:**462–465, **6:**471, **6:**474, **7:**503, **7:**504, **7:**511, **7:**546, **7:**547, **8:**565, **8:**594, **8:**597, **8:**602, **9:**652–653, **9:**654, **9:703–706,** **10:**750, **10:**752, **10:**754, **10:**769, **10:**772, **10:**775

Spice Islands (Moluccas) **2:**130, **2:**131, **2:**142, **3:**213, **5:**347, **5:**349, **6:**422–423, **6:**426, **6:**475, **7:**515, **7:**551, **7:**552, **8:**574, **8:**576, **9:**704
Spitsbergen **1:**66, **1:**67, **2:**101, **2:**102, **3:**235, **3:**236, **3:**237, **4:**254, **6:**461, **7:**507, **7:**508, **7:**509, **7:**510, **7:**513, **7:**518, **7:**554, **8:**612, **8:**614, **8:**627, **10:**745, **10:**751
King's Bay **2:**119
Sri Lanka (Ceylon) **3:**167, **4:**257, **5:**347, **5:**359, **10:**750
Stadacona **2:**152, **2:**153, **2:**154, **4:**272
Staten Landt **10:**734
Stornoway **6:**418
Strait of Belle Isle **2:**151
Strait of Gibraltar **5:**328
Strait of Magellan **2:**98, **2:**148, **3:**217, **3:**227, **4:**266, **6:**424, **6:**425, **6:***426,* **7:**505, **9:**687, **9:**705
Straits of Mackinac **6:**436, **6:**437
Stromness **8:**638
Su-chou **8:**610
Sudan **9:**709, **9:**710, **9:**715, **10:**745
Suez Canal **9:**712
Suffolk **4:**264
Sulawesi **10:**779
Sumatra **3:**166, **3:**167, **5:**346, **5:**348, **5:**349, **5:**358, **7:**533, **8:***574*
Sumer **5:**377
Sunda Strait **7:**504
Sutter's Fort **2:**146
Svalbard archipelago **2:**101, **7:**507, **7:**513
Sweden **2:**87, **4:**250, **6:**461, **7:**507–510, **10:**773
Switzerland **10:**791
Sydney **2:**84, **2:**85, **2:**86, **4:**268
Syene **4:**245
Syria **1:**76, **1:**77, **2:**115, **2:**117, **5:**358, **5:**359, **5:**360, **9:**647
Syrian Desert **1:**76, **10:**788, **10:**789
Szechwan **2:**93

Tabasco **3:**204, **3:**206
Tabora (Kezeh) **2:**116, **9:**708
Tadoussac **3:**178
Tagus River **3:**223
Tahiti **1:**69, **2:**98, **2:**99, **3:**197, **3:**198, **3:**199, **3:**200, **3:**218, **4:**252, **6:**471
Taiwan **4:**300
Tajikistan **9:**663, **10:**793
Takla Makan Desert **5:**379, **8:**586, **9:**661, **9:**663
Tampa Bay **6:**464
Tangier **5:**358
Tanzania **4:**314, **9:**708, **9:**712

Taos **2**:145
Tashkent **9**:661
Tasmania **4**:268, **4**:303, **9**:687, **9**:688,
 10:733, **10**:734 *see also* Van
 Diemen's Land
Tavistock **3**:226
Taxila **4**:259
Tehran **2**:93
Tennessee **1**:56, **9**:684
Tenochtitlán **3**:204, **3**:206–208,
 6:464, **9**:706
Ternate **6**:475
Terra Australis **3**:197, **6**:*425*, **7**:529,
 7:556, **8**:593, **8**:594, **8**:595, **9**:654,
 9:656, **10**:734 *see also* Australia;
 southern continent
Terra da Vera Cruz **2**:134
Terrebonne **10**:738
Texas **2**:122–125, **2**:147, **3**:201,
 3:202, **5**:384, **5**:386, **6**:410, **7**:547,
 7:548, **9**:684, **9**:*693*
Thailand **3**:166, **8**:*574*
Thule **4**:246, **4**:*247*, **8**:627, **9**:717,
 9:718
Thunder Bay **5**:396
Tibet **2**:91, **4**:314, **5**:341, **8**:585,
 8:586, **8**:588, **8**:613, **9**:707, **9**:709,
 10:731, **10**:789, **10**:793,
 10:794–795
Tidore **6**:475
Tien Shan Mountains **4**:258, **8**:586
Tierra del Fuego **1**:69, **3**:216, **3**:217,
 3:226, **3**:227, **4**:264, **4**:*265*, **4**:*266*,
 6:*426*, **9**:687
Tigris River **1**:16, **5**:338, **6**:*429*
Timbuktu **2**:143, **4**:252, **4**:273,
 4:274, **5**:361, **7**:533–534, **7**:536,
 8:602
Timia **2**:142
Timor **3**:214
Tirol **5**:373
Tlaxcala **3**:208
Tombouctou *see* Timbuktu
Tomsk **8**:612
Tonga **10**:734
Tordesillas **2**:131, **3**:176, **4**:261,
 4:263, **4**:272, **6**:423, **6**:448, **9**:704
Toronto **7**:548
Torquay **2**:113
Torres Strait **10**:734
Toulon **3**:209
Toulouse **8**:605
Tralee **2**:104, **2**:105
Traversay Islands **2**:85
Trent **6**:448–449
Trieste **2**:115, **2**:117
Trinidad **3**:185
Tripoli **10**:746

Trois-Rivières, Quebec **5**:394, **5**:396
Troms0 **7**:509
Troy **7**:527
Tsangpo River **10**:794
Tsien Tang River **10**:741
Tsing Hai (Lake Koko Nor) **8**:586
Tuamoto atolls **2**:85
Túcume **5**:336, **5**:338
Turkey **1**:15, **1**:76, **1**:77, **2**:86, **5**:342,
 5:358, **8**:565, **9**:716, **10**:747,
 10:752, **10**:775, **10**:791 *see also*
 Asia Minor
Turkistan **8**:585, **8**:586, **8**:588
Tuscany **9**:716, **10**:782
Tyre **1**:15, **1**:16

Udyana **4**:259
Uganda **9**:710, **9**:715
Ujiji **6**:414, **6**:417, **9**:712
Ukerewe **9**:708
Ukraine **9**:707, **9**:712
Ulan Bator **8**:586
Ulm, Germany **8**:589
United Kingdom *see* Great Britain
United States **1**:27–29, **1**:30–32,
 1:33–36, **1**:37–42, **2**:90, **2**:91,
 2:120, **3**:191, **3**:202, **4**:256,
 4:279–283, **5**:355, **5**:380,
 6:408–412, **6**:466, **7**:495, **7**:496,
 8:577–580, **8**:613, **8**:620,
 9:664–667, **9**:690–692,
 9:695–702, **10**:728, **10**:730,
 10:735–738
 border with Canada **10**:736,
  10:737, **10**:738
 southwestern **7**:523–526
 western **9**:664–667
Upper Norwood, London **4**:264
Uppsala **8**:626
Ural Mountains **2**:87, **7**:507, **8**:612
Urga **8**:586
Uruguay **2**:*99*, **3**:217, **10**:772
Uruguay River **7**:552
Usk, Wales **10**:777
U.S.S.R. *see* Soviet Union
Ussuri **8**:586, **8**:613
Ussuri River **8**:585
Utah **2**:109, **2**:145, **5**:380
Utah Desert **7**:543
Uzbekistan **8**:564, **8**:565, **9**:661

Valladolid **3**:185, **3**:189, **6**:462
Vancouver, British Columbia **1**:24,
 4:313
Vancouver Island **3**:227, **10**:762,
 10:763, **10**:*764*
Vancouver, Washington **8**:615
Van Diemen's Land **4**:268, **10**:733

see also Tasmania
Vanuatu **1**:71, **8**:596, **9**:687, **9**:688
Varanasi **4**:259
Venezuela **3**:188, **5**:355, **8**:599,
 8:600, **10**:770
Venice **2**:126, **2**:129, **6**:476, **8**:564,
 8:565, **8**:566, **8**:568, **9**:663,
 10:748–749
Veracruz **3**:204, **3**:206, **5**:374
Verina **5**:*356*
Vermont **3**:209
Versailles **1**:*61*
Victoria, South Australia **2**:110
Victoria Falls **6**:414, **6**:416
Victoria Land **7**:554, **7**:557
Victory Point, King William Island
 4:277
Vienna **5**:392, **10**:746
Vietnam **3**:166, **3**:167, **4**:274, **4**:295,
 4:296–297
 South **8**:567
Vineyard Sound **10**:768
Vinland **4**:317–318, **6**:407, **7**:549,
 7:550
Virginia **1**:30, **2**:94, **2**:118, **3**:177,
 3:182, **3**:213, **4**:281, **4**:*312*, **4**:313,
 5:326, **6**:454, **6**:455, **6**:456, **8**:598,
 8:599, **9**:668–671
Virgin Islands **3**:187
Vostock Island **2**:86

Wadi Hammamat **6**:427
Wales **2**:105, **9**:711, **9**:712, **10**:777,
 10:779
Wapakoneta, Ohio **1**:27
Ward Hunt Island **8**:627
Warsaw **10**:783
Washington, DC **3**:193, **4**:253,
 4:256, **5**:390, **6**:411, **6**:454, **6**:457,
 9:671, **9**:672, **9**:673, **10**:789
Washington State **1**:33, **1**:34, **4**:279,
 4:280, **8**:615, **10**:737, **10**:788
Waterloo **2**:100
Weddell Sea **8**:627
Wellington Channel **4**:276
West Africa **1**:70, **2**:115, **2**:117,
 2:143, **3**:183, **3**:213, **3**:222, **4**:252,
 4:273, **4**:274, **4**:284, **4**:302, **4**:314,
 5:328–330, **5**:332, **6**:431, **6**:470,
 7:533–536, **8**:602, **9**:650, **9**:651,
 9:654, **10**:788, **10**:790
Western Sahara **3**:175
West Indies **1**:70, **2**:126, **2**:155,
 3:187, **3**:205, **3**:226, **4**:247, **4**:287,
 4:298, **6**:443
West Virginia **8**:632
Wetheringsett, Suffolk **5**:324
Whitby **3**:196

White Nile **10**:745
White Sea **2**:89
Wilkes Land **7**:556
Willamette River valley **9**:665
Williamstown, Ontario **10**:738
Willoughby, Lincolnshire **9**:668
Winchester, Virginia **2**:118
Wind River Mountains **4**:280
Winnipeg **5**:395
Winnipeg River **5**:397
Wisconsin River **5**:371, **6**:437
Wounded Knee, South Dakota
 1:26
Wyoming **1**:32, **2**:108, **5**:398, **8**:578,
 8:*618*, **9**:664

Yakutsk **2**:88, **2**:90, **8**:612
Yang-chou **8**:567
Yangtze River **2**:93, **3**:166, **8**:567,
 8:586
Yasshüyük **1**:15
Yellow River **4**:257, **4**:258, **8**:586
Yellowstone National Park **2**:107,
 2:109, **8**:*580*
Yellowstone River **1**:57, **6**:408,
 6:412
Yemen **5**:358
Yenisei River **7**:508
Yiyang **8**:567
York, Canada **7**:548
Yorkshire, England **2**:91, **4**:284,
 4:287
Yucatán **3**:204, **3**:205, **6**:462
Yucatán Peninsula **7**:551
Yukon **9**:675
Yumurtalik **8**:565
Yunnan Province **3**:164, **3**:167,
 4:296, **4**:297, **8**:567

Zacatecas **7**:523
Zambezi River **6**:414, **6**:416, **9**:*652*
Zanzibar **6**:417, **9**:712
Zayton **5**:361
Zeeland **10**:734
Zhaoqing **8**:610

INDEX OF SCIENCE AND TECHNOLOGY

Page numbers in *italic type* refer to illustrations. **Boldface** numbers preceding a colon indicate the volume number. Page numbers entirely in **boldface** type refer to main articles.

Admiral Fitzroy's Barometer **4**:267
aerial photography **1**:62–63, **1**:65, **2**:121, **4**:305, **6**:428, **6**:432, **8**:605, **8**:606, **10**:729, **10**:730
aerial sextant **2**:121, **2**:159
aeronautics **1**:27, **1**:29, **1**:79, **6**:468, **6**:479
aging research **4**:308
agriculture **4**:288, **10**:728
aircraft **1**:59–65, **6**:432
air pressure **3**:173, **3**:174, **4**:266, **4**:267
airships **1**:18, **1**:21, **1**:60, **3**:236–237
alcohol **8**:581, **8**:582
alidade **7**:499, **10**:728, **10**:729
alloy **6**:476, **6**:479
almanacs **7**:496, **10**:742
animal transport **5**:376, **5**:377, **5**:378, **5**:381
anthropology **1**:22–26, **5**:336, **5**:399, **6**:459
Apollo project **1**:28–29, **1**:38, **1**:39, **1**:48, **6**:432, **6**:466, **6**:467, **9**:644, **9**:645, **9**:646, **9**:692, **9**:696, **9**:697
Aqua-Lung **3**:173, **3**:209–210, **3**:211, **10**:758–759, **10**:760
archaeology **1**:76–78, **4**:318, **5**:338, **6**:453, **9**:660, **9**:663, **10**:747
  aerial **1**:63
  underwater **10**:724
Arecibo radio telescope, Puerto Rico **1**:46, **1**:54, **8**:632, **8**:633, **8**:634
armillary sphere **5**:343
assayers **4**:285
asteroid belt **9**:681, **9**:700, **9**:719
asteroids **1**:53, **1**:54, **9**:676, **9**:681, **9**:719
astrolabe **1**:43, **3**:232, **5**:343, **5**:344, **5**:345, **5**:392, **5**:399, **7**:491, **7**:494, **7**:497, **7**:499–500, **9**:695, **10**:729, **10**:770
  plane **5**:343, **5**:345
astronauts **1**:27–29, **1**:37–42, **1**:47, **3**:195, **4**:288, **4**:306–308, **5**:382
  clothing **3**:173–174

training **1**:42, **9**:644, **9**:645, **9**:646
  see also cosmonauts
astronomical instruments **1**:43–48
astronomical tables **7**:485
astronomy **1**:49–54, **3**:185, **3**:233, **4**:252, **4**:300, **6**:429, **7**:484
  radio **1**:46
  and search for extraterrestrial intelligence **8**:632
atmosphere **6**:479
atmospheric pressure **10**:782
aurora borealis **2**:101, **2**:102, **2**:159, **3**:238
autonomous underwater vehicle (AUV) **10**:727
aviation **1**:59–65, **2**:103, **2**:118–121, **3**:235–238
  first flight **1**:59, **8**:606
  long-distance **8**:615
  modern uses in exploration **1**:65

back staff **1**:67, **7**:494, **7**:500–501
ballast **10**:725, **10**:799
balloons **6**:432, **8**:627
  cameras attached to **8**:605
  flights **1**:59, **1**:61, **1**:62, **10**:725, **10**:784
barometer **3**:239, **4**:266, **4**:267, **10**:782, **10**:784
  Admiral Fitzroy's Barometer **4**:267
  Fitzroy's Remarks **4**:267
barometric pressure **3**:233, **3**:239
bathymetric map **10**:760
bathyscaphe **3**:210, **3**:239, **10**:724–725, **10**:726, **10**:799
bathysphere **10**:724, **10**:726, **10**:799
bearing **6**:447, **6**:479, **10**:799
Beaufort Wind Scale **4**:266, **10**:783
bends, the (decompression sickness) **3**:173, **3**:239, **10**:759
big bang theory **1**:54, **9**:677
binnacle **7**:498
biology **3**:218, **3**:219
birds **1**:55–58, **7**:487
  banding **1**:56, **1**:57
  endangered **1**:58
  in navigation **7**:491
bireme **5**:329
black box **10**:726
black hole **1**:52, **1**:53, **1**:79
book production **8**:592

botany **1**:69–71, **3**:197, **3**:198, **4**:253, **4**:314, **5**:354, **5**:355, **5**:365, **6**:452, **7**:484, **7**:486–487, **7**:559, **8**:587, **8**:626, **10**:744
botulism **4**:278, **4**:319
breathing apparatus **3**:209–210
bronze **6**:476, **10**:747
Buran space shuttle **9**:692

calendars **3**:207
camcorders, digital **8**:601, **8**:604
cameras **1**:23, **1**:65, **4**:277
  attached to balloons **8**:605
  attached to homing pigeons **8**:605, **8**:606
  digital **7**:541, **8**:604
  distortion **1**:65
  movie **1**:24
canoes **5**:371, **5**:380, **5**:647, **9**:653–654, **10**:743
  birch-bark **5**:396, **5**:397, **10**:735
caravel **2**:137, **2**:159, **3**:222, **3**:225, **4**:291, **4**:293, **5**:331, **5**:332, **5**:334, **5**:399, **9**:648–650, **9**:651, **9**:654
caravela redonda **9**:649, **9**:651
carracks *see* naos
carbon dioxide **9**:678
cartography **3**:230–231, **4**:247, **4**:265, **4**:279, **4**:295, **4**:300, **4**:319, **5**:345, **6**:427–432, **6**:433–435, **6**:444–447, **6**:452, **6**:479, **7**:503, **8**:574, **8**:591, **8**:592, **8**:639
  and remote sensing **8**:607
  and satellites **8**:622
carvel-built hulls **9**:648–649, **9**:719
catamaran **6**:461, **6**:479, **10**:792, **10**:799
caulking **9**:649, **9**:719
cellular phones **3**:194
Chagas disease **3**:219
Chandra X-ray Observatory **1**:48, **9**:674
chariots **5**:377
charts **4**:265, **7**:492, **7**:494, **7**:503
  navigational, as records **6**:428, **8**:601
  synoptic **4**:267
chip log **3**:220, **3**:221
chlorofluorocarbons (CFCs) **8**:607
cholera **2**:113, **2**:159, **9**:706
chronometer **1**:43, **3**:168–169, **3**:217, **3**:221, **3**:232, **4**:266, **4**:309, **5**:388, **5**:392–393, **7**:494, **7**:495,

7:559
H1 **3**:169
H4 **3**:168, **3**:169
K1 **3**:169
circumnavigation of the world **2**:84, **2**:97–99, **2**:131, **2**:148–150, **3**:213, **3**:226–228, **4**:302, **6**:422–426
civil engineering **4**:311
clay tables **8**:601
climate **3**:232–233, **4**:250
  change and coral reefs **10**:759
  zones **9**:686
climatology **5**:356
clinker-built hulls **9**:648–649, **9**:719
clocks at sea **3**:168–169, **5**:392–393
clothing **3**:170–174
  desert **3**:172
  freezing climate **3**:171–172
  sea **3**:172–173
  space **3**:173–174
  underwater **3**:173, **10**:756, **10**:759
cloud types **10**:785
coal-tar naphtha **3**:172, **3**:239
coastlines, changing **8**:607
cogs **9**:649, **9**:719
collections **1**:24–26, **8**:587
  exploration and **9**:674–675
  museum **6**:453–457
collectives **4**:288
colliers **3**:196, **3**:239
Columbia space shuttle **1**:39, **1**:40, **6**:468, **9**:692–693, **9**:697, **10**:791
comets **1**:53, **9**:676, **9**:681, **9**:719
communication **3**:190–191
  distress signals **3**:192
  satellite **3**:191, **3**:194, **3**:195, **4**:311, **6**:468, **8**:620, **8**:621
  telephone **3**:194
  underwater **3**:195
  wireless **3**:192–193
  without speech **3**:191–192
communication devices **3**:190–195**
  underwater **3**:195
compass **3**:185, **4**:303, **7**:492–493, **7**:497–498, **7**:498
  magnetic **3**:220, **3**:232, **4**:302, **4**:309, **7**:498, **10**:729
  pivoting ship's **7**:493, **7**:498
  variation problem **3**:220, **7**:498

compass points **7**:489
compass rose **7**:*489*
computers
   handheld **8**:601, **8**:604
   high-speed digital **6**:432
   laptop **8**:604
   map projections **6**:435
conic projections **6**:435
conservationism **3**:211
Conshelf projects **3**:210
constellation **7**:489
construction **3**:231
   surveying for projects
      10:728–730
continental shelf **3**:210, **3**:239,
   10:756, **10**:761
coordinates (map) **4**:301, **8**:591
copper **6**:477, **10**:747
copperplate engraving **6**:447
coral **3**:198, **3**:216, **9**:662
coral reefs **3**:218, **4**:*312*, **10**:759,
   10:761
corona **9**:719
corvette **2**:84, **2**:159
cosmography **6**:445, **10**:772
cosmonauts **1**:37–42, **4**:288–290,
   4:306 *see also* astronauts
cotton **6**:441, **6**:453
crane **6**:431, **6**:479
crop rotation **3**:179
cross-staff **7**:494, **7**:500
cultural anthropology **1**:22
cultural geography **4**:300, **4**:305
cumulus **7**:491, **10**:785
curragh **2**:105, **2**:159, **9**:658
currents **7**:508, **8**:*571*, **8**:572,
   10:**739–743**
  defined **10**:739
  world's main **10**:*742*
cyclones **7**:505
cylindrical projections **6**:434–435

Dacron **3**:174
Daguerre camera **7**:*541*
daguerrotype **7**:542
dark matter **1**:53
Davis quadrant **1**:*67*
dead reckoning **3**:168, **3**:**220–221**,
   3:232, **7**:492, **7**:494, **7**:496
decompression chamber **3**:173
deductive reasoning **7**:485
Deep Space Network **8**:632, **9**:701,
   9:702
deforestation **1**:64
dehydration **3**:174
delta **9**:709, **9**:719
desalination **8**:597
dhow **5**:359, **5**:399, **9**:647, **9**:648

diamonds **6**:477, **6**:478
diesel power **9**:648, **9**:650
digital photography **7**:541, **7**:544
direct observation **7**:485
diseases **3**:181–182, **3**:197,
   5:366–370, **9**:669, **9**:670, **9**:706
  brought by colonizers **3**:180,
     3:181–182, **3**:208
  carried by explorers **3**:181–182,
     3:187, **5**:370
  of the cold **5**:368–370
  dietary **8**:583, **8**:584
  European **6**:472
  vitamin deficiency **8**:583
distress signals **3**:192
diving **10**:758–759
  communication devices **3**:195
  decompression sickness (the
    bends) **10**:759
  suits **3**:173, **3**:209, **10**:*756*, **10**:759
Dornier flying boats **3**:235
draft **10**:799
drifting research stations **8**:614
drinking supplies **8**:581–582
  freshwater **8**:581, **8**:582, **8**:597,
    10:757
dry suits **3**:173
dwarf stars **1**:52
dysentery **3**:228, **4**:296, **4**:319,
   5:366, **5**:368, **6**:417

Earth **3**:229–234, **5**:343, **5**:345, **7**:484,
   7:486, **9**:676, **9**:678, **9**:679, **9**:695,
   10:752
  beneath the surface of **3**:231
  as center of the universe **1**:49,
    3:233, **8**:590, **9**:676
  circumference of **4**:244,
    4:245–246, **4**:298, **4**:299, **4**:300,
    4:302, **4**:303, **5**:364, **8**:593
  crust **10**:779
  dimensions of **4**:305
  as flat **3**:185, **3**:229, **4**:300
  magnetic field of **4**:253, **7**:492,
    7:508
  mantle and core of **3**:231
  mapping **3**:230–231, **8**:606–607
  orbiting **4**:288–290, **4**:306–308,
    4:319
  as part of a heliocentric
    universe **1**:49, **3**:233, **8**:591,
    9:676
  photos from space of **6**:428,
    6:432, **6**:435, **6**:469
  polar circumference of **1**:50
  revolutionary ideas about **3**:233
  as a sphere **4**:299
  statistics of **3**:231

earthquakes **3**:217, **3**:231
Earth Resources Technology
   Satellite *see Landsat*
Eckert projection **6**:435
eclipse of the moon **4**:299, **6**:451
eclipse of the sun **1**:51, **3**:197,
   5:344
ecology **6**:477
economics **6**:439–443
ecosystems **10**:724, **10**:727, **10**:759
ejector seat **4**:289
electric telegraph **3**:190, **3**:192
electromagnetic radiation **3**:193,
   3:239, **9**:677
electromagnetic spectrum **1**:46,
   1:48, **1**:50, **1**:79, **8**:605–606,
   8:633, **8**:639
electronic maps **4**:311
electronic navigation **7**:494–496
elevation **4**:310
energy **7**:497
engraving **6**:447
entomology **10**:777, **10**:778
environmentalism **4**:256, **9**:675
  and satellites **8**:622
equator **5**:389, **5**:390, **9**:715, **10**:743
equinoxes, precession of the
   5:343, **5**:399
ethnography **1**:23, **5**:363
ethnology **1**:22, **8**:578, **8**:580
European Remote-Sensing
   Satellite (ERS-1) **8**:*605*
evolution **1**:22, **10**:777–780
  Darwin's theory of **3**:216,
    3:217–218, **3**:219, **4**:264, **4**:267,
    7:487
evolutionary theory **3**:216, **3**:219,
   7:487
excavations **2**:90, **5**:338
expedition data,
   publication of **8**:601
   record keeping **8**:**601–604**
experimentation **7**:485
extraterrestrial **1**:41, **1**:46, **1**:49,
   1:54, **1**:79, **7**:531, **8**:632–634,
   8:639
  transport **5**:382
Extravehicular Mobility Unit
   (EMU) **3**:174

factories **6**:413
Ferguson tractors **5**:381
fiber-optic cable **3**:191, **3**:194,
   3:239
field research **1**:24, **4**:251
film strip **7**:541, **7**:542
flares, distress signals **3**:192
flora and fauna **1**:69–70, **8**:603

food
  pickling in brine **8**:582
  preservation **3**:179, **8**:582
  production **3**:179, **3**:182
  salted **8**:582, **8**:583
fossils **3**:217, **7**:508, **10**:731, **10**:753
foundry **2**:90, **2**:159
free trade **6**:440, **6**:442, **6**:443
freshwater **8**:596, **8**:597, **10**:755
frostbite **1**:20, **3**:171, **5**:366, **5**:*368*,
   5:368, **5**:370, **7**:537, **8**:630, **8**:639

gabardine **3**:171, **3**:239
Galata observatory **4**:*300*
galaxies **1**:52, **9**:677
Galileo mission **9**:691, **9**:697,
   9:700–701
galleon **9**:650, **9**:651, **9**:719
galleys **9**:647, **9**:658
gangrene **2**:138, **2**:159, **5**:368,
   8:630, **8**:639
Gemini Project **1**:27, **1**:28, **1**:39,
   6:466, **6**:467, **6**:*468*, **9**:692, **9**:697
geocentric view of the universe
   1:49, **3**:233, **8**:590, **9**:676
geographical societies **4**:251–256,
   8:586
Geographic Information System
   (GIS) **6**:428
geography **3**:185, **3**:230–231,
   4:244–247, **4**:252–253,
   4:298–305, **5**:324, **5**:344–345,
   5:354–357, **5**:363, **6**:427–429,
   6:445, **6**:447, **7**:484, **8**:585,
   8:591–593, **8**:595, **9**:716–718
  first textbook **4**:304, **4**:305
geological surveys **3**:231, **3**:235,
   6:475, **8**:578, **8**:580, **10**:730–731
geology **3**:231, **3**:235, **4**:253, **4**:311,
   4:319, **5**:354, **5**:399, **7**:508, **8**:578,
   8:580, **10**:753, **10**:756, **10**:779
  and satellites **8**:622
geomagnetic field **5**:357
geophysics **2**:121
Geosat **10**:742
geostationary satellites **4**:311,
   8:623, **10**:785, **10**:799
GIS (Geographic Information
   System) **6**:428
glacier **2**:102–103, **2**:118, **2**:159
glider flight **1**:59
Global Orbiting Navigation
   Satellite System (GLONASS)
   4:309
Global Positioning System (GPS)
   1:43, **4**:309–311, **5**:388, **5**:*389*,
   5:393, **7**:495, **7**:496, **8**:620,
   8:622–623

satellites **4:**309, **4:**310, **4:**311
GLONASS *see* Global Orbiting
　　Navigation Satellite System
GLORIA sonar device **10:**760
gnomon **9:***695*
gnomonic projection **6:**434
GOES weather satellite **10:**781
gold mining **3:**182, **4:**284
Gore-Tex **3:**174
GPS *see* Global Positioning
　　System
gradient **10:**729, **10:**799
gravitation **1:**51, **1:**52
gravity **1:**50, **1:**52, **1:**79, **5:**393, **8:**619,
　　9:677, **9:**719, **10:**742
　and the moon **10:**739
　zero **1:**38, **1:**41
gravity assist **9:**691
Great Trigonometrical Survey of
　　India **10:**731, **10:**794
greenhouse effect **9:**678, **9:**719
Greenwich Mean Time **3:**168–169
Greenwich meridian **3:**168, **4:**266,
　　5:389, **5:***391*, **5:**392
Greenwich Royal Observatory
　　5:388, **5:***390*, **5:**391, **5:**393
grid **4:**247, **4:**300, **4:**302, **4:**319,
　　5:345, **6:**447, **10:**730
gunpowder **1:**30, **1:**71
Gunter's chain **10:**729, **10:**730
gyrocompass **7:**502
gyroscope **7:**502

Halley's comet **1:**53
handheld maneuvering unit
　　(HHMU) **1:**38
hardtack **8:**582–583
heliocentric view of the universe
　　1:49, **3:**233, **8:**591, **9:**676
heliograph **3:**192
heliopause **9:**702
Helios 1 **9:**702
Helios 2 **9:**696, **9:**702
helium **9:**677
hemisphere **1:**53, **1:**79, **6:**433, **6:**446
hovercraft **9:**658
Hubble Space Telescope (HST)
　　1:41, **1:**46, **1:**47, **1:**51, **8:**620,
　　8:622
hybrid remotely operated vehicle
　　(HROV) **10:**727
hydrogen **1:**61, **9:**677
hydrographic survey **6:**451
hydrography **4:**313, **4:**319, **5:**371,
　　6:452, **10:**733, **10:**760, **10:**799
Hydrolab **10:**761
hydrothermal vents **10:**727
hygrometer **10:**782

hypothermia **3:**173, **3:**239, **5:**366,
　　5:370

icebreakers **7:**512, **7:***514*, **8:**612,
　　8:614, **8:**615, **9:**650, **9:**655, **9:***658*
illness and disease **5:**366–370
immersion suits **3:**173
India rubber **3:**172
inductive reasoning **7:**485
Industrial Revolution **6:**413
infrared rays **1:**47, **1:**48, **1:**65
internal combustion engine
　　5:376, **5:**378
international date line **5:**389
International Space Station (ISS)
　　1:39, **6:**466, **6:**468, **6:***469*, **8:**620,
　　9:692, **9:**694
Internet **8:**604
　and SETI **8:**634
interrupted homosoline
　　projection **6:**435
inventions **1:**71, **3:**172
　communications **3:**190–195
　the wheel **5:**376, **5:**377
iron firebox **8:**582
irrigation **10:**728
Italia (airship) **1:**18, **1:**21, **3:**238

James Webb Space Telescope
　　1:48
jet aircraft **1:**59
junks **3:***164*, **9:**647

karst **10:**754, **10:**755
kayak **4:**285, **4:**287, **6:**460
Keck I and II telescopes **1:**45, **1:**46
keel **9:**719
keelboat **6:**410, **6:**479
Kevlar **3:**174
knarr **6:**407, **9:**648
knots (nautical miles per hour)
　　3:221, **7:**492

lacquerware **9:**662
Lambert conformal conic
　　projection **6:**435
land claims and record keeping
　　8:601
land management **8:**580
landmarks **7:**491
Landsat (Earth Resources
　　Technology Satellites) **6:**432,
　　6:468, **6:**469, **8:**606, **8:**607, **8:**622
land surveying **10:**728–730
land transport **2:**139–143,
　　5:376–382
land vehicles, remote-controlled
　　on Mars **1:**65

laser **10:**729
lateen **4:**293, **9:**648, **9:**651, **9:**719
latitude **1:**43, **3:**185, **3:**232, **4:**299,
　　4:300, **4:**302, **4:**310, **5:**342, **5:**345,
　　5:364, **5:**388–393, **5:**399, **6:**428,
　　6:447, **7:**491, **7:**494, **7:**499, **8:**591,
　　8:592
　defined **5:**389
latitude sailing **6:**406, **7:**492
lead and line **7:**494, **7:**497, **7:**498
life preservers **3:**173
linen cloth **9:**662
lithograph **4:**276
logbooks **8:***601*, **10:**767, **10:**799
logline **3:**220
longitude **3:**168, **3:**197, **3:**221,
　　3:232, **4:**266, **4:**299, **4:**300, **4:**302,
　　4:310, **5:**342, **5:**345, **5:**364,
　　5:388–393, **5:**399, **6:**428, **6:**447,
　　6:451, **7:**496, **8:**591
　defined **5:**389
　lunar distance method **1:**67
　problem **1:**43, **3:**168–169, **7:**494,
　　7:495
long ship **6:***407*, **8:***624*, **9:**648
Luna 1 **9:**695, **9:**696
Luna 2 **9:**691, **9:**692, **9:**695
Luna 3 **9:**695
lunar distance method **1:**67, **7:**496
lunar eclipse **4:**299, **6:**451
lunar month **5:**344, **10:**742
Lunar Rover **5:**377, **5:***382*, **6:**469
lunar roving vehicle (LRV) **9:***696*

mackintosh raincoat **3:**172
Magellan Venus space probe
　　9:700
magnetic compass **3:**220, **3:**232,
　　4:302, **4:**309, **6:**428, **10:**729
magnetic field **2:**103
magnetic storms **5:**354, **5:**357,
　　5:399
magnetism
　of the earth **4:**253
　and radio communication **2:**103
magnetite **7:**498, **7:**559
magnetosphere **8:**620, **8:**639
malaria **1:**17, **2:**116, **5:**356, **5:**366,
　　5:368, **5:**369, **5:**399, **6:**415, **7:**559,
　　8:595, **10:**771, **10:**772, **10:**779
manned maneuvering unit
　　(MMU) **1:**38
mantle **3:**231, **3:**239
mapmaking **2:**102, **2:**130–131,
　　3:231, **4:**299, **6:**427–432, **7:**492,
　　7:506
　medieval **5:**362, **5:**364–365
　and surveying **10:**729

mapping the seabed **10:**760
map projection **4:**247, **4:**299,
　　4:319, **5:**345, **6:**427, **6:**428, **6:**429,
　　6:433–435, **8:**592
　conic projections **6:***433*, **6:**435
　cylindrical projections **6:***433*,
　　6:434–435
　gnomonic projection **6:**434
　Mercator projection **4:**303,
　　6:428, **6:**429, **6:**434–435, **6:**444,
　　6:446,–447, **7:**504, **7:**506
　Peters projection **6:**434
　plane projection **6:**433, **6:**434
　pseudocylindrical **6:**435
map referencing **5:**388, **5:**393
　latitude and longitude **5:**388–393
maps **4:**298, **4:**299, **4:**303, **4:**304
　in the ancient world **6:**427–428,
　　6:447
　dual function **6:**427
　electronic **4:**311
　first world map printed in
　　England **7:***515*
　medieval **5:**362, **6:**428, **7:**528,
　　7:529
　names and claims **6:**432
　pioneers **5:**390
　as records **8:**601
　standardized **5:**390
　T and O renderings **6:**428
　see also world maps
marine archaeology **9:**656
marine biology **7:**488
marine conservation **3:**211
Mariner space probes **9:**678, **9:**691,
　　9:696, **9:**698, **9:**700
marine science **9:**674, **10:**757–758
Mars 2 **9:**698
Mars 3 **9:**698
Mars Global Surveyor (*MGS*) 1:65,
　　6:466, **9:**678, **9:**697, **9:**699
Mars orbital laser altimeter
　　(MOLA) **9:**699
mathematics **4:**244–247, **4:**265,
　　4:299, **5:**342–345
　instrument making **6:**447
　and map projection **6:**433–435,
　　6:445
　reasoning **7:**485
Mayday distress signal **3:**192
measles **3:**181, **5:**370, **9:**706
medicine **3:**179
meltwater **6:**411, **6:**479
mercantilism **6:**439–443, **7:**503,
　　10:750
　and the nation-state **6:**441–442
Mercator projection **4:**299, **4:**303,
　　6:428, **6:**429, **6:**434–435, **6:**444,

Mercator projection *(cont.)*
6:446–447, 7:504, 7:506
merchant companies 7:515, 9:659,
10:747
Mercury space program 3:174,
6:466–467, 9:644–645, 9:674,
9:692, 9:697
meridian 3:168, 3:197, 3:239, 4:266,
5:389, 5:390, 5:399, 6:434, 6:435
Greenwich 5:389, 5:390–391,
5:399
Messenger (Mercury Surface,
Space Environment,
Geochemistry and Ranging)
space probe 9:678, 9:697, 9:700
metallurgy 6:452
meteorites 1:53, 1:54, 9:678, 9:681
meteoroids 1:53, 9:681
meteorology 3:232–233, 3:239,
4:264, 4:267, 8:623, 8:633, 8:639,
10:781–785
microbes 7:486
micrometeorite 8:639
micrometeoroids 1:38, 3:174
migration 3:182, 7:527, 10:787
military planning, aerial
photography and 6:432
mineralogy 5:354, 6:452, 7:507
mineral resources 6:439,
6:476–477
mining 1:30, 3:231, 4:284, 4:286,
10:728, 10:752
mining school 5:354
Mini Remote-Operated Vehicle II
(MR2) 10:*726*
Mir space station 1:41, 8:615, 9:694
modules 4:289, 4:319
monopoly 2:142, 2:158, 2:159,
5:384, 5:396, 5:399, 6:441, 7:504,
8:574, 10:750
moon 1:28, 1:46, 5:355, 5:393,
8:619, 9:*676*
distance from the earth 5:344
eclipses of the 4:299, 6:451
exploration 6:466, 6:467, 6:469
first landing on the 1:28–29,
3:194, 7:541, 7:*544*
first spacecraft to reach the
9:691
first walk on the 1:27–29, 1:28,
1:29, 1:38, 1:39
gravitational pull of the 10:739,
10:742
missions to the 9:644, 9:646,
9:692, 9:696
radio-controlled lunar vehicles
5:377
space station on 9:699

and the tides 10:740, 10:742
moons 9:676, 9:679, 9:701
motion, Newton's laws of 1:49,
1:51, 3:233, 9:677
motor vehicles 5:376, 5:377, 5:381
extraterrestrial transport 5:382
mountain transport 5:382
multispectral scanner 8:606, 8:639
mummification 1:22
museums 1:23, 1:24–26, 6:453–457,
9:672–675
Mylar 3:174

names for new botanical
discoveries 7:485, 7:487
naos 9:650, 9:*653*
NASA (National Aeronautics and
Space Administration) 1:27,
1:28, 1:29, 4:308, 6:466–469,
6:478, 9:645, 9:674, 9:677, 9:678,
9:692, 9:696, 9:699, 9:700
natural history 6:455, 7:485–486,
10:777–780
natural philosophy 7:485
natural resources 3:231, 6:474–478
food 6:474
land 6:474
minerals 6:476–478
spices 6:474–476
natural sciences 6:454, 7:484–488
natural selection 3:216, 3:219
nautical charts 6:428, 8:601
navigation 3:168–169, 3:232,
7:489–496, 7:498
celestial 1:43, 1:49, 1:67, 3:232,
5:343, 5:392, 7:484, 7:489–491,
7:496, 9:678, 9:695
dead reckoning 3:220–221
electronic 7:494–496
Global Positioning System
4:309–311
landmarks 7:491
mapmaking and 6:429, 6:447
and map referencing 5:388–393
radio-based 4:309
satellite-based 4:309–311
tides and currents 10:739–743
use of chronometer 4:266
winds in 7:489–491
navigational instruments
7:492–496, 7:497–502
chronometer 3:168–169, 4:266
Navstar 1 (GPS satellite) 4:309
negative (photographic) 7:541,
7:559
dry-plate 7:541, 7:542, 7:543
neoprene 3:173, 3:174
neutron stars 1:52

nimbus 10:785
Nimbus (weather satellite) 8:607,
8:620, 8:623, 10:785
Norge (airship) 1:18, 1:21, 1:60,
1:62, 2:119, 3:236–237
North Pole 1 (drifting research
station) 8:614
nuclear powered ships 9:650,
9:651
nutrition 3:179, 8:584

observatories 5:354, 5:357, 5:*390*,
5:391, 9:674
ocean drilling program 7:486
oceanography 3:234, 4:311, 4:319,
6:461, 10:743, 10:756–761
remote-sensing studies 8:605,
8:607, 8:620
ocean ridge systems 7:486, 7:488
oceans, depth sounding
10:756–757
observing from space 10:761
octant 7:494, 7:495, 7:501
oil pipelines 10:724
oil prospecting 6:475, 6:477,
10:730–731
oil tanker 7:519
Opportunity space rover 9:678,
9:697, 9:699
orbit 6:468, 8:619, 8:623, 9:676,
9:681
retrograde 9:679
ores, testing 4:285
Orion lunar module 9:*696*
ornithology 1:55–58, 10:745
ozone layer 8:607

paleontology 10:753
parallels 4:247, 5:389, 5:390, 5:399,
6:434
Parkes telescope 8:634
patent 1:79
Pathfinder space probe 6:469,
6:*478*, 9:678, 9:699
PDAs (personal digital assistants)
8:604
Peters projection 6:434
philology 4:244, 4:319
philosophy 4:244, 4:299, 9:686
photogrammetry 10:729
photography 1:23, 1:62–63, 1:65,
2:92, 2:*93*, 2:101, 2:102,
7:541–544, 8:604
aerial 1:62–63, 8:605, 8:606
digital 7:544
dry-plate glass negatives 1:22
flexible film strip 7:541, 7:542
and printing 7:542

satellite 1:63, 1:65, 3:*229*, 3:230
wet collodion process 7:541,
7:542
photointerpretation 8:605
physical anthropology 1:22
physical geography 4:305
phytoplankton 10:761
pinnace 3:227, 4:285, 4:319
pirogue 4:296, 6:410, 6:479
pitch 6:441
plane projections 6:433–434
plane table 10:*728*, 10:729
planets 1:51, 4:252, 5:391, 6:468,
7:485, 9:676, 9:678, 9:680–681,
9:698–702
far 9:680–681
giant 9:680
gravitational pull of 9:691
hot 9:678
movement of 3:233
orbits 1:50
red 9:678–679
supporting life 9:678
planisphere 5:364, 5:399
plankton 5:357
plants 1:69–70, 6:455, 8:599, 8:617,
8:624, 8:626
classification of 7:486, 7:487
plumb line 3:185
polar exploration 7:553–558
drifting research stations 8:614
provisioning 8:*581*, 8:583
transport 5:381, 8:629
population 3:182
growth 6:443, 6:474
Malthus's theory 7:488, 10:779
world 3:182
portage 5:371, 5:399, 6:438, 6:479
portolan charts 6:*423*, 7:492
postal service,
Chinese system 8:568
first transatlantic 2:121
precession of the equinoxes
5:343
pressure ridge 6:479
prevailing wind 9:650, 9:703,
9:719, 10:743
prime meridian 5:388, 5:390–391,
5:399
printing,
invention of 6:429
and photography 7:542
Project FAMOUS (French-
American Mid-Ocean
Undersea Study) 10:727
projection *see* map projection
Project Mercury *see* Mercury
space program

Project Ozma (SETI) **8**:632
Project Phoenix (SETI) **8**:633, **8**:634
prominence **9**:677
propeller **9**:648, **9**:650, **9**:719
provisioning **8**:581–584
pulsars **1**:52, **9**:702
pyramids **7**:*542*, **10**:730

quadrant **1**:43, **3**:185, **7**:494,
    7:499–500
  Davis **1**:*67*
quasars **1**:53
quinine **5**:366, **5**:369

radar **1**:43, **1**:63, **1**:64, **1**:65, **7**:495,
    7:*496*, **10**:728, **10**:784, **10**:799
radar mapping **3**:230, **3**:231, **3**:239
radiation **8**:607, **8**:620, **8**:639
radio **3**:*190*, **3**:192, **3**:193, **3**:194,
    4:289
radio astronomy **1**:46
radio communication **3**:190,
    3:192, **3**:193, **3**:194, **4**:289, **7**:496
  and magnetism **2**:103
radio waves **4**:309, **4**:310
rafts **9**:647, **9**:648, **9**:651, **9**:658
railroads **2**:109, **4**:283, **5**:380, **10**:728
reconnaisance **1**:59, **1**:79, **5**:399,
    8:605
record keeping **8**:601–604
  classic visual records **8**:603
  classic written accounts
      8:602–603
  modern **8**:604
  purpose of **8**:601
reflecting telescopes **1**:45, **1**:46,
    1:50
refracting telescopes **1**:44–45,
    1:46, **1**:50
refractor **1**:44–45, **1**:79
relativity theories **1**:50–51, **1**:79,
    9:677
remotely operated vehicle (ROV)
    1:65, **10**:726–727
  hybrid (HROV) **10**:727
Remote Manipulator System **1**:*47*
remote sensing **6**:432, **6**:468–469,
    6:*478*, **6**:479, **8**:605–607, **9**:675
  aerial photography **8**:605
  early developments **8**:605
  electromagnetic spectrum
      8:605–606
  mapping the earth **8**:606–607
  satellites **8**:605–607
  research centers **9**:672
rhumb lines **6**:447
Robinson projection **6**:435
robotics **10**:760

rocket power **9**:690, **9**:695
rocket science **1**:37
rudder **9**:648, **9**:649

safety lamp **5**:354
saltpeter **1**:30
sandglass **3**:220, **7**:*492*
satellite communication **3**:191,
    3:194, **3**:195, **4**:311, **6**:468, **8**:620,
    8:621
satellite photography **1**:63, **1**:65,
    3:*229*, **3**:230
satellites **1**:41, **1**:63, **1**:79,
    4:309–311, **4**:319, **5**:393, **6**:432,
    6:466, **6**:468, **6**:469, **7**:496,
    8:619–623
  exploring the universe **8**:622
  the first **8**:620
  geostationary **4**:311, **8**:623,
      10:*785*
  mapping the earth **8**:606–607,
      10:729
  natural **8**:619
  navigation **4**:309–311
  networks of **8**:623
  observation from space **8**:622,
      10:761
  orbiting **4**:309–311, **8**:619, **8**:623,
      9:690, **9**:695
  remote-sensing **8**:605–607
  in sea mapping **3**:234
  weather **8**:606, **8**:620, **8**:623,
      10:781, **10**:784–785
Saturn rockets **9**:*691*, **9**:692
scale (maps) **6**:427
science **5**:354, **7**:485
scientific collections **9**:672–675
scientific exploration **4**:305, **6**:452,
    6:454, **8**:577–580
scientific knowledge **7**:485
scientific revolution **4**:251,
    7:484–485
screw propeller **9**:648, **9**:650
scuba **3**:209–210, **10**:758
scurvy **1**:18, **2**:89, **2**:98, **2**:111, **2**:112,
    2:149, **2**:152, **2**:153, **2**:156, **2**:159,
    3:197, **3**:217, **4**:269, **4**:278, **4**:292,
    4:293, **5**:347, **5**:352, **5**:366–368,
    5:370, **5**:399, **6**:425, **7**:512, **7**:513,
    7:557, **7**:558, **8**:629, **8**:635, **8**:639,
    9:655
  remedies for **8**:584, **10**:763,
      10:764
sea
  clocks at **3**:168–169, **5**:392–393
  clothing for exploration at
      3:172–173
  communication signals **3**:192

time at **7**:492, **7**:495, **7**:559
seabed
  mapping the **3**:234, **10**:760
seamarks **7**:491
seaplanes **1**:*60*, **3**:237
Seasat **8**:607, **8**:620
seismic measurement **1**:65, **3**:231,
    3:239
seismic test **10**:731
semaphore **3**:190, **3**:191
SETI (Search for Extraterrestrial
    Intelligence) **1**:54, **8**:632–634
  instruments **8**:634
  projects **8**:633, **8**:634
  radio waves and interference
      8:633
sextant **1**:43, **1**:46, **3**:232, **3**:239,
    4:309, **5**:345, **5**:392, **5**:399, **7**:*494*,
    7:495, **7**:496, **7**:501, **7**:502,
    10:735, **10**:737
shipbuilding **2**:86, **2**:90, **3**:167,
    6:441, **6**:443, **7**:503, **9**:647–650
  design **6**:429, **6**:459
  early **9**:647
  materials **9**:648, **9**:650
ships **9**:651–658
  measuring speed of **3**:220, **7**:492
  reconstructing ancient **9**:658
signal fires **3**:191
sign language **4**:287
silk **3**:175, **4**:296, **6**:478, **9**:659,
    10:748, **10**:797, **10**:798
skiing **7**:518
Skylab space station **1**:38, **6**:466,
    6:468, **8**:*623*, **9**:691, **9**:692, **9**:694
sled boat **7**:517, **7**:518
sleds **1**:20, **5**:376, **5**:381, **7**:519,
    7:538, **7**:554, **7**:555, **7**:557, **7**:558,
    7:559, **8**:*629*
sloop **2**:149, **2**:159
smallpox **3**:176, **3**:180, **3**:181, **3**:182,
    3:208, **5**:366, **5**:370, **9**:669, **9**:706
SnoCats **5**:*381*
snow blindness **3**:171
socialism **10**:780
Solar and Heliospheric
    Observatory (SOHO) **9**:677,
    9:702
solar eclipse **1**:51, **1**:59, **3**:197,
    5:344
solar flares **9**:677, **9**:719
solar system **1**:49, **1**:52, **3**:233,
    6:468, **8**:590, **8**:591, **8**:619, **8**:632,
    8:639, **9**:676–681
  origins of the **9**:677
solar wind **9**:702, **9**:719
solar year **5**:342, **5**:344
solstice **4**:245, **4**:319

sonar **1**:65, **3**:234, **3**:239, **7**:494,
    7:495, **7**:559, **10**:728, **10**:760
sonic device **2**:103
SOS signal **3**:192
sound recording **1**:24
Soyuz 4 **1**:38
Soyuz 5 **1**:38
space
  observing oceans from **10**:761
  pictures of the earth from **6**:428,
      6:432, **6**:435, **6**:469
space capsule **4**:307
spacecraft **4**:288, **4**:289, **9**:690–694
  first manned **1**:28–29, **4**:306,
      9:692
space exploration **1**:27–29,
    1:37–42, **4**:288–290, **4**:306–308,
    6:466–469, **6**:477, **7**:531, **7**:544,
    9:644–646, **9**:695–702
  clothing **3**:173–174
  docking in space **1**:27, **1**:39
  international projects **1**:39
  living and working in space
      1:40–41
  manned spaceflight programs
      6:466–467
  remote control **6**:432,
      6:468–469, **6**:*478*, **6**:479
  satellites **6**:432, **6**:466, **6**:468,
      6:469
  walking in space **1**:38–39
Spacelab mission **9**:697
space oblique Mercator (SOM)
    projection **6**:435
space probes **6**:468–469, **6**:479,
    9:678, **9**:700
space shuttles **1**:29, **1**:39, **1**:41,
    4:308, **6**:466, **6**:468, **8**:620, **8**:622,
    9:692–694
space sickness **1**:41
space stations **1**:38–39, **1**:39, **1**:41,
    6:468, **8**:615, **8**:620, **8**:*623*, **9**:691,
    9:692, **9**:694, **9**:699
space suits **1**:38, **3**:173–174, **4**:*306*
space telescopes **1**:47–48, **8**:620,
    8:622
speleology **10**:755
Spirit space rover **6**:469, **9**:678,
    9:697, **9**:699
SPOT satellite **8**:606
spruce beer **10**:763, **10**:764, **10**:799
Sputnik 1 **4**:310, **6**:466, **8**:614, **8**:615,
    8:620, **9**:690, **9**:692, **9**:695
stars **1**:49, **1**:52–53, **5**:342–343,
    5:393, **7**:484, **7**:489, **8**:634
  catalogs of **1**:50, **5**:342, **5**:343,
      8:589
  shooting or falling **9**:681

steam-powered locomotives
5:378
steamships 9:648, 9:650, 10:743
stratosphere 1:61, 1:79
submarines 3:195, 9:648
    nuclear-powered 9:650, 9:651
submersibles 3:234, 10:724–727
    autonomous 10:727
    unmanned 10:726–727
sun 1:43, 1:46, 1:49, 3:233, 8:590,
    8:591, 9:676, 9:677, 9:702
    and celestial navigation 7:489,
        7:491
    as center of the universe 7:484,
        7:486
    eclipse of the 1:51, 1:59, 3:197,
        5:344
    measuring height of 7:499
sundials 4:298, 7:491, 10:799
sunspots 1:44, 1:49, 5:357, 9:677,
    9:719
supernovas 1:52
surveyor's chain see Gunter's
    chain
surveys 4:311, 10:728–731
    aerial 1:65, 4:305
    in the ancient world 10:730
    geological 3:231
    instruments 10:735
    methods 6:419, 6:452
    for oil 10:730–731
    purpose of 10:728–729
    technology 10:729
    underwater 10:729
    of the United States 10:730,
        10:735–738
survival of the fittest 3:219,
    7:487–488, 10:779
synoptic chart 4:267
synthetic fabrics 3:174

tacking 2:149, 2:159, 9:648, 9:719
taxonomy 7:559
tectonic plates 10:779
Teflon 3:174
Tektite project (NASA) 10:761
telegram 3:190, 3:192, 3:193
telegraph 4:267, 5:380
    electric 3:190, 3:192, 3:193
transatlantic cable route 10:743,
    10:757, 10:760
telegraphy, wireless 3:190, 3:193
telemetry 3:190, 3:195
telephone 3:190, 3:192, 3:194
    cellular 3:194
    mobile system 3:191
    underwater 3:234
    video service 3:191

telescopes 1:44–48, 1:49, 1:50,
    1:54, 3:191, 5:342, 5:343, 9:695,
    10:735
    Galileo's 7:484, 7:532
    radio 1:46, 1:47, 1:54, 8:632–634
    reflecting 1:45, 1:50
    refracting 1:44–45, 1:50
    space 1:47–48, 8:620, 8:622
television 3:194
    underwater cameras 3:210
Telstar 3:191, 3:194, 6:468, 8:620,
    8:621
termination shock 9:702
test pilots 4:288, 4:306, 9:644,
    9:645
theodolite 10:731
thermal imaging 1:63, 1:79
thermometer 10:782
tidal bore 10:741, 10:799
tide clocks 10:742
tide predictors 10:740, 10:741
tides 10:739–743
    defined 10:739
    measuring of 10:741–742
time at sea 3:168–169, 5:392–393,
    7:492, 7:495, 7:559
tin 6:474, 6:477, 10:747
TIROS (weather satellite) 8:606,
    8:620, 8:623, 10:784
tobacco 3:182, 3:186, 3:226, 3:228,
    6:440, 6:441, 8:599
topography 3:239, 4:279, 4:319,
    8:591, 8:605, 8:639
T and O renderings 6:428
total ozone mapping
    spectrometer (TOMS) 8:607
tourism 9:660, 9:661
    space 9:694
transit 1:69, 1:79, 4:252, 5:380
transport 3:179
    animals 5:378
    extraterrestrial 5:382
    land 5:376–382
    land survey for 10:728
    in the mountains 5:382
traverse board 3:220, 3:221
trigonometry 5:344, 5:345, 6:435,
    6:479
trireme 5:329
typhoid 4:296, 4:319, 5:368, 9:670,
    9:706

UAVs (unmanned aerial vehicles)
    1:63, 1:65
ultraviolet rays 1:47, 1:65, 3:172,
    3:239
underground exploration 10:728,
    10:752–755

undersea observatories 10:724,
    10:761
undersea telegraph cable 10:757
underwater exploration
    3:210–211, 3:234, 4:274,
    10:724–727, 10:756–761
    breathing 10:759
    clothing 3:173
    communication devices 3:195,
        3:234
universe 3:230
    big bang theory 1:54, 9:677
    geocentric theories 1:49, 3:233,
        8:590
    heliocentric theory 1:49, 8:591
    Newton's laws of motion 1:51

Van Allen radiation belt 8:620
Van der Grinten projection 6:435
vehicles
    four-wheel drive 5:382
    lightweight tracked 5:381
    radio-controlled lunar 5:377
    remote-controlled land 5:382
    wheeled 5:376, 5:377
    wind-powered 5:381
Venera Venus space probes 9:700
Very Large Array (VLA) radio
    telescope, 1:46, 1:47
videophone 3:191, 3:194
Viking space mission 9:691, 9:696,
    9:698–699
vitamin deficiency 8:583, 8:584,
    10:763
volcanoes 2:92, 2:106, 3:217, 3:218,
    3:231, 5:329, 7:557, 8:602, 8:606,
    10:785
    on Jupiter 9:700
    thermal monitoring 8:607
    underwater 10:727, 10:761
Voskhod 2 1:38
Vostok (spacecraft) 1:37, 4:288,
    4:289, 4:290, 8:615, 9:692, 10:791
Voyager (spacecraft) 8:619, 9:676,
    9:697, 9:700, 9:701, 9:702
vulcanized rubber 3:172, 3:239

Wallace's Line 10:779
water clock 10:783, 10:799
water pressure 3:173, 3:195
waterproofing 3:172
water supplies 8:581, 8:582
weapons 8:576
weather 3:232–233
    charts 9:673
    the science of 10:782–783
weather forecasting 4:267, 8:623,
    10:781–785

in the air 10:784
by satellites and computers
    3:229, 8:606, 8:620, 8:623,
    10:781, 10:784–785
early 10:781–782
weather observation network
    10:782–783
weightlessness 1:40, 1:42, 4:289,
    4:307, 4:308
wet collodion process 7:541,
    7:542
wet suits 3:173
wheel, invention of the 5:376,
    5:377
wind-drift instrument 2:121, 2:159
wind-powered vehicles 5:381
winds
    measurement of 2:121, 2:159,
        4:266, 4:267
    in navigation 7:489–491, 7:505
wind vane 10:781, 10:783, 10:799
Winkel Tripel projection 6:435
wireless communication 3:190,
    3:192–193
woolen cloth 9:662
world maps 3:230, 4:245,
    4:246–247, 4:299, 5:332, 5:345,
    6:430–431, 6:435, 6:444, 6:446
World Ocean Circulation
    Experiment 10:760
World Wide Web 10:727

X-15 program (NASA) 6:468

zoology 6:455, 6:461, 7:484, 8:587,
    10:745
zoos 6:455

COMPREHENSIVE INDEX

Page numbers in *italic type* refer to illustrations. **Boldface** numbers preceding a colon indicate the volume number. Page numbers entirely in **boldface** type refer to main articles.

abominable snowman **5:**340, **5:**341
aboriginal people **3:**180
aborigines, Australian **2:**112, **3:**198, **4:***270,* **6:**470, **6:**473
Abu Inan, Sultan **5:**358, **5:**361
Abyssinia **9:**711 *see also* Ethiopia
Acadia **4:**272, **6:**450
Acapulco **2:**137, **8:**594, **8:**597
Aceh **5:**346, **5:**349
Acla **7:**521
Acoma, New Mexico **3:***203*
Adams, George **10:**737
Adams, John Couch **9:**681
Adelaide **2:**110, **3:**180, **4:**269
Admiralty, British **4:**313, **4:**314
   Corps of Surveying Officers **4:**265, **4:**266
Adriatic Sea **10:**753, **10:**754
aeronautics **1:**27, **1:**29, **1:**79, **6:**468, **6:**479
Afghanistan **1:**16, **5:**358, **5:**359, **8:**566, **9:***660,* **10:**793, **10:**794
Afonso V **5:***331,* **8:**574
Africa **2:**113, **2:**114–117, **2:**131, **2:**133, **2:**139, **2:**143, **3:**181, **3:**222, **3:**230, **4:**253, **4:**256, **4:**271, **4:**291, **4:**299, **4:**304, **4:**312, **5:**377, **5:**380, **6:**428, **6:**443, **6:**476, **6:**477, **6:**478, **9:**650, **9:**658, **9:**674, **9:**686, **9:**717, **10:**743, **10:**744–746, **10:**747, **10:**749, **10:**786
   Livingstone's coast-to-coast crossing **6:**415–417, **6:**452
   Moffat's mission **6:**452
   Portuguese exploration of **3:**175, **7:**528, **8:**573–574, **8:**593
   Portuguese settlements in **8:**576
   slave trade **6:**440–441, **6:**472–473
   as the "white man's grave" **5:**368
   see also Central Africa; East Africa; South Africa; southern Africa; West Africa
African Association **1:**70, **1:**71, **4:**251–252, **4:**255, **4:**312, **7:**533, **7:**534

Africus (wind) **7:**491
Age of Discovery **3:**230, **4:**260, **6:**429, **6:**476, **7:**531, **8:**581, **8:**589, **9:**651, **9:**686, **10:**748
Age of Exploration **4:**302–303, **5:**390, **7:**484
Agulhas current **10:***742*
aircraft **1:**59–65, **6:**432
air pressure **3:**173, **3:**174, **4:**266, **4:**267
airships **1:**18, **1:**21, **1:**60, **3:**236–237, **3:**237
Alabama **9:**685
Alaminos, Anton de **8:**569
Alarcón, Hernando de **3:**202
A-la Shan (plateau) **8:**585
Alaska **2:**87–90, **2:***90,* **3:**196, **3:**200, **3:**237, **7:**538, **7:**539, **8:**607, **8:**612, **8:**613, **8:**614, **8:**624, **9:**675, **10:**763
Alborg **10:***776*
Albuquerque, Afonso de **8:**574, **8:**576
alcohol **8:**581, **8:**582
Aldrin, Buzz (Edwin Eugene, Jr.) **1:**28, **1:**29, **1:**38, **1:**39, **6:**466, **7:**544, **9:**692, **9:**696
Ales Stener (Stones of Ale), Sweden **10:***773*
Aleutian Islands **2:**87, **2:**90
Alexander VI, Pope **3:**175, **4:**271, **6:**423, **6:**448
Alexander I, Czar **2:**84
Alexander II, Czar **9:**675
Alexander the Great **1:**14–17, **4:**246, **4:**300, **5:**377, **6:**455, **6:**474, **8:**589, **9:**659, **9:**660, **9:**661, **10:**797
Alexander, William **4:**313
Alexander Island **2:**84, **2:**86
Alexander Mosaic, Pompeii **1:***17*
Alexandria **1:**15, **1:**16, **1:**17, **4:***245,* **4:**300, **5:**390, **8:**589, **8:**592, **9:**716
   library **4:**244, **4:**245, **8:**589, **9:**717
Alexandria, Minnesota **8:**625
Algarve **5:**331
Algiers **10:**746
Algonquins **2:**158, **5:**353, **8:***603,* **9:**653, **9:**670
alidade **7:**499, **10:***728,* **10:**729
Allen Telescope Array **8:**634
Allouez, Claude **6:**450, **6:**451
Almagro, Diego de **1:**73
almanacs **7:**496, **10:***742*
Almeida, Charles de **2:**138
Almeida, Francisco de **6:**422, **8:**574

alpaca **5:***378*
Alpine Club **4:**253
Alps **1:**76, **1:**77, **10:**790
Altai Mountains **8:**587
Altamira **10:**754
altitude **6:**479
   sickness **5:**356
   of stars **3:**185
Altun Shan range **8:**586
Alvarado, Luis de Moscoso **9:**684–685
Alvin **3:**234, **10:**726, **10:**727
Amaseia **9:**716
Amazon Basin **1:**60, **1:**63, **1:**64–65, **10:**777, **10:**778–779
Amazon River **5:**355, **6:**455, **7:**486, **7:**487, **7:**551, **7:**552, **9:**652, **9:**654, **10:**770
amber **6:**453, **6:**479, **9:**662
Amboina **5:**349
Ambon **6:**475
America **2:**129–131, **7:**514, **7:**515, **7:**522
   explorers **3:**235–238, **4:**279–283, **7:**537–540
   naming of **6:**431, **10:**769, **10:**772
   Russians in **8:**613
   southwestern United States **7:**545–548
   women explorers of **10:**787–788
   see also Central America; North America; South America
American Fur Company **1:**34
American Geographical Society **2:**103, **2:**119, **4:**252
American Indians *see* Native Americans
American Museum and Library of Natural History, New York **1:**22, **1:***23,* **1:**24, **1:**25
American River **9:**666
American Telephone and Telegraph Company (AT&T) **8:**621
American West **1:**30–32, **4:**279–283, **8:**577–580
Americas **3:**176, **3:**181, **3:**184, **3:**226, **3:**230, **5:**380, **10:**749, **10:**752, **10:***772*
   British in the **4:**312
   Christianity in the **6:**448, **6:**470
   medieval maps of the **7:**528
   slavery in the **3:**176
   see also New World

amidships **8:**639
Amsterdam **5:**346, **5:**347, **5:***348,* **5:**351, **7:***503,* **10:**732
Amu Darya River **10:**794
Amundsen-Ellsworth expedition (1926) **3:**236–237
Amundsen, Roald **1:**18–21, **1:**60, **1:**62, **2:**101, **2:**119, **3:**171, **3:**231, **3:**235, **3:**236, **3:**238, **4:**315, **5:**339, **5:**340, **5:**381, **7:***502,* **7:**515, **7:**518–519, **7:**539, **7:**543, **7:**555, **7:**558, **8:**625, **8:**627, **8:**628–629, **8:**636, **9:**655
Anastasia Island **3:***179*
Anatolia **10:**752
Anaximander of Miletus **4:***298,* **4:**299, **9:**686
Andes Mountains **1:**73, **1:**74, **1:**75, **3:**177, **3:**217, **3:**235, **4:**256, **5:**356, **7:**486, **7:**487, **9:**652, **9:**682, **9:**705
Andrée, Salomon August **1:**61, **1:**62, **8:**627
Andronicus of Cyrrhus **10:**783
Angola **6:**415
animals
   extinct **3:**183
   species **7:**486, **7:**487, **7:**488
animal transport **5:**376, **5:**377, **5:**378, **5:**381
Anna, empress of Russia **2:**88
annedda tree ("tree of life") **2:**152, **2:**153
Anson, George **5:**366–367
Antarctic **1:**61–62, **1:**71, **3:**231, **3:**238, **4:**255, **5:**368–370, **6:**477, **7:**506, **7:**539, **7:**553, **7:**554, **7:**556–557, **8:**581, **8:**602, **8:**607, **8:**613, **8:**614, **8:**625, **8:**628–631, **8:**635–638, **9:**656, **9:***658,* **9:**689, **10:**757, **10:**762, **10:**792
   aerial mapping of **4:**305
   Amundsen's voyage **1:**18, **1:**20–21
   Byrd's expeditions **2:**118–121
   circumnavigation of (1819–1821) **2:**84–86
   Cook's circumnavigation **2:**86, **3:**196, **3:**199, **3:**200
   exploration by air **1:**60, **1:**61–62
   first flight over **3:**238
   first motor vehicle crossing **5:**377
   first sighting of **2:**85
   geophysical survey of **2:**121

Antarctic (cont.)
  Hillary's expedition 5:339, 5:340
  mapping of 2:86, 2:120–121,
    6:430, 6:432, 7:556–557
  scientific bases set up 7:555
  Scott's expeditions 3:170, 3:190,
    4:253, 4:315, 7:558, 8:581,
    8:629–630
  Shackleton's voyage 7:543,
    7:557, 8:635
Antarctic Circle 2:85, 3:196, 3:199,
  9:688
anthropology 1:22–26, 5:336,
  5:399, 6:459
  collectors and museums
    1:24–26
  development in Europe and
    North America 1:24
  early roots 1:22–23
  and Western society 1:26
Anticosti Island 2:151, 2:152
Antilles, Lesser 8:569
Apache 2:147, 5:375, 5:379
Apalachee Bay 2:123
Apalachee people 6:464
Apollo project 1:28–29, 1:38, 1:39,
  1:48, 6:432, 6:466, 6:467, 7:542,
  7:544, 9:644, 9:645, 9:646, 9:692,
  9:696, 9:697
Apollo-Soyuz Test Project 6:466,
  6:468
Appa Glacier 10:753
Appalachian Mountains 2:94,
  9:685
Apure River 5:356
Aqua-Lung 3:173, 3:209–210,
  3:211, 10:758–759, 10:760
aquariums 6:455, 7:486, 7:488
Aquarius 10:761
Arab empire 4:301, 5:363
Arabia 1:76–77, 2:114, 2:115, 5:359,
  5:363, 6:477, 10:741
Arabian Gulf 8:576
Arabian Sea 1:17, 10:745
Arabs
  astronomers 1:43, 8:590, 10:740
  libraries 8:591
  merchants 6:474
  navigators 4:298
  shipbuilders 9:647, 9:648
  traders 2:133, 2:135, 2:143, 7:505
Aragon 4:260–263, 8:569, 8:639
Arcata, California 10:729
archaeology 1:76–78, 4:318, 5:338,
  6:453, 9:660, 9:663, 10:747
  aerial 1:63
  underwater 10:724
Archer, Colin 6:459

Archer, Frederick Scott 7:541,
  7:542
Arctic 1:60, 2:101–103, 2:118,
  3:231, 5:368–370, 6:458–461,
  6:473, 7:553, 8:583, 8:612, 8:614,
  8:627, 10:749, 10:757, 10:790
  Amundsen's voyage 1:18, 1:19
  Baffin's voyages 1:66–68
  Barents's voyages 7:503, 7:504,
    7:512, 7:513, 7:554, 7:556
  British expedition (1875) 5:367
  Canadian 7:514, 7:515–519
  clothing for the 3:171–172
  Ellsworth's expedition
    3:235–238
  exploration by air 1:60
  Franklin's expeditions 4:275–278
  Frobisher's voyage 4:286–287
  Nordenskiöld's voyage
    7:507–510
  Peary's exploration 7:537–540
  Ross's expedition (1829) 8:583
  Russian 7:507–514, 9:650, 9:653
Arctic Circle 4:247, 5:381, 7:507,
  9:717
Arctic drift 7:554, 7:555
Arctic Ocean 1:60, 3:237,
  6:418–419, 6:458–461, 8:614,
  8:625, 8:627, 10:736
Arecibo radio telescope 1:46, 1:54,
  8:632, 8:633, 8:634
Arethusa 8:571
Argentina 1:69, 2:97, 2:125, 2:131,
  4:264, 6:424, 7:552, 10:772
Argo 7:527, 9:658, 10:726
Argo-Jason 7:542, 7:544
Arikara Indians 1:31, 1:79
Aristarchus of Samos 1:50
Aristotle 1:14, 4:299, 6:428, 6:444,
  7:484, 7:485, 9:686, 10:781
arithmetic 3:185
Arizona 2:145, 3:201, 5:373, 5:374,
  5:375
Arkansas 9:684
Arkansas River 5:371, 5:386, 7:546,
  9:684
Armenia 9:716
armillary sphere 5:343
Armstrong, Neil 1:27–29, 1:38, 1:39,
  6:466, 7:544, 9:692, 9:696
Arrest, Heinrich Louis d' 9:681
Arrian 1:17
Artika 8:614, 8:615, 9:655
artists, official 8:603–604
Arundel, Isabel 2:113
Ascension Island 2:98, 3:214, 3:218
Ashley, William Henry 1:30–32,
  2:107, 9:664, 9:665, 9:666

Ashmole, Elias 6:457
Ashmolean Museum, Oxford
  6:454, 6:457
Asia 1:15, 1:16, 1:22, 2:87, 2:113,
  2:139, 2:141, 2:143, 3:181, 3:185,
  4:246, 4:259, 4:271, 4:300, 5:350,
  5:377, 5:394, 6:423, 6:428, 6:430,
  6:431, 6:432, 6:448, 6:474, 6:477,
  7:504, 7:511, 7:514, 7:515, 8:564,
  9:660, 9:717, 10:749, 10:779
  expeditions in central
    8:585–588, 8:612, 10:793
  Marco Polo's maps of 8:568
  Portuguese exploration in 3:175
  routes to 9:652–653, 9:705
  trade with Europe 10:748
Asia Minor 1:14, 1:16, 1:76, 1:77,
  5:358 see also Turkey
Asimov, Isaac 7:532
Assiniboine Indians 5:397
Assiniboine River 5:395, 5:397
Association of American
  Geographers 4:253
asteroids 1:53, 1:54, 9:676, 9:681,
  9:700, 9:719
Astor, Caroline Schermerhorn
  1:36
Astor, George 1:33
Astor, John Jacob 1:33–36, 9:664
Astor, John Jacob, II 1:36
Astor, John Jacob, IV 1:36
Astor, Nancy Witcher Langhorne
  1:36
Astor, William Backhouse 1:36
Astor, William Waldorf 1:36
astrolabe 1:43, 3:232, 5:343, 5:344,
  5:345, 5:392, 5:399, 7:491, 7:494,
  7:497, 7:499–500, 9:695, 10:729,
  10:770
astronauts 1:27–29, 1:37–42, 1:47,
  3:195, 4:288, 4:306–308, 5:382
  clothing 3:173–174
  training 1:42, 9:644, 9:645, 9:646
  see also cosmonauts
astronomer royal 5:393
astronomical instruments 1:43–48
astronomical observation 6:429
astronomical tables 7:485
astronomy 1:49–54, 3:185, 3:233,
  4:252, 4:300, 7:484
  Arabic 1:43, 8:590
  Babylonian 5:343
  European 8:590–591
  Greek 1:43, 1:50, 5:342–345,
    7:499
  Ptolemy's 8:589–590
  radio 1:46
  and search for extraterrestrial

intelligence 8:632
Asunción 2:123, 2:125
Aswan 4:245, 9:716
Atahualpa, Incan king 6:478,
  9:682, 9:683, 9:705
Atbara River 9:709
Athabasca country 10:736
Athens 4:244, 10:783
Atlantic Ocean 1:59, 2:104–106,
  2:126–128, 2:129, 2:133–134,
  2:151, 2:155, 3:178, 3:184, 3:185,
  3:186, 3:234, 4:247, 4:275, 4:298,
  4:300, 4:307, 5:336, 5:337, 5:349,
  5:351, 7:515, 7:529, 7:551, 8:606,
  8:621, 9:644, 9:650, 9:651, 9:652,
  9:653, 9:669, 9:714, 10:725,
  10:743, 10:749, 10:757, 10:765,
  10:766–767, 10:770
  first female solo flight across
    10:788, 10:789
  first flight across (1919) 2:118
  see also North Atlantic; South
    Atlantic
Atlantis 7:529, 7:530
atlas 6:429, 6:447, 7:506
  al-Idrisi's 5:365
  Berghaus's 4:255
  Catalan 4:301, 8:565
  Ortelius's 7:506
  Ptolemy's 5:390
Audubon, John James 1:55–58
Augustus 4:300
aurora borealis 2:101, 2:102, 2:159,
  3:238
Australia 1:70–71, 2:92, 2:110–112,
  3:180, 3:196, 3:198, 3:218, 3:231,
  5:349, 5:380, 9:655, 10:732,
  10:733, 10:734, 10:763, 10:779,
  10:789
  British in 3:180, 3:200, 3:212
  Burke and Wills's crossing 4:299,
    4:314
  circumnavigation 4:268–270
  colonization of 4:269
  convicts as colonists 4:269
  Cook's voyage 3:198–200
  Dampier's voyage to 3:214
  Dutch discovery 4:303, 7:504
  Flinders's circumnavigation
    4:269, 4:275, 4:314
  naming of 1:71, 4:270
  see also New Holland; southern
    continent; Terra Australis
aviation 1:59–65, 2:103, 2:118–121,
  3:235–238
  first flight 1:59, 8:606
  long-distance 8:615
Avilés, Pedro Menéndez de 8:572

Avon River, Bristol **6**:473
Azores **2**:105, **3**:175, **5**:332, **5**:333, **5**:335, **7**:549, **7**:550, **10**:747
Aztec Empire **3**:182, **3**:204, **3**:205, **3**:206–208
Aztecs **3**:176, **3**:181, **3**:206–207, **5**:*370*, **6**:440, **6**:464, **7**:523, **7**:559, **9**:704, **9**:705, **10**:752

Babylon **1**:16, **1**:17
Babylonia **6**:427
Babylonians **3**:231, **5**:343, **8**:602
Bachman, John **1**:57
Backhuysen, Ludolf **7**:503
Back River **4**:276
back staff **1**:*67*, **7**:494, **7**:500–501
Bacon, Francis **7**:485, **7**:486
Bactria **10**:796, **10**:797, **10**:798
Badajoz **7**:520, **9**:683
Badakhshan **8**:566
Baffin, William **1**:**66–68**, **5**:325, **7**:516
Baffin Bay **1**:66, **1**:67, **1**:68, **7**:516
Baffin Island **1**:67, **4**:286, **4**:317, **6**:406, **6**:470, **7**:515, **7**:516, **7**:518, **8**:603
Bafing River **7**:*535*
Bagamoyo **9**:712, **9**:714
Baghdad **1**:76, **1**:77, **1**:78, **2**:139, **2**:140, **5**:358, **5**:361, **5**:390, **10**:773, **10**:775, **10**:790
Bahamas **2**:105, **3**:186, **3**:189, **4**:307
Bahr al-Ghazal **10**:745
Baie de Chaleur **2**:151, **2**:154
Baines, Thomas **9**:652
Baird, Spencer Fullerton **9**:673–674, **9**:675
Bakewell, Lucy **1**:55, **1**:56
Bali **5**:346, **5**:348, **10**:779
Ballantyne, J. M. **7**:530
Ballard, Robert **4**:311, **7**:544, **10**:726–727
balloons **6**:432, **8**:627
    cameras attached to **8**:605
    flights **1**:59, **1**:61, **1**:62, **10**:725, **10**:784
Baltic Sea **2**:84, **7**:514, **8**:624, **10**:775
Bamako **7**:535, **7**:536
Bamian, Afghanistan **9**:*660*
Banana **9**:714, **9**:715
Bancroft, Ann **7**:555, **7**:558, **10**:792
Banks, Joseph **1**:**69–71**, **2**:85, **3**:197, **3**:198, **4**:251, **4**:270, **4**:314, **6**:454, **7**:486, **7**:533, **7**:534, **10**:764
Bantam **5**:348, **7**:504
Barents, Willem **7**:503, **7**:504, **7**:512, **7**:513, **7**:554, **7**:556
Barents Sea **1**:60, **7**:512
Barison, Giuseppe **6**:455

barometer **3**:239, **4**:266, **4**:267, **10**:782, **10**:784
    Admiral Fitzroy's **4**:267
    barometric pressure **3**:233, **3**:239
Barros, João de **3**:225, **4**:291
Barrow, John **4**:254, **4**:275
Barton, Otis **10**:724
Batavia (Jakarta) **2**:150, **3**:214, **7**:504, **10**:732, **10**:733, **10**:734
Bates, Henry Walter **7**:487, **10**:777, **10**:*778*, **10**:779
bathymetric map **10**:760
bathyscaphe **3**:210, **3**:239, **10**:724–725, **10**:726, **10**:799
bathysphere **10**:724, **10**:726, **10**:799
Bavaria **1**:71, **5**:373, **5**:394, **8**:605, **8**:606
Bay of Bengal **5**:359
Bay of Cambay **10**:*748*
Bay of Fundy **10**:739
Bay of Whales **1**:20, **1**:62, **2**:120
Beardmore Glacier **7**:*553*, **7**:557, **8**:629
Bear Island **2**:103, **7**:513
Beaufort, Francis **10**:783
Beaufort wind scale **4**:266, **10**:783
Beaufoy, Henry **4**:251, **4**:252
Beauharnois, Charles de **5**:395, **5**:396
beavers **1**:31, **5**:398, **10**:735, **10**:*750*, **10**:751
Bechuanaland **6**:414
Beebe, William **10**:724, **10**:725, **10**:726
Beechey Island **4**:276, **4**:277, **4**:278
Behaim, Martin **4**:303, **6**:429
Beijing **8**:564, **8**:565, **8**:566, **8**:567, **8**:586, **8**:610, **8**:611, **9**:660, **10**:749
Belalcázar, Sebastián de **1**:**72–75**, **9**:704
Belalcázar (town) **1**:72
Belém (Pará) **10**:779
Belgium **6**:444–445, **9**:711, **9**:714–715
Bell, Alexander Graham **3**:190, **3**:192
Bell, Gertrude **1**:**76–78**, **10**:788, **10**:790
Bell, Mark **10**:793
Bella Coola Indians **6**:420, **6**:421
Bella Coola River **6**:420, **6**:*421*
Bellingshausen, Fabian Gottlieb von **2**:**84–86**, **7**:554, **7**:556, **8**:613, **8**:614, **9**:656, **9**:689
Bellingshausen Sea **2**:86, **9**:656
Benalcázar *see* Belalcázar, Sebastián de
Benares **4**:259

bends, the (decompression sickness) **3**:173, **3**:239, **10**:759
Bennett, Floyd **1**:60, **1**:62, **2**:103, **2**:119, **3**:237
Bennett, Gordon **9**:711
Bent, Charles **2**:145
Benton, Thomas Hart **4**:279, **4**:280
Bent's Fort **2**:*145*
Berghaus, Heinrich **4**:252–253, **4**:254, **4**:255
Bering, Vitus Jonassen **2**:**87–90**, **7**:512, **7**:514, **8**:612, **8**:614, **8**:624, **8**:626–627
Bering Island **2**:88, **2**:89, **2**:90
Bering Sea **3**:200
Bering Strait **2**:90, **5**:389, **7**:512, **8**:612
Berkner Island **8**:627
Berlin **4**:252, **4**:254, **4**:305, **5**:354
    Oceanographical Museum **3**:223
Bermuda **2**:105, **6**:455, **10**:724
Bernoulli, Daniel **10**:742
Berrio, Antonio de **8**:600
betel leaves **5**:361
Beuningen, Gerrit van **5**:348
Bhutan **10**:731
big bang theory **1**:54, **9**:677
Big Horn Mountains **5**:395, **5**:398
Billings, Joseph **8**:613
Bilma **2**:142
Bimini **8**:569, **8**:571
Bingham, George Caleb **2**:95
Bingham, Hiram **4**:256
Bird, Isabella Lucy *see* Bishop, Isabella Lucy
Bird Banding Society (US) **1**:57
birds **1**:55–58, **7**:487
    of America **1**:58
    banding **1**:56, **1**:57
    in navigation **7**:491
bireme **5**:329
Bishop, Isabella Lucy **2**:**91–93**, **10**:788, **10**:789
Bismarck, North Dakota **6**:410, **8**:617
bison **2**:123, **6**:438
Bitterroot Mountains **6**:410, **6**:411
Bjaarland, Olav **1**:21
Bjarni Herjolfsson **6**:406
Bjorn, son of Gudrid **4**:318
Black Hills of South Dakota **9**:664
black hole **1**:52, **1**:53, **1**:79
Black River **10**:736
Black Sea **3**:176, **5**:359, **7**:*527*, **9**:712, **9**:716, **10**:751
Blaeu, Jan, world map **9**:*687*, **10**:*733*

Blanchard, Jean-Pierre **1**:62
Blantyre **4**:314, **6**:413
Blériot, Louis **1**:*59*
Blessing, Henrik **7**:554
Bligh, William **4**:268, **9**:656
Block Island **10**:767–768
Blue Nile **9**:709, **10**:745
Board of Longitude **3**:169, **5**:393
Boas, Franz **1**:23, **1**:24, **1**:25
boats *see* ships
Bobadilla, Francisco de **3**:185, **3**:189
Bologna **5**:388, **10**:783
Bonpland, Aimé **5**:355–357, **7**:486, **7**:487
book production **8**:592
Boone, Daniel **2**:**94–96**
Boonesborough **2**:94, **2**:95, **2**:96
Boothia Peninsula **4**:313
Borinquen **8**:570
Borneo **10**:779
Bosporus **7**:527
Boston, as prime meridian **5**:390
botany **1**:69–71, **3**:197, **3**:198, **4**:253, **4**:314, **5**:354, **5**:355, **5**:365, **6**:452, **7**:484, **7**:486–487, **7**:559, **8**:587, **8**:626, **10**:744
Botany Bay **1**:70, **3**:198, **4**:269
Botswana **6**:414, **6**:415
botulism **4**:278, **4**:319
Boudeuse **2**:98, **2**:99, **9**:655
Bougainvillea spectabilis **7**:486
Bougainville, Hyacinthe **2**:100
Bougainville, Louis-Antoine de **2**:**97–100**, **4**:273, **4**:274, **6**:471, **7**:486, **9**:655
Boullé, Hélène **2**:157
Bounty, HMS **1**:70, **1**:71, **9**:656
Bourdillon, Tom **5**:339
Bouvet de Lozier, Jean-Baptiste Charles **9**:688
Bouvet Island **9**:688
Bowers, Henry **8**:629
Boxer, C. R. **10**:751
Boyd, Louise Arner **2**:**101–103**, **10**:788, **10**:790
Boyle, Robert **10**:756, **10**:760
Boyne, Battle of the (1690) **5**:367
Bozeman Trail **2**:109
Bradbury, Ray, *Fahrenheit 451* **7**:530, **7**:532
Braddock, James **2**:94
Brahe, Tycho **1**:49
Brahe, William **2**:111, **2**:112
Brahmaputra River **10**:794
Bransfield, Edward **2**:85, **9**:689
Brattahlid **4**:250, **4**:316
Braun, Wernher von **9**:690

Brazil **1**:69, **2**:115, **2**:117, **2**:123, **2**:125, **2**:133–134, **3**:182, **3**:214, **3**:217, **3**:225, **4**:252, **6**:471, **7**:*529*, **7**:549, **7**:551, **8**:574, **8**:576, **10**:*742*, **10**:743, **10**:767, **10**:768, **10**:770, **10**:771, **10**:779
breathing apparatus **3**:209–210
Bremen **9**:*650*
Brendan **2**:104–106
Bressant, Father **6**:451
Brest **2**:97, **4**:287, **4**:296
Bridger, Jim **1**:31, **2**:107–109, **2**:145, **9**:667
Bridger's Pass **2**:109
Bristol **2**:127, **2**:129
Britain *see* Great Britain
British
in Australia **3**:180, **3**:198, **3**:212
colonization in North America **3**:177–178, **8**:598–600
explorers **1**:66–68, **1**:69–71, **1**:76–78, **2**:113–117, **3**:226–228, **4**:264–267, **4**:268–270, **4**:275–278, **4**:284–287, **4**:312–315, **10**:749
in Oregon **9**:665
polar exploration **8**:629–630, **8**:635–637
scientists **3**:216–219
British Admiralty **10**:757
British Antarctic Survey **8**:607
British Columbia **1**:24, **6**:421, **9**:674, **10**:737, **10**:753
British Empire **4**:312, **5**:391, **8**:585
and the Russian Empire **10**:795
British Everest Expedition **4**:315, **5**:339–340, **10**:795
British Foreign Office **2**:117
British High Commission, Iraq **1**:77, **1**:78
British Isles *see* Great Britain
British Meteorological Office **4**:264, **4**:267
British Museum **4**:315, **6**:454, **6**:456, **10**:790
British National Antarctic Expedition (1901-1904) **4**:255, **8**:628–631, **9**:657
British naval expeditions **7**:517–518
British Royal Navy **3**:169, **3**:196–197, **3**:213, **4**:264, **4**:265, **4**:267, **4**:268–270, **4**:275, **4**:276, **5**:326, **5**:366, **5**:368, **5**:391, **5**:393, **7**:517, **8**:584, **8**:630, **9**:655, **10**:743, **10**:762, **10**:783
Hydrographic Office 760, **10**:760
British Trans-Antarctic Expedition

(1957 and 1958) **5**:381
Brittany **2**:97, **2**:105, **4**:287, **4**:296
Bronze Age **9**:658
Brouage **2**:155, **2**:156
Broughton, Lieutenant **10**:763
Brouwer, Hendrik **7**:504, **7**:505, **10**:734
Brulé, Étienne **2**:157
Brussels **10**:757
Bry, Theodore de **7**:505, **8**:570
Bryan, Rebecca **2**:94, **2**:96
buccaneer **3**:213, **3**:239, **4**:313
Bucephala **1**:17
Buchan, David **4**:313
Buchanan, James **3**:193
Buckingham, duke of **6**:455
Buddh Gaya **4**:259
Buddhism **4**:257–259, **4**:299, **8**:588, **9**:660–661, **9**:661, **9**:663, **10**:795
buffalo **3**:183, **5**:384
Bukhara **8**:564
bull, papal **3**:175–176, **6**:470, **6**:472
Buran space shuttle **9**:692
Bureau of Ethnology (U.S.) **8**:578, **8**:580
Bureau of Land Management (U.S.) **8**:580
Burke, Robert O'Hara **2**:110–112, **4**:299, **4**:314, **6**:470, **6**:473
Burke and Wills Expedition (1860–1861) **2**:*110*, **2**:111–112
Burma **5**:358, **6**:430, **8**:567, **8**:*574*, **10**:794
Burr, Aaron **7**:547
Burton, Richard Francis **2**:113–117, **4**:253, **4**:255, **4**:314, **5**:366, **5**:368, **6**:417, **9**:707–708, **9**:709, **9**:710
Buru, Indonesia **2**:98
Bush, George W. **9**:699
Bussa **7**:536
Button, Thomas **7**:516, **7**:518
Buzzards Bay, Massachusetts **3**:182
Bykovsky, Valery **8**:*615*
Bylot, Robert **1**:67, **1**:68, **7**:516, **7**:518
Byrd, Richard E. **1**:60, **1**:62, **2**:103, **2**:118–121, **3**:237, **7**:555
Byron, John **2**:148
Byzantine Empire **9**:659, **10**:747

Cabeza de Vaca, Alvar Núñez **2**:122–125, **3**:201, **6**:463, **6**:464, **6**:465
Cabot, John **2**:126–128, **2**:129, **2**:131, **3**:177, **3**:220, **5**:324, **6**:406, **6**:474, **9**:652, **9**:654, **10**:751, **10**:765

Cabot, Sebastian **2**:127, **2**:129–132, **3**:220, **5**:324, **6**:406, **7**:511
Cabral, Pedro Álvares **2**:133–135, **3**:223, **3**:225, **4**:293, **8**:574, **10**:743
Cabrillo, Juan Rodríguez **2**:136–138
Cabrillo National Monument, San Diego Bay **2**:138
Cadamosto, Alvise da **5**:332, **5**:335
Cadiz **3**:184, **3**:185, **3**:228, **10**:770
Caillié, René-Auguste **4**:252, **4**:273, **4**:274, **7**:536
Cairo **1**:77, **1**:78, **2**:139, **2**:141, **2**:143, **5**:338, **5**:358, **9**:709, **10**:744, **10**:745, **10**:746, **10**:748
conference (1921) **1**:76, **1**:77
Cajamarca, battle of **5**:379, **9**:682, **9**:683
Calabar coast **4**:314
calendars, Aztec **3**:207
Calicut **2**:135, **3**:167, **4**:292, **4**:293, **4**:294, **5**:358, **6**:476, **8**:*575*
California **2**:101, **2**:136–138, **2**:145, **2**:146–147, **3**:226, **3**:227, **3**:228, **4**:281, **4**:282, **4**:283, **5**:324, **5**:374, **5**:375, **6**:437, **7**:526, **8**:615, **9**:645, **9**:665, **9**:666, **9**:692, **9**:701, **10**:*729*, **10**:785, **10**:788
charting the coast **10**:763
Callimachus of Cyrene **4**:244
calotype **7**:541, **7**:542
Cambay **10**:*748*
Cambodia **4**:295
Cambridge, England **3**:216, **5**:391
camcorders, digital **8**:601, **8**:604
camel caravans **2**:139–143, **5**:379, **8**:*565*, **8**:573, **9**:661
camels **5**:378, **5**:379, **5**:380
Arabian **2**:141
Bactrian **2**:141
wild **8**:587
cameras **1**:23, **1**:24, **1**:65, **4**:277, **7**:541, **8**:604
attached to balloons **8**:605
attached to homing pigeons **8**:605, **8**:606
Camino Real (de Tierra Adentro) **7**:523
Camões, Luis Vaz de **8**:575
Campbell, John **7**:495, **7**:502
Camp Fortunate **6**:411
Canada **2**:91, **2**:97, **2**:126–128, **2**:151–154, **2**:155–158, **3**:196, **4**:271, **4**:275, **5**:350, **5**:353, **5**:371–372, **5**:377, **6**:408, **6**:418–421, **6**:443, **6**:450–451, **6**:473, **6**:478, **7**:548, **8**:627, **9**:653, **9**:675, **10**:735–738, **10**:739, **10**:751, **10**:771

border with United States **10**:736, **10**:737, **10**:738
British claim to **2**:126
the British in **4**:312, **4**:313
Christianizing **3**:179
French claim to **2**:151, **2**:155, **2**:156
the French in **4**:271–273
fur trade **10**:735–738
Harleian Map **2**:*154*
Hudson's exploration **5**:351–353
Jolliet's exploration **5**:371–372
La Vérendrye's exploration **5**:394–398
map **5**:*352*
Canadian navy **7**:519
Canary Islands **2**:105, **3**:187, **5**:390, **6**:464, **9**:703
Canberra **9**:701
cannibalism **3**:187, **3**:206, **4**:275, **4**:277, **4**:315, **7**:528, **10**:767, **10**:768, **10**:790
canoes **5**:*371*, **5**:380, **9**:647, **9**:654, **10**:743
birch-bark **5**:396, **5**:*397*, **10**:*735*
Native American **9**:653–654
Canton **6**:449, **8**:574
Cão, Diogo **3**:223, **3**:224, **8**:574, **8**:575
Caparra **8**:569
Cape Arctichesky **8**:627
Cape Bauld **2**:127
Cape Blanc **5**:332, **5**:335
Cape Bojador **5**:332, **5**:335
Cape Breton **2**:127
Cape Cabrillo **10**:763
Cape Canaveral, Florida **1**:27, **4**:307, **6**:468, **9**:*645*, **9**:*698*
Cape Chelyuskin **8**:612
Cape Cod **10**:726, **10**:768
Cape Colony **8**:626
Cape Cross **3**:*223*, **3**:224
Cape Fear **10**:767
Cape Henry **9**:670
Cape Horn **2**:137, **3**:197, **3**:213, **3**:214, **4**:264, **7**:504–505, **7**:511, **10**:764
Cape Kennedy Space Center, Florida **9**:696
Cape Non **5**:332
Cape of Good Hope **2**:134, **3**:214, **3**:218, **3**:222, **3**:223, **3**:224, **3**:225, **3**:228, **4**:291, **4**:292, **4**:293, **4**:299, **4**:302, **6**:474, **7**:500, **7**:504, **7**:511, **8**:573, **8**:575, **8**:593, **9**:654, **9**:687
Cape Town **2**:98, **7**:504, **7**:505
Cape Verde Islands **3**:184, **3**:217, **3**:224, **4**:291, **5**:332, **5**:390, **6**:423,

8:*606,* 9:704, **10:**770
Cape Vert **5:**332, **5:**335
Cape York Peninsula **3:**198
caravan **2:**126, **2:139–143,** **5:**332, **5:**379, **10:**798
caravanseries **2:**140
caravel **2:**137, **2:**159, **3:**222, **3:***225,* **4:**291, **4:**293, **5:**331, **5:**332, **5:***334,* **5:**399, **9:**648–650, **9:**651, **9:**654
caravela redonda **9:**649, **9:**651
Carcassone **2:**154
Cárdenas, García López de **3:**202, **3:**203
Caribbean islands **3:**176, **3:**182
Caribbean Sea **2:**128, **3:**226, **5:**337, **6:**472, **7:**552, **8:**569, **8:***570,* **8:**603, **9:**652, **9:**682, **9:**683, **9:**704, **10:**761, **10:**762, **10:**765, **10:**768, **10:**769
  Cortés's journeys **3:***205*
  tides **10:**739
Caribs **3:**187
Carlsberg Ridge **10:**761
Carolina Outer Banks **10:**767
Carolinas **3:**228, **6:**441, **9:**684
Caroline County, Virginia **6:**410
Carpenter, M. Scott **9:**645
carracks *see* naos
Carson, Kit (Christopher) **2:144–147,** **4:**280
Cartagena, Colombia **1:**74, **1:**75
Carte Pisane **3:**220, **7:**494
Carteret, Philip **2:148–150,** **9:**655
Carthage **5:**328, **5:**329, **5:**330, **8:**602
Cartier, Jacques **2:151–154,** **2:**155, **3:**220, **4:**271, **4:**272, **4:**273, **10:**764
cartography **3:**230–231, **4:**247, **4:**265, **4:**279, **4:**295, **4:**300, **4:**319, **5:**345, **6:**427–432, **6:**433–435, **6:**444–447, **6:**452, **6:**479, **8:**591, **8:**592, **8:**639
  Dutch **7:**503
  Portuguese **8:**574
  and remote sensing **8:**607
  and satellites **8:**622
carvel-built hulls **9:**648–649, **9:**719
Casa de las Indias (House of the Indies), Seville **10:**772
Caspian Sea **9:**659, **9:**716
Cassini, Dian Domenico **9:**680
Cassini mission **9:**691, **9:**692, **9:**697, **9:**701
Castile **4:**260–263, **6:**462
Catalan Atlas (1375) **4:***301*
Catalonia **8:**565
catamaran **6:**461, **6:**479, **10:**792, **10:**799
Cathay *see* China

Cathay Company of London **4:**286, **4:**287
Catherine the Great (Catherine II) **8:**613
Catholicism **3:**205
cattle, as transport **5:**376
cave paintings **10:**753–754
caves **10:**752–755
Cave of the Thousand Buddhas, Dunhuang **9:**663
cedar **9:**647, **10:**747
cellular phones **3:**194
Center for Earth and Planetary Studies (U.S.) **9:**675
Central Africa **4:**299, **9:**713
Central America **2:**137, **3:**176, **3:**204, **3:**226, **5:**354, **7:**520–522, **9:**703, **9:**706, **10:**765
Central Pacific Railroad **5:**380
Ceram **6:**475
Ceuta **3:**175, **5:**331, **5:**332, **5:**363, **8:**573, **8:**574
Ceylon (Sri Lanka) **3:**167, **4:**257, **4:**259, **5:**358, **5:**359
Chaeronea, Battle of **1:**14
Chagas disease **3:**219
Challenger, HMS **3:**234, **10:**743, **10:**758, **10:**760
Challenger space shuttle **9:**693, **10:**791
  disaster (1986) **1:**29, **6:**468
Champlain, Samuel de **2:155–158,** **3:**179, **4:**272, **5:**353, **5:**366, **9:**653, **9:**655
Chancellor, Richard **7:**511–512
Chandra X-ray Observatory **1:**48, **9:**674
Chang'an **4:**258, **10:**796, **10:**797, **10:**798
Chang Chi'en *see* Zhang Qian
Channel Islands **2:**137, **2:**148, **2:**149
Chappe, Claude **3:**190, **3:**191
Charbonneau, Toussaint **6:**410, **8:**616–618
Charlesbourg-Royal **2:**153
Charles I, king of England **3:**178
Charles II, king of England **4:**264, **5:**391
Charles I, king of Spain **1:**72, **6:**422, **6:**463, **6:**464 **9:**682, **9:**683, *see also* Charles V, Holy Roman Emperor
Charles IV, king of Spain **5:**355
Charles V, Holy Roman Emperor **2:**131, **6:**463
Charles, Jacques **10:**784
Charner, Léonard **4:**295
Charrúa Indians **7:**552

charts **4:**265, **7:**492, **7:**494
  Barents's of the Russian Arctic **7:**503
  navigational, as records **6:**428, **8:**601
  synoptic **4:**267
Chaves, Jeronimo de **9:**685
Cheng Ho **3:164–167,** **3:**191, **6:**454, **6:**455
Chesapeake Bay **9:**669, **9:**670, **9:**675
Cheyenne Peak **7:**548
Cheyenne River **5:**398
Chibcha people **1:**75
Chicago **1:**26, **3:**190, **3:**236, **6:**438
Chickahominy River **9:**669
Chi Hoa, Battle of (1861) **4:**295, **4:**296
Chihuahua **7:**548
Chile **1:**73, **2:**117, **2:**132, **2:**149, **2:**150, **3:**177, **3:**214, **3:**217, **4:**264, **7:**530, **9:**705
Chimborazo **5:**356
China **1:**22, **1:**59, **2:**93, **2:**126, **2:**142, **3:**175, **3:**182, **3:**184, **4:**257, **4:**295, **4:**300, **4:**301, **5:**347, **5:**350, **5:**351, **5:**358, **5:**360, **5:**361, **5:**379, **5:**383, **6:**428, **6:**430, **6:***452,* **6:**478, **7:**543, **8:**564–568, **8:**576, **8:**585, **8:**586, **8:**602, **9:**659–663, **9:***663,* **10:**731, **10:**741, **10:**748, **10:**749, **10:**751, **10:**788, **10:**789, **10:**793, **10:**796–798
  Christian missionaries in **6:***449,* **6:***452,* **8:**608–611
  and India **4:**259
  mapmaking **4:**300
  trade route to **4:**295–297
  trade with **1:**34
  treasure fleet **3:**165–167
Chinese
  astronomy **10:**740
  explorers **4:**257–259, **10:**796–798
  geography **4:**300, **9:**661
  invention of compass **3:**220, **3:**232, **7:**492, **7:**494, **7:**497, **10:**729
  language **8:**608, **8:**609
  navigation **3:**164–167, **3:**190, **3:**191
  Russian treaty with **10:**794
  shipbuilding **3:**167, **9:**647, **9:**648
  society **8:**568
  writing **8:**568
Chino (or Chini), Eusebio Francisco *see* Kino, Eusebio Francisco
chip log **3:**220, **3:**221

Chkalov, Valery **8:**615
chlorofluorocarbons (CFCs) **8:**607
cholera **2:**113, **2:**159, **9:**706
Cho Lon **4:**295, **4:**296
Cholulans **3:**207, **3:**239
Chomolungma *see* Mount Everest
Christianity **2:**104–106, **5:**335, **6:**404
  in the Americas **6:**448
  in China **6:**449, **6:**452, **8:**564
  and colonization **6:**416–417, **6:**470–472
  conversion of Africans to **4:**252
  conversion of Native Americans to **3:**176, **3:**187, **3:**206, **9:**669
  and geography **4:**300
  in Iceland **4:**316
  and Islam **5:**363–364, **8:**573
  and theory of evolution **3:**218–219, **4:**264, **4:**267, **10:**780
  see also evangelical Christianity; missionaries; missions
Christian maps **6:**430–431
Christmas Harbour, Kerguelen's Land **9:***688*
Christy, Henry **10:**753, **10:**754
chronometer **1:**43, **3:168–169,** **3:***169,* **3:**217, **3:**221, **3:**232, **4:**266, **4:**309, **5:**388, **5:**392–393, **5:***393,* **7:**494, **7:**495, **7:**559
Chu Chan-chi **3:**167
Chu Kao-chih **3:**167
Chumash tribe **2:**137
Chumi Shengo **10:**794
Church Hill, near Tralee **2:**104
Churchill, Winston **1:***76*
Churchill River **10:***735,* **10:**736
Church of Jesus Christ of the Latter-day Saints *see* Mormons
Chu Ti, Prince **3:**164, **3:**165, **3:**166, **3:***167*
Cibola **7:**529
  Seven Golden Cities of **3:**201
Cimaroons **3:**226
cinchona tree **5:**356, **5:**366, **5:***369*
cinnamon 748, **5:**347, **9:**662, **10:**748
circumnavigation of the world **2:**84, **2:**97–99, **2:**131, **2:**148–150, **3:**213, **3:**226–228, **4:**302, **6:**422–426
Citlaltépetl volcano **10:**791
civil engineering **4:**311
Clark, William **6:408–412,** **8:**616–618, **8:**625, **9:**654, **10:**783, **10:**787
Clarke, Arthur C. **3:**195, **7:**532

classical learning **8**:591

Claudius, Emperor **8**:589

clay tables **8**:601

Clement IV, Pope **8**:564

Clement VII, Pope **4**:271, **4**:272, **6**:448, **6**:450

Clement VIII, Pope **8**:595

Clerke, Charles **3**:200

climate **3**:232–233, **4**:250

climate change, and coral reefs **10**:759

climate zones **9**:686

climatology **5**:356

clinker-built hulls **9**:648–649, **9**:719

clocks at sea **3**:168–169, **5**:392–393

Clonfert **2**:105

clothing **3**:170–174

  desert **3**:172

  freezing climate **3**:171–172

  sea **3**:172–173

  space **3**:173–174

  underwater **3**:173, **10**:*756*, **10**:759

cloud types **10**:785

cloves **5**:347, **6**:423, **6**:426, **6**:475, **7**:504, **10**:748, **10**:750

coal-tar naphtha **3**:172, **3**:239

coastlines, changing **8**:607

Cochin **2**:135, **4**:293, **4**:294

Cochin China **4**:295, **4**:297, **8**:567

Cockerell, C. R. **6**:457

cod fishing **2**:128, **6**:474, **10**:749, **10**:751

Coen, Jan Pieterszoon **7**:504

cogs **9**:649, **9**:719

Colbertisme **6**:443

Colbert, Jean-Baptiste **6**:440, **6**:442, **6**:*443*

Coleridge, Samuel Taylor **8**:567

Colla Micchati **5**:336

collections,

  exploration and **9**:674–675

  museum **6**:453–457

collectors **1**:24–26, **8**:587

Collins, Eileen **10**:791

Collins, Michael **1**:28, **1**:29

Colombia **1**:72, **1**:74, **1**:75, **5**:355, **5**:356, **7**:520, **7**:526

colonies **1**:69, **1**:71, **1**:79, **3**:177–178, **6**:441, **6**:443, **6**:449, **6**:474

  British in Australia **1**:71

  British in North America **8**:598–600

  convicts in the **4**:269

  missions in **6**:449–451

  Phoenician **3**:176

  Spanish **1**:72

colonization **3**:175–180, **6**:416, **6**:448, **6**:470–473

  of Australia **4**:269

  British in America **9**:668–671

  causes and results of **3**:178–180

  Christianity and **6**:471–472

  English **3**:177–178

  French **3**:178

  mercantilism and **10**:750

  Portuguese **3**:175

  Spanish **3**:175–177, **3**:205

  Viking **4**:250

Colorado **2**:92, **2**:93, **2**:144, **2**:145, **4**:283, **7**:547

Colorado River **3**:202, **4**:304, **5**:374, **5**:375, **7**:524, **7**:526, **8**:577–580, **9**:666

Columbian Exchange **3**:181–183

Columbia River **1**:34, **2**:146, **4**:280, **6**:408, **6**:410, **6**:412, **10**:737

Columbia space shuttle **1**:39, **1**:40, **6**:468, **9**:692–693, **9**:697, **10**:791

Columbus, Bartolomeo **3**:188

Columbus, Christopher **2**:105, **2**:126, **2**:127, **3**:175, **3**:176, **3**:181, **3**:182, **3**:184–189, **3**:204, **3**:220, **3**:223, **3**:231, **3**:232, **4**:260–263, **4**:302, **4**:303, **5**:338, **5**:370, **6**:422, **6**:429, **6**:431, **6**:451, **6**:453, **6**:454, **6**:462, **6**:470, **6**:474, **7**:494, **7**:515, **7**:522, **7**:549–550, **7**:551–552, **8**:568, **8**:593, **8**:603, **9**:704, **10**:749

  brings Christianity to New World **8**:594

  final voyage (1502–1504) **3**:189, **4**:263

  first voyage (1492–1493) **3**:186–187, **4**:247, **4**:298, **4**:*302*, **4**:303 **9**:650, **9**:651, **9**:654, **9**:658, **9**:718

  second voyage (1493–1496) **3**:187–188, **4**:263, **8**:569, **8**:570

  third voyage (1498–1500) **3**:188–189, **4**:263

  gifts of plants from the New World **8**:599

  map of voyages **3**:*188*

  meets Bartolomeu Dias **3**:223

  Spanish support for **4**:260–263

  on the Taino **8**:572

  and Vespucci **10**:769, **10**:771, **10**:772

Columbus, Diego **3**:189, **6**:462

Columbus, Hernando **2**:127

Columbus (steamship) **9**:*650*

Comanches **2**:147, **9**:667, **9**:719

comets **1**:53, **9**:676, **9**:681, **9**:719

Commander Island Group **2**:89

Commerson, Philibert de **7**:486

Commonwealth Trans-Antarctic Expedition **5**:339, **5**:340

communication **3**:190–191

  distress signals **3**:192

  satellite **3**:191, **3**:194, **3**:195, **4**:311, **6**:468, **8**:620, **8**:621

  telephone **3**:194

  underwater **3**:195

  wireless **3**:192–193

  without speech **3**:191–192

communication devices **3**:190–195

Compagnie Van Verre **5**:347, **5**:349

Company of Merchant Adventurers **2**:132, **7**:511

compass **3**:185, **4**:303, **7**:492–493, **7**:497–498, **7**:*498*

  magnetic **3**:220, **3**:232, **4**:302, **4**:309, **7**:498, **10**:729

  pivoting ship's **7**:*493*, **7**:498

  variation problem **3**:220, **7**:498

compass points **7**:489

compass rose **7**:*489*

computers

  handheld **8**:601, **8**:604

  high-speed digital **6**:432

  laptop **8**:604

  map projections **6**:435

Concepción **6**:424, **6**:426

Condoy, Julio Garcia **7**:551

Congo **2**:115

  Belgian **9**:711, **9**:713, **9**:714–715

  Democratic Republic of **9**:715

  Congo River **4**:304, **6**:417, **9**:713, **9**:714, **10**:745, **10**:746

conquest **3**:175–180, **6**:470

  causes and results **3**:178–180

  defined **3**:175

  mercantilism and **10**:750

conquistadores **1**:72, **1**:74, **1**:79, **3**:176, **3**:201, **5**:370, **5**:379, **6**:462, **7**:520, **7**:523, **8**:569–572, **8**:639, **9**:683, **9**:706, **10**:752, **10**:799

Conshelf *see* Continental Shelf

Constantinople (Istanbul) **3**:175, **8**:591, **10**:747, **10**:748, **10**:773, **10**:775

construction **3**:231

  surveying for projects **10**:728–730

Continental Divide **6**:411

continental shelf **3**:210, **3**:239, **10**:756

Continental Shelf (Conshelf) **3**:210, **10**:761

conversion **3**:176, **6**:448–452, **8**:611

convicts **1**:71, **3**:180, **4**:292

  as colonists **4**:269

Cook, Frederick Albert **4**:255, **7**:539–540

Cook, James **2**:84, **2**:85, **2**:86, **3**:169, **3**:180, **3**:196–200, **3**:212, **4**:252, **4**:269, **4**:270, **4**:299, **4**:303, **4**:314, **5**:368, **6**:430, **6**:470, **6**:471, **7**:486, **7**:502, **7**:554, **7**:556, **8**:626, **9**:651, **9**:655, **9**:656, **9**:688–689, **10**:733

  first Pacific voyage (1768–1771) **1**:69, **1**:70–71, **3**:197–198

  map of three voyages (1768–1779) **3**:*197*

  second Pacific voyage (1772–1775) **3**:199, **10**:757, **10**:762

  third Pacific voyage (1776–1780) **3**:200, **10**:762

Cooper, James Fenimore **2**:96

Cooper, L. Gordon, Jr. **9**:645

Cooper's Creek **2**:111, **2**:112, **6**:473

coordinates (map) **4**:301, **8**:591

Copernicus, Nicolaus **1**:44, **1**:49, **3**:233, **7**:484, **7**:486, **8**:591, **9**:676, **9**:680

copperplate engraving **6**:447

coral **3**:198, **3**:216, **9**:662

coral reefs **3**:218, **4**:*312*, **10**:759, **10**:761

Cordoba **5**:363

  Great Mosque **5**:*362*

Cornwall **10**:739

Cornwallis Island **4**:276

Coronado, Francisco Vásquez de **3**:201–203, **6**:477, **7**:525

Coronelli, Vincenzo, map of New France **6**:*438*

Corry, Captain **6**:431

Corsica **2**:100

Cortés, Hernán **2**:136, **3**:182, **3**:204–208, **5**:376, **6**:439, **6**:455, **6**:462–464, **6**:478, **7**:522, **7**:523, **9**:*704*, **9**:705, **9**:706

  map of journeys in the Caribbean **3**:*205*

Cortés, Martín **3**:206

Cortés, Tolosa **7**:523

corvette **2**:84, **2**:159

cosmography **6**:445, **10**:772

cosmonauts **1**:37–42, **4**:288–290, **4**:306 *see also* astronauts

Costa Rica **3**:185, **3**:189

Cotton, Robert **6**:456

Council of the Indies **1**:74, **1**:75, **6**:463, **9**:704

Courten, William **6**:456

Cousin, Jean **7**:549

Cousteau, Jacques-Yves **3:209–211,** **4:**274, **10:**758, **10:**760, **10:**761

Cousteau Society **3:**211

Crean, Thomas **8:**638

creation
  Bible story **7:**487
  evolutionary theory **3:**216, **3:**219, **7:**487

Cree Indians **5:**353, **5:**397, **6:**473, **10:**737, **10:**799

Crévecoeur **5:**386

Crimea **5:**358, **9:**712

Crimean War (1854–1856) **2:**115, **9:**707, **9:**709

Cromwell, Oliver **6:**440

Cronin, Vincent **8:**611

crop rotation **3:**179

Crosby, Alfred **3:**181

cross-staff **7:**494, **7:**500

Crozier, Francis **4:**276, **4:**277, **4:**278

Crusades **4:**319, **5:**331, **5:**339, **9:**648

Cuba **3:**176, **3:**185, **3:**186, **3:**188, **6:**440, **6:**462, **8:**569, **8:**570, **8:**571, **9:**682
  Cortés's conquest of **3:**205

cultural anthropology **1:**22

cultural geography **4:**300, **4:**305

cultural relativism **1:**24

Cunningham, Alan **1:**70, **4:**314

curragh **2:**105, **2:**159, **9:**658

currents **7:**508, **10:739–743**
  and conquests **10:**743
  defined **10:**739
  Gulf Stream **8:**571, **8:**572
  world's main **10:**742

Curzon, George **10:**794

Cuzco **1:**72, **9:**682, **9:**683

cylindrical projections **6:434–435**

Cyrene **4:244–247**

Dablon, Claude **6:**438, **6:**450, **6:**451

Dacron **3:**174

Daguerre camera **7:**541

Daguerre, Louis-Jacques-Mandé **7:**541, **7:**542

daguerrotype **7:**542

Dakar **5:**392

Dakota **5:**397, **5:**398
  Black Hills of South **9:**664

Dalai Lama **8:**588, **10:**794

Dalrymple, Alexander **9:**689

Damascus **1:**76, **1:**77, **2:**115, **2:**117, **5:**360

Dampier, William **2:**149, **3:212–215,** **4:**313, **9:**651, **9:**655

Dampier Archipelago **3:**213

Dampier Strait **3:**213, **3:**214

Dance, Lieutenant **1:**19

Dandonneau du Sablé, Marie-Anne **5:**394, **5:**396

Danes **10:**775

Dannett, Captain **4:**276

Danskøya Island **1:**61, **1:**62

Dare, Virginia **8:**603

Darién **1:**72, **3:**226, **7:**520, **7:**521, **7:**522

Darius III, king of the Persians **1:**15, **1:**16

Dark Ages **8:**591

dark matter **1:**53

Darwin, Charles **3:**212, **3:216–219,** **4:**264, **4:**265, **4:**266, **4:**267, **5:**357, **7:**486, **7:**487–488, **7:**494, **10:**777, **10:**780

Darwin, Emma **3:**219

Darwin, Erasmus **3:**216

David, Jacques-Louis **1:**55, **2:**100

Dávila, Pedro Arias **1:**72, **7:**521, **7:**522, **9:**683

Davis, John **1:**67, **1:**68, **7:**494, **7:**500, **7:**516, **7:**518

Davis quadrant **1:**67

Davis Strait **1:**67, **1:**68, **7:**516, **7:**518

Daxia *see* Bactria

Daza, Louis de **1:**74

dead reckoning **3:**168, **3:220–221,** **3:**232, **7:**492, **7:**494, **7:**496

Dease, Peter **7:**519

Deception Island **1:**61

decompression chamber **3:**173

Deep Space Communications Center, Mojave Desert **8:**632

Deep Space Network **9:**701, **9:**702

Defoe, Daniel, *Robinson Crusoe* **3:**213, **3:**214, **3:**215, **4:**268, **7:**530

De Geer Glacier **2:**102

Delaporte, Louis **4:**295

de la Roche, Antoine **9:**688

de las Casas, Bartolomé **6:**472

Delaware **8:**624, **8:**625

del Conte, Jacopino **8:**609

de le Torre, Bernard **10:**743

Delhi **5:**358, **5:**359

Dellenbaugh, Frederick **8:**579

Delphi **4:**247

de Monts, Sieur *see* Gua, Pierre du

de Moucheron **5:**349

Denbigh, north Wales **9:**711, **9:**712

Denmark **2:**87, **2:**88, **4:**250, **8:**624, **10:**773, **10:**776

Denver and Rio Grande Railroad **5:**380

Deptford **3:**228, **4:**285

Desceliers, Pierre **2:**154, **6:**431

Deseret *see* Utah

Desolation Islands **9:**688

de Solís, Juan Díaz **7:**551, **7:**552

Devon **3:**226

Devon Island **1:**63, **1:**65

Devonport, England **3:**216, **8:**630

Dezhnyov, Semyon **8:**612, **8:**614

Dge-lugs-pa (Yellow Hat) order of lamas **8:**588

dhow **5:**359, **5:**399, **9:**647, **9:**648

diamonds **6:**477, **6:**478

Diamond Sutra **9:**663

Dias, Bartolomeu **2:**133, **3:222–225,** **4:**291, **4:**293, **4:**299, **6:**474, **7:**500, **8:**574, **8:**575, **8:**593, **10:**743, **10:**749
  meets Columbus **3:**223
  route around Africa **3:**224

Dias, Dinis **5:**332, **5:**335

Dicaearchus of Messina **5:**388

Dieppe **7:**549, **10:**766, **10:**767, **10:**768

diesel power **9:**648, **9:**650

digital photography **7:**541, **7:**544

dinosaurs **1:**54

Din, Rashid al-, *Jami at-tawarikh* **9:**662

direct observation **7:**485

Discovery **1:**41, **4:**308, **8:**622, **9:**694

diseases **3:**181–182, **3:**197, **5:366–370,** **9:**669, **9:**670, **9:**706
  brought by colonizers **3:**180, **3:**181–182, **3:**208
  carried by explorers **3:**181–182, **3:**187, **5:**370
  of the cold **5:**368–370
  dietary **8:**583, **8:**584
  European, among slaves **6:**472
  vitamin deficiency **8:**583

distress signals **3:**192

diving **10:758–759**
  communication devices **3:**195
  decompression sickness (the bends) **10:**759
  suits **3:**173, **3:**209, **10:**756, **10:**759

Djibouti **5:**338, **9:**707

Dodge, Grenville **2:**109

dodo **6:**456, **6:**479

dogs, sled **1:**20

doldrums **3:**188, **3:**239

Dollier, François **5:**384

Dolomites **10:**791

Dolphin, HMS **2:**148, **2:**150

Dominica **3:**187, **8:**569

Dominican Republic **3:**186

Doña Marina *see* La Malinche

Donington **4:**268

Donnacona **2:**151

Dornier flying boats **3:**235

Dorset **10:**779

Down, Kent **3:**218

Drake, Francis **3:226–228,** **4:**285, **4:**287, **4:**312, **5:**326, **5:**366, **6:**440, **8:**598, **8:**599, **9:**651, **9:**654, **9:**687, **9:**706
  secret ships **3:**227

Drake, Frank **8:**632

drifting research stations **8:**614

drinking supplies **8:**581–582
  freshwater **8:**581, **8:**582, **8:**597, **10:**757

dry suits **3:**173

Dublin **10:**775

Dudley, Ambrose, earl of Warwick **4:**285

Duisburg **6:**444, **6:**446, **6:**447

Dundee **4:**314

Dunhuang **9:**663

Dupré, Marie-Jules **4:**296–297

Dupuis, Jean **4:**296, **4:**297

Durham **1:**76, **1:**77, **4:**264, **4:**267

Durrance, Samuel **1:**40

Dutch colonies **2:**150

Dutch East India Company **5:**346, **5:**348, **5:**349, **7:**504, **8:**574, **8:**576, **10:**732–733, **10:**750–751

Dutch exploration **3:**198, **5:**346–349, **5:**351, **7:**503–506, **7:**512–513, **9:**654–655, **9:**687, **10:**749, **10:**786

Dutch mapmakers **6:**429, **7:**506

Dutch West India Company **7:**504, **7:**506

Dvina River **7:**512

dwarf stars **1:**52

dysentery **3:**228, **4:**296, **4:**319, **5:**366, **5:**368, **6:**417

Eagle lunar landing module **1:**28, **1:**29

Eannes, Gil **5:**332, **5:**335

Earhart, Amelia **10:**788, **10:**789

Earle, Sylvia **10:**759

Earth **3:229–234,** **5:**343, **5:**345, **7:**484, **7:**486, **9:**676, **9:**678, **9:**679, **9:**695, **10:**752
  beneath the surface of **3:**231
  as center of the universe **1:**49, **3:**233, **8:**590, **9:**676
  circumference of **4:**244, **4:**245–246, **4:**298, **4:**299, **4:**300, **4:**302, **4:**303, **5:**364, **8:**593
  crust **10:**779
  dimensions of **4:**305
  as flat **3:**185, **3:**229, **4:**300
  magnetic field **4:**253, **7:**492, **7:**508
  mantle and core **3:**231
  mapping **3:**230–231, **8:**606–607

Earth (cont.)
orbiting **4**:288–290, **4**:306–308, **4**:319
as part of a heliocentric universe **1**:49, **3**:233, **8**:591, **9**:676
photos from space of **6**:428, **6**:432, **6**:435, **6**:469
polar circumference of **1**:50
revolutionary ideas about **3**:233
satellite **8**:619
as a sphere **4**:299
statistics **3**:231
earthquakes **3**:217, **3**:231
Earth Resources Technology Satellite (ERTS) *see Landsat*
East Africa **3**:166, **3**:167, **4**:292, **5**:358, **7**:528, **9**:707–715, **10**:744
Burton and Speke's exploration (1857–1858) **2**:114–117
East Asia **2**:143, **3**:167, **10**:748
Easter Island **3**:199, **5**:336, **5**:338
Eastern Europe **10**:775
East Indies **2**:150, **3**:227, **6**:455, **7**:503, **7**:504, **8**:573, **8**:576, **9**:653, **9**:654–655, **9**:687, **10**:732–733, **10**:751
Houtman's voyage to the **5**:346–349
Spanish **4**:285
Eastman, George **7**:541, **7**:542
East Pacific Rise **7**:*488*
ebony **6**:477, **6**:479
Ecbatana **1**:16
Eckert projection **6**:435
eclipse of the moon **4**:299, **6**:451
eclipse of the sun **1**:51, **3**:197, **5**:344
economics **6**:439–443
ecosystems **10**:724, **10**:727, **10**:759
Ecuador **1**:*64*, **1**:72–73, **5**:355, **9**:705
Edinburgh **1**:56, **1**:58, **2**:91, **2**:93
Edwards Airbase, California **9**:692
Edwards, William Henry, **10**:777
Egmont Island **2**:150
Egypt **1**:15, **1**:16, **1**:77, **2**:115, **2**:141, **2**:142, **4**:244–245, **5**:359, **5**:360, **5**:377, **5**:390, **7**:497, **7**:543, **8**:565, **8**:589, **8**:592, **9**:709, **9**:710, **9**:712, **9**:717, **10**:730, **10**:747, **10**:752
ancient **5**:337, **5**:338
Egyptians **6**:474, **6**:477, **8**:589
exploration **8**:602
mapmakers **6**:*427*
mummification **1**:22
shipbuilding **9**:647, **9**:648
surveyors **10**:730
tomb painting **10**:*747*

Eielson, Carl Ben **1**:61, **1**:62
Einstein, Albert **1**:50–51, **9**:677
ejector seat **4**:289
Elcano, Sebastián de **6**:426
El Dorado **1**:72, **1**:74, **1**:75, **6**:477, **7**:*524*, **7**:525, **7**:526, **7**:529, **8**:598, **8**:599, **8**:600, **10**:752
map of **7**:*524*
electric telegraph **3**:190, **3**:192
electromagnetic radiation **3**:193, **3**:239, **9**:677
electromagnetic spectrum **1**:46, **1**:48, **1**:50, **1**:79, **8**:605–606, **8**:633, **8**:639
electronic maps **4**:311
electronic navigation **7**:494–496
Elephant Island **4**:315, **8**:636, **8**:637, **8**:638
Elizabeth I **3**:226, **3**:228, **4**:285, **4**:312, **5**:325, **5**:326, **6**:*440*, **6**:441, **8**:598, **8**:600, **9**:669
Elizabeth II **5**:340
Ellesmere Island **2**:118, **5**:370, **8**:627
Ellsworth, Lincoln **1**:18, **1**:21, **1**:60, **1**:62, **2**:119, **3**:235–238
Elmina **3**:222, **3**:224
El Paso (del Rio del Norte) **7**:524
Emery, Josiah **7**:495
Emin Pasa Relief Expedition **9**:713, **9**:715
empire **6**:441, **6**:452, **10**:750
and land claims **8**:601
Encounter Bay **4**:269
Endeavour (Cook's ship) **1**:69, **2**:86, **3**:197–198, **5**:368, **7**:486, **8**:626, **9**:651, **9**:655
Endeavour (space shuttle) **1**:41, **1**:47
Endurance **4**:315, **7**:543, **8**:635, **8**:636–638, **9**:*656*
England **2**:113, **2**:127, **2**:132, **2**:148, **3**:182, **3**:184, **3**:196, **4**:268, **5**:363, **5**:390, **6**:451, **9**:671, **9**:713, **9**:715, **10**:740–741, **10**:742, **10**:750, **10**:774, **10**:775, **10**:793
Elizabethan **6**:441, **6**:470, **6**:473
English Channel **3**:190
balloon flights **1**:59, **1**:62
English explorers **5**:350–353, **7**:511–512, **7**:517–518, **9**:652–653, **9**:668–671, **9**:707–710
English navy, provisions **8**:583
Enlightenment **6**:456–457, **6**:479
Enterprise of England **9**:706
entomology **10**:777, **10**:778
environmentalism **4**:256, **9**:675

and satellites **8**:622
equator **5**:389, **5**:390, **9**:715, **10**:743
equinoxes, precession of the **5**:343, **5**:399
Eratosthenes of Cyrene **1**:50, **4**:244–247, **4**:298, **4**:299, **5**:345, **5**:390
world map **4**:245, **4**:246–247, **5**:345, **5**:390
Erbil, Iraq **1**:16
Erik the Red **4**:248–250, **4**:316, **6**:404, **10**:774, **10**:775
Eriksfjord **4**:248, **4**:249
Escalante River **8**:579
Espíritu Santo **8**:596, **8**:597
Estero Bay **8**:571
Estrada, Beatriz **3**:201
Ethiopia **9**:707, **9**:709
ethnography **1**:23, **5**:363
ethnology **1**:22, **8**:578
Euler, Leonhard **10**:742
Euphrates River **1**:16, **1**:77, **6**:*429*
Europe **1**:24, **1**:34, **2**:113, **2**:143, **3**:181, **4**:251, **4**:283, **4**:291, **4**:300, **5**:377, **6**:428, **6**:430, **6**:441, **6**:453, **7**:511, **7**:515, **8**:564, **9**:659, **9**:660, **9**:662, **9**:717, **10**:749, **10**:776
colonization **3**:179
northern **9**:648–649
Renaissance **8**:591
trade with Asia **10**:748
European Geographical Society (EUGEO) **4**:253, **4**:256
European Remote-Sensing Satellite (ERS-1) **8**:*605*
European Space Agency **6**:469, **9**:677
evangelical Christianity **2**:91, **2**:104–106, **2**:159
Evans, Charles **5**:339
Evans, Edgar **8**:629, **8**:630
Everest, George **5**:341, **10**:731
evolution **1**:22, **10**:777–780
Darwin's theory of **3**:216, **3**:217–218, **3**:219, **4**:264, **4**:267, **7**:487
Évora, Portugal **8**:594, **8**:596
excavations **2**:90, **5**:338
exchange of goods **3**:182
expeditionary force **4**:295, **4**:319
expedition data, publication **8**:601
record keeping **8**:601–604
extraterrestrial **1**:41, **1**:46, **1**:49, **1**:54, **1**:79, **7**:531, **8**:632–634, **8**:639
extraterrestrial transport **5**:382
Extravehicular Mobility Unit

(EMU) **3**:174
Eyre, Edward John **6**:473

factories **6**:413
Faeroe Islands **2**:105, **4**:250, **7**:491, **8**:624, **10**:775
Fa-hsien *see* Faxian
Fairness Point **1**:67
Faisal I, king of Iraq **1**:78
Falkland Islands **2**:97, **2**:98, **2**:148, **3**:217
Falmouth **3**:218, **10**:762
famine **4**:249
famine relief **6**:461
Fang **4**:315
Far East **9**:718
Fatu Hiva **5**:336
Faxian **4**:257–259, **4**:*299*, **4**:300, **9**:660
Fo Kuo Chi **4**:259
route through South and Southeast Asia (399–414) **4**:*258*
Fedorov, Eugeny **8**:614
Ferdinand, king of Spain **3**:184, **3**:185, **3**:186, **3**:187, **3**:188, **4**:260–263, **4**:303, **6**:463, **8**:569, **8**:571, **9**:703, **9**:704
Ferguson tractors **5**:381
Ferrelo, Bartolomé **2**:138
Fertile Crescent **5**:377
feudalism **10**:773, **10**:799
Fez **5**:361
fiber-optic cable **3**:191, **3**:194, **3**:239
Fichtel Mountains **5**:354
field research **1**:24, **4**:251
Fiennes, Ranulph **4**:255, **4**:315
Fiji **10**:732, **10**:734
Filson, John **2**:95
Fimbul Ice Shelf **2**:85, **7**:556
Findlay, John **2**:94–95
Finisterre **4**:267
Finland **7**:507, **8**:624
Fisher, George **3**:214
Fitzroy, Robert **3**:216–217, **3**:218, **4**:264–267, **7**:486, **7**:487
fjords **2**:102, **2**:159, **4**:250
Flamsteed, John **5**:393
Flanders **6**:444
flares, distress signals **3**:192
Flatheads **2**:108
Flemish tapestry **8**:*575*
Flinders, Matthew **1**:71, **4**:268–270, **4**:275, **4**:314
map of voyages around Australia **4**:*269*
flood moons **10**:742

flora and fauna **1:**69–70, **8:**603
Florence **6:***453,* **10:**765, **10:**769,
    10:770, **10:**771, **10:**783
Florida **1:**27, **1:**56, **1:**57, **2:**94,
    2:122–125, **3:***179,* **3:**182, **3:**211,
    3:234, **4:**307, **6:**462, **6:**463, **6:**464,
    6:468, **6:**470, **8:**569, **8:**570, **8:**572,
    9:*645,* **9:**682, **9:**683, **9:**684, **9:***685,*
    9:692, **9:**696, **10:**767, **10:**768
Florida Keys **8:**571, **10:**761
Fogo **8:***606*
folklore **10:**782, **10:**799
food **3:**182–183, **8:**582
    daily ration **8:**583
    dried **8:**582
    pickling in brine **8:**582
    preservation **3:**179, **8:**582
    production **3:**179, **3:**182
    resources **6:**474
    salted **8:**582
    in space **1:**40
    supplies **8:**582–583, **8:**638
fool's gold *see* iron pyrite
Forbidden City *see* Lhasa
ford **7:**559
Ford, Edsel **2:**118
Forest, Lee de **3:**193
Forest Service (U.S.) **8:**580
Forster, Johann Georg Adam
    7:*486*
Forster, Johann Reinhold **7:**486
Fort Astoria **1:**34, **1:**35
Fort Bourbon **5:**395, **5:**398
Fort Bridger **2:**108, **2:**109
Fort Chipewyan **6:**418, **6:**420
Fort Churchill **10:**735
Fort Crozon **4:**287
Fort Cumberland **10:**735
Fort Dauphin **5:**395, **5:**398
Fort Duquesne **2:**94
Fort Fork **6:**419
Fort Kaministikwia **5:**396
Fort Laramie **2:**146
Fort Rouge **5:**395, **5:**397
Fort Mandan **6:**410, **6:**411, **8:**616
Fort Manuel **8:**618
Fort Maurepas **5:**394, **5:**397
Fort Resolution **6:***419*
Fort Saint-Charles **5:***394,* **5:**396,
    5:397
Fort Saint-Pierre **5:**394, **5:**396
Fort William **5:***398*
fossils **3:**217, **7:**508, **10:**731, **10:**753
Foulshiels **7:**533
Fountain of Youth **8:**570, **8:**571
Four Hundred **1:**36
Foxe, Luke **4:**287, **7:**516, **7:**518
Foxe Basin **1:**67, **7:**518

Foxe Channel **7:**516
Fox River **5:**371, **6:**437
Fox Talbot, W. H. **7:**541, **7:**542
Fram **1:**19–20, **1:**21, **6:**458,
    6:459–460, **7:**554, **7:**555, **8:**624,
    8:627
Framheim **1:***21*
France **1:**55, **2:**97–100, **2:**114,
    2:151–154, **2:**155–158, **3:**209,
    3:231, **4:**246, **4:**271–274, **4:**287,
    5:363, **5:**394, **6:**436–438, **6:**441,
    6:442, **6:**443, **6:**447, **6:**448, **6:**450,
    7:543, **8:**624, **10:**750, **10:**753,
    10:756, **10:**761, **10:**765, **10:**775,
    10:776
    becomes a republic **2:**100
    and Britain **3:**196, **4:**265, **4:**269,
        4:313
Franciscans **3:**179, **5:**385, **5:**399,
    9:662–663
Francisco River **3:**227
Francis I, king of France **2:**151,
    2:152, **2:**153, **2:**154, **4:**271, **6:**448,
    10:765, **10:**766, **10:**767, **10:**768
Francis I, Holy Roman emperor
    10:753
Franco-German War (1870–1871)
    4:296
Franklin, John **4:**252, **4:**275–278,
    4:313, **7:**517, **7:**518, **7:**519
    map of expeditions to the
        Canadian Arctic **4:***277*
Franklin Strait **4:**276
Franks **6:**448
Franz Josef Land **2:**101, **2:**102,
    3:238
Fraser, Simon **4:**313
Fraser River **6:**419, **6:**420
Fray Marcos de Niza **3:**201, **3:**202
Frederick Jackson Island **6:**458,
    6:460
Frederikshåb **4:**250
free trade **6:**440, **6:**442, **6:**443
Freiberg **5:**354
Frémont, Charles **4:**279
Frémont, Jessie Benton **4:**279,
    4:280, **4:**281, **10:**788
Frémont, John Charles **2:**145–146,
    2:147, **4:**279–283
    map of expeditions **4:***282*
    the Pathfinder **4:**280–281, **10:**788
French **3:**177, **9:**652–653
    in Canada **3:**179
    colonization in North America
        3:178
    explorers **3:**209–211, **4:**271–274,
        4:295–297, **5:**371–372,
        5:383–387, **10:**749

navigation **2:**97–100
French and Indian War
    (1754–1763) **2:**94, **4:***272,* **4:**273
French empire **4:**295
French navy **3:**209
    Undersea Research Group **3:**210
French Revolution **2:**100, **2:**150,
    6:442
freshwater **8:**596, **8:**597, **10:**755
Freuchen, Peter **8:**627
Freydis Eriksdottir **4:**248, **4:**316,
    6:407
Frisius, Gemma **6:**444, **6:**445, **7:**495
Frith, Francis **7:**542, **7:**543
Frobisher, Martin **3:**172, **4:**284–287,
    4:313, **6:**470, **6:**473, **7:**515, **7:**518,
    8:603
    map of search for Northwest
        Passage **4:***285*
Frontenac, Comte de (Louis de
    Buade) **5:**384, **5:**386
frontier exploration **6:**408–412
frontiersmen **2:**94–96, **2:**107–109,
    2:144–147, **4:**280
frostbite **1:**20, **3:**171, **5:**366, **5:***368,*
    5:370, **7:**537, **8:**630, **8:**639
Fuchs, Vivian **5:**340
Fuegians **4:***266*
Fukien, China **2:***92*
Fulton, Robert **9:**648
Furneaux, Tobias **3:**199
fur trade **1:**30–32, **1:**33–36, **2:**90,
    2:155, **2:**156, **2:**158, **3:**178, **4:**271,
    4:273, **4:**313, **5:**371, **5:**384–385,
    5:394–396, **6:**418–421, **6:**473,
    6:474, **6:**475, **6:**478, **7:**512, **7:**517,
    9:653, **9:**662, **9:**664–667, **9:**689,
    10:735–738, **10:**749
    beaver **6:**419, **6:**421, **10:***750,*
        10:751
    trapping **2:**107–109, **2:**145, **8:**612,
        8:613
Fury and Hecla Strait **7:**517, **7:**518
Fury Beach **8:**583

gabardine **3:**171, **3:**239
Gabon **4:**315, **10:**788, **10:**790
Gaffarel, Jacques **10:**752–753,
    10:754
Gagarin, Yury **1:**37, **1:**38, **1:**40,
    4:288–290, **4:**306, **8:**615, **9:**644,
    9:692, **9:**695, **9:**696, **10:**791
Gagnan, Émile **3:**209, **3:**210, **10:**758,
    10:760
Galápagos Islands **3:**216, **3:**217,
    3:*218,* **5:**336, **5:**338, **7:**487
Galata observatory **4:***300*
galaxies **1:**52, **9:**677

Galilei, Galileo **1:**44, **1:**49, **1:**50,
    3:233, **7:**484, **7:**532, **9:**680, **10:**782
Galileo mission **9:**691, **9:**697,
    9:700–701
Galinée, René de **5:**384
Galle, Johann Gottfried **9:**681
galleon **9:**650, **9:**651, **9:**719
galleys **9:**647, **9:**658
Galton, Francis **4:**256
Galveston Island, Texas **2:**123
Gama, Paolo da **4:**291
Gama, Vasco da **2:**133, **2:**135,
    2:143, **3:**222, **3:**223, **3:**224, **3:**231,
    4:291–294, **4:**298, **4:**302–303,
    5:366, **6:**476, **8:**574, **8:**575, **9:**650,
    9:651, **9:**654, **9:**660, **9:**686–687,
    10:749, **10:**751
    voyage to India **4:**291–293
Gambia River **5:**332, **5:**335, **7:**534,
    8:574
Gandhara **4:**259
Ganges River **1:**17, **4:**246
gangrene **2:**138, **2:**159, **5:**368,
    8:630, **8:**639
Ganswindt, Hermann **9:**690
Garcia, Stephanus, world map
    (1076) **3:***230*
Garden of Intelligence **6:**455
Garnier, Francis **4:**274, **4:**295–297
    Mekong River expedition
        (1866–1868) map **4:***296*
Gaspar à Myrica **6:**444, **6:**447
Gaspé Bay **4:***271*
Gaspé Peninsula **2:**151
Gates, Horatio **6:**409
Gaugamela, Battle of **1:**16
Gaul **3:**176
Gaza people **1:**23
Gazelle River (Bahr al-Ghazal)
    10:745
Gemini Project **1:**27, **1:**28, **1:**38,
    1:39, **6:**466, **6:**467, **6:***468,* **9:**692,
    9:697
Genesis, Book of **3:**216, **3:**219
Genghis Khan **3:**190, **3:**191, **9:**661
Genoa **2:**126, **3:**184, **10:**748–749
    war with Venice **8:**566, **8:**568
Gentz, Wilhelm **10:**744
geocentric view of the universe
    1:49, **3:**233, **8:**590, **9:**676
geographical societies **4:**251–256,
    8:586
Geographic Information System
    (GIS) **6:**428
geography **3:**185, **3:**230–231,
    4:298–305, **5:**324, **5:**354–357,
    5:363, **5:**390, **6:**427–429, **6:**445,
    6:447, **7:**484, **8:**585, **9:**717

geography (cont.)
first textbook **4**:304, **4**:305
in Germany **4**:252–253
Greek **4**:244–247, **4**:298, **4**:299,
5:344–345, **8**:595, **9**:716–718
Ptolemy's **8**:591–593
Strabo's definition **4**:301
Geological Survey (U.S.) **8**:578,
8:580
geological surveys **3**:231, **3**:235,
6:475, **8**:578, **8**:580, **10**:730–731
geology **3**:231, **3**:235, **4**:253, **4**:311,
4:319, **5**:354, **5**:399, **7**:508, **8**:578,
8:580, **10**:753, **10**:756, **10**:779
and satellites **8**:622
geomagnetic field **5**:357
geophysics **2**:121
George III **1**:52, **1**:71, **6**:420, **6**:421
George Medal **5**:340
Georgia **2**:94, **4**:279, **4**:281, **6**:470,
9:684
geostationary satellites **4**:311,
8:623, **10**:785, **10**:799
German explorers **10**:745
German Geographical Society
4:252, **4**:255
Germany **1**:24, **1**:33, **1**:34, **1**:71,
4:299, **5**:354–357, **6**:447, **6**:463,
9:*650*, **9**:690, **9**:702, **10**:743
geography in **4**:252–253, **4**:255
post office **3**:191
geysers **2**:107, **3**:231
Ghana **2**:115, **2**:143, **3**:222, **4**:284,
5:365
Gibraltar **4**:247
Gila River **5**:374, **5**:375
Gilbert, Humphrey **7**:515
GIS (Geographic Information
System) **6**:428
Giza **7**:542
Gjøa **1**:18–19, **7**:518, **9**:655
glacier **2**:102–103, **2**:118, **2**:159
Glaisher, James **10**:784
Glasgow **1**:23, **1**:26
Glenn, John **1**:37, **1**:38, **4**:306–308,
9:645
glider flight **1**:59
Global Orbiting Navigation
Satellite System (GLONASS)
4:309
Global Positioning System (GPS)
1:43, **4**:309–311, **5**:388, **5**:*389*,
5:393, **7**:495, **7**:496, **8**:620,
8:622–623
globe **4**:299, **4**:303, **5**:324, **6**:427,
6:429, **6**:444, **6**:446
GLONASS (Global Orbiting
Navigation Satellite System)

4:309
GLORIA sonar device **10**:760
gnomonic projection **6**:434
Goa **8**:576, **8**:608, **8**:610
Gobi Desert **4**:258, **8**:565, **8**:566,
8:585, **8**:586, **8**:587, **9**:659, **9**:663,
10:793, **10**:794, **10**:796
Goddard, Robert **1**:37, **1**:38, **9**:690
Godthåb (Nuuk) **4**:250
GOES weather satellite **10**:781
gold **2**:142, **2**:143, **2**:153, **3**:175,
3:186, **4**:283, **4**:285, **4**:287,
6:439–440, **6**:453, **6**:464, **6**:474,
6:477–478, **7**:515, **8**:569, **8**:573,
9:662, **9**:684, **9**:706, **10**:749,
10:750, **10**:752
cities of **3**:201, **4**:252, **7**:523,
7:525, **7**:529, **7**:533, **8**:598,
8:600
Incan **7**:521
mining **3**:182, **4**:284
Gold Coast **3**:222, **6**:478
Golden Bay **10**:733
Goldin, Dan **4**:308
Golding, William, *Lord of the Flies*
7:530
Goldstone **9**:701
Gomes, Fernão **8**:574
Gondokoro **10**:745
gonfalonier **10**:771, **10**:799
Goodacre, Glenna **8**:618
Goode, J. Paul **6**:435
Gordian Knot **1**:15
Gordium, Temple of Zeus **1**:15
Gore-Tex **3**:174
Gosnold, Bartholomew **3**:182
Gosse, Philip Henry **7**:488
Goths **6**:448
Gouda **5**:346
governorship **4**:262, **4**:267
GPS *see* Global Positioning
System
gradient **10**:729, **10**:799
Graham Land **1**:61
Granada **4**:*263*, **5**:358, **5**:359, **8**:569,
8:570, **9**:704
fall of (1492) **4**:260, **4**:261
Grand Canyon **3**:202, **3**:203,
8:577–580
Grand Master of the Order of
Christ **5**:331
Grand Portage **10**:737
Granicus River, Battle of **1**:15
Grant, James Augustus **9**:707,
9:709
gravitation **1**:51, **1**:52
gravity **1**:50, **1**:52, **1**:79, **5**:393, **8**:619,
9:677, **9**:719, **10**:742

and the moon **10**:739
zero **1**:38, **1**:41
gravity assist **9**:691
Gray, Charles **2**:111
Great Barrier Reef **3**:198, **4**:268,
4:269, **4**:270, **9**:656
Great Basin **2**:107, **2**:109, **2**:146,
4:280, **4**:281, **9**:665, **9**:666, **9**:667
Great Bear **7**:489, **7**:553
Great Britain **1**:56, **3**:169, **3**:176,
4:246, **4**:312–315, **6**:477, **8**:624,
9:706, **9**:717, **9**:718, **10**:739,
10:747
first telegraph **3**:190
and France **3**:196, **4**:265, **4**:269,
4:273, **4**:313
free trade **6**:440, **6**:443
Mercator's map **6**:446
Royal Navy **2**:148
and the United States **1**:33
Great Fish River **3**:224
Great Lakes
(East Africa) **9**:708, **9**:709
(U.S.) **2**:155, **5**:371, **5**:384, **6**:436,
6:450, **7**:545
Great Northern Expedition
(1733–1741) **2**:88–89, **7**:514
Great Northern War **2**:87
Great Ocean Sea **4**:299
Great Plains **3**:183, **3**:203, **5**:398,
8:616
Great Plains Indians **7**:546
Great Pyramid, Giza **7**:*542*
Great Pyramid of Khufu **10**:730
Great Salt Desert **9**:666–667,
Great Salt Lake **2**:107, **2**:109, **2**:146,
9:665, **9**:666, **9**:667
Great Slave Lake **6**:418, **6**:*419*
Great Southern Continent **4**:303
Great South Land **9**:689
Great Trigonometrical Survey of
India **10**:731, **10**:794
Greece **1**:14, **6**:428, **6**:447, **8**:565,
9:659
Greeks **1**:14–17
astronomy **1**:43, **1**:50, **5**:342–345,
7:499, **8**:589–590, **10**:740,
10:783
geography **4**:244–247, **4**:298,
4:299, **5**:344–345, **8**:595,
9:716–718
mapmakers **5**:390, **6**:428, **10**:729
mathematics **4**:244–247, **4**:299,
5:342–345
meteorology **10**:781
myths **7**:527, **8**:571
philosophy **4**:299, **9**:686
trading posts **3**:176

Green Bank equation **8**:632
Green Bay, Lake Michigan **2**:158,
5:371, **6**:437, **6**:438
Greene, Henry **5**:353
greenhouse effect **9**:678, **9**:719
Greenland **1**:66, **1**:67, **2**:101, **2**:102,
2:118, **4**:248–250, **4**:276, **4**:285,
4:300, **4**:316–318, **5**:353, **5**:377,
6:404, **6**:406–407, **6**:458–461,
7:491, **7**:507, **7**:508, **7**:509, **7**:510,
7:516, **7**:517, **7**:537–538, **7**:555,
7:558, **8**:625, **8**:627, **10**:743,
10:747, **10**:773, **10**:774, **10**:781,
10:787, **10**:788
colonization of **4**:249–250,
10:775
Green River **1**:30, **1**:32, **2**:145, **8**:578
Greenwich **7**:496
Greenwich Mean Time **3**:168–169
Greenwich meridian **3**:168, **4**:266,
5:389, **5**:*391*, **5**:392
Greenwich Royal Observatory
5:388, **5**:*390*, **5**:391, **5**:393
Gregory X, Pope **8**:565
Grenville, Richard **8**:598, **8**:*599*
Greve **10**:765, **10**:767
grid **4**:247, **4**:300, **4**:302, **4**:319,
5:345, **6**:447, **10**:730
Grinnell, George Bird **1**:58
Grissom, Virgil "Gus" **4**:306, **9**:645
Gromov, Mikhail **8**:615
Guadeloupe Island **6**:443
Guam **3**:213, **6**:426
Gua, Pierre du (Sieur de Monts)
2:156
Guarani Indians **2**:125
Guatemala **2**:137
Guayaquil **1**:73, **1**:74
Guayas River **5**:*355*
Gudrid (Gudridur
Thorbjarnarsdottir) **4**:316–318,
10:787, **10**:788
Guinea **5**:330, **6**:455, **6**:478, **8**:574,
8:602
Gulf of Bengal, sea chart (1518)
8:*574*
Gulf of Cadiz **10**:770
Gulf of California **5**:375, **7**:524, **7**:526
Gulf of Cambay **10**:741
Gulf of Carpentaria **2**:111, **4**:269,
10:734
Gulf of Mexico **2**:122, **3**:189, **3**:*205*,
3:213, **5**:371, **5**:372, **5**:386, **6**:437,
8:571, **10**:739, **10**:743, **10**:771
Gulf of Panama **7**:521
Gulf of Paria **3**:188
Gulf of Saint Lawrence **2**:151,
2:154, **10**:771

Gulf of San Miguel **7**:522
Gulf of the Ganges **10**:770
Gulf of Urabá **7**:520
Gulf Stream **8**:569, **8**:*571*, **8**:572,
    10:739, **10**:*742*, **10**:743
Gulliver, Lemuel **7**:529
Gungunhana **1**:23
Gunnbjörn's Skerries **4**:249
Gunnbjörn Ulf-Krakason **4**:249
gunpowder **1**:30, **1**:71
Gunter, Edmund **10**:729, **10**:730
Gunter's chain **10**:729, **10**:730
Gunung Mulu National Park,
    Sarawak **10**:*755*
gyrocompass **7**:502
gyroscope **7**:502

Haakon VII, king of Norway **2**:101
Hadley, John **1**:46, **7**:495, **7**:501
Haggard, H. Rider, *King Solomon's
    Mines* **6**:477
Hague, The **10**:744
Haida **9**:674
Haiti **1**:55, **1**:56, **3**:186, **4**:262, **6**:440
hajj (pilgrimage) **2**:143, **2**:159,
    5:358, **5**:361, **5**:363
Hakluyt, Richard **5**:324–327
Hakluyt Society **5**:324
Halicarnassus **1**:22
Hall, Charles **9**:674
Hall, James **1**:66
Halley, Edmond **1**:53, **4**:252, **9**:688
Halley's comet **1**:53
Hallveig Einarsdottir **4**:316
Hancock, Thomas **3**:172
handheld maneuvering unit
    (HHMU) **1**:38
Han dynasty **10**:796
Hanno of Carthage **5**:328–330,
    8:602
Hanoi **4**:296, **4**:297
Hanssen, Helmer **1**:21
Harappan civilization **10**:741
Harbaugh, Gregory **1**:*47*
hardtack **8**:582–583
Harer **2**:114–115
Harley, Robert **6**:456
Harold, king of England **1**:53
Harriot, Thomas **8**:598, **8**:603
Harrison, John **1**:43, **3**:168–169,
    3:232, **5**:388, **5**:391, **5**:393, **7**:495
Harun al-Rashid, caliph **2**:140
Harvard College Observatory
    9:674
Harvey's Lake **3**:209
Harwich **4**:286
Hassel, Sverre **1**:21
Hasselborough, Frederick **9**:689

Hastings, Battle of (1066) **1**:*53*
Hatshepsut **6**:474, **6**:477
Hatteras Indians **8**:599
Havana **6**:462
Hawaii **1**:45, **2**:92, **3**:196, **3**:200,
    10:759, **10**:789
Hawaiian Islands **6**:470, **6**:471
Hawkins, John **3**:182, **3**:226, **4**:312
Hayes Barton, England **8**:599
Hayes River **10**:736
Hearne, Samuel **10**:735, **10**:*736*
Hebrides **1**:70, **1**:71, **6**:404, **8**:624
Hecataeus, *A Tour Around the
    World* **4**:298, **4**:299
heliocentric view of the universe
    1:49, **3**:233, **8**:591, **9**:676
heliograph **3**:192
heliopause **9**:702
Hellespont **1**:14, **1**:16
Helluland **4**:317, **6**:407
Helsinki **7**:507
hemisphere **1**:53, **1**:79, **6**:433, **6**:446
Hennepin, Father Louis, *New
    Discovery of a Vast Country in
    America* **5**:384, **5**:385, **5**:387
Henry VII, king of England **2**:126
Henry VIII, king of England **2**:130,
    7:511
Henry IV, king of France **2**:155,
    3:178, **4**:272
Henry the Navigator **3**:175, **4**:298,
    4:302, **5**:331–335, **8**:573, **8**:574,
    9:650, **9**:651, **9**:654
Henry, Andrew **1**:30, **9**:665
Henry, Joseph **3**:190, **3**:192, **9**:673,
    9:675, **10**:783
Henry Mountains **8**:579
Henslow, John **3**:216
Henson, Matthew **5**:370, **7**:538,
    7:539
Heracles (Hercules) **9**:718
herbals **7**:485
Herbert, Wally **4**:255
herbs **6**:453
heresy **6**:444, **6**:446, **6**:479
Herodotus **1**:22, **4**:298, **4**:299,
    4:300, **5**:330, **6**:428, **7**:494, **7**:497,
    9:718
Herschel, William **1**:50, **1**:52, **9**:680
Heuglin, Theodor von **10**:745
Hevelius, Johannes **1**:43, **7**:532
Heyerdahl, Thor **5**:336–338, **9**:658
hidalgo **6**:462, **6**:474, **6**:479, **7**:559
Hidatsa people **6**:411, **8**:616, **8**:617,
    8:618
Hierro, Canary Islands **3**:187
Higueruela, Battle of **9**:*703*
Hillary, Edmund **3**:192, **4**:253,

4:315, **5**:339–341, **7**:543
Himalayan Trust **5**:340, **5**:341
Himalayas **1**:60, **1**:62, **4**:247, **5**:339,
    5:382, **8**:588, **9**:707, **9**:709,
    10:731, **10**:793, **10**:794
Himilco **6**:474, **6**:477
Hindu Kush Mountains **1**:16,
    5:359, **8**:566, **9**:660, **10**:794
Hipparchus **1**:50, **5**:342–345, **8**:590
    star catalog **5**:342, **5**:343
Hippocrates, *Airs, Waters and
    Places* **10**:781
Hispaniola **3**:176, **3**:184, **3**:185,
    3:186, **3**:187, **3**:188, **3**:204, **4**:262,
    6:443, **7**:520, **7**:521, **7**:550, **8**:569,
    8:570, **8**:572, **9**:653
Hochelaga **2**:152
Hoffman, Jeffrey **1**:*40*
Holbein, Ambrosius **7**:531
Holland 734, **10**:734
Hollandsche Kerckhoff **5**:348
Hollick-Kenyon, Herbert **1**:62,
    3:236, **3**:238
Holy Island (Lindisfarne) **10**:740
Holy Land **7**:528, **9**:648
Holy Roman emperor **6**:463
Holy Roman Empire **1**:71
Holy War **8**:573
Homer, **7**:489, **7**:527, **7**:528
homing pigeons **3**:190, **3**:191,
    8:605
Hondius, Jodocus,
    Atlas Minor **7**:506
    map **3**:228
Honduras **3**:185, **3**:189, **3**:204,
    3:208
Hong Kong **6**:449
Hood Canal **10**:763
Hood, Robert **4**:275
Hoorn **7**:505
Hop **4**:318
Hormuz **8**:576
Horn of Africa **5**:338, **9**:707, **10**:745
Horsens **2**:87, **2**:88
horses **3**:182, **3**:183, **3**:*204*, **5**:*376*,
    5:377, **5**:378, **5**:379, **5**:380, **5**:381
    history of **5**:379
    Manchurian ponies **8**:629
    Przhevalsky's horse **8**:587
    wild **8**:587
Houston, Texas **9**:*693*, **9**:697
Houtman, Cornelis **5**:346–349,
    7:504, **9**:654
Houtman, Frederik **5**:346–347,
    5:349, **9**:654
Houtman's Abrolhos **5**:349
hovercraft **9**:658
Howard, Charles **9**:*706*

Howard, Luke **10**:785
Howse Pass, Rocky Mountains
    10:736, **10**:737
Hsiung Nu **10**:796, **10**:797
Hsüan-tsang **4**:300, **9**:660, **9**:661,
    9:663
Hubble, Edwin **1**:47, **1**:51, **9**:677
Hubble Space Telescope (HST)
    1:41, **1**:46, **1**:47, **1**:51, **8**:620,
    8:622
Hudson, Henry **1**:66–67, **4**:313,
    5:325, **5**:350–353, **7**:504, **7**:506,
    7:512, **7**:513, **7**:516, **7**:518, **7**:553,
    7:554
Hudson, John **5**:351
Hudson Bay **1**:66, **2**:155, **4**:273,
    4:275, **5**:350, **5**:352–353, **5**:372,
    5:395, **7**:516, **7**:518, **7**:553,
    10:735, **10**:736
Hudson River **5**:350, **5**:351
Hudson's Bay Company **7**:517,
    7:519, **9**:664, **9**:666, **10**:735–736,
    10:*738*, **10**:751
Hudson Strait **1**:67, **2**:130, **5**:352,
    7:518
humanitarian work **6**:448, **6**:461
Humboldt, Alexander von **3**:233,
    4:252–253, **4**:254, **4**:255, **4**:305,
    5:354–357, **6**:452, **6**:454,
    7:486–487, **10**:745
    Kosmos **4**:252, **4**:299, **4**:305, **5**:354,
    5:357
    Personal Narrative **7**:487
Humboldt current **5**:357
Hungerford, Henry **9**:672
Hunt, John **4**:315, **5**:339
hunter-gatherers **3**:180
Hurd, Thomas **4**:265
Hurley, Frank **7**:542, **7**:543, **8**:604,
    8:636
Huron Indians **2**:157, **3**:179, **9**:653
Hurricane Fran **10**:*781*
huskies **5**:381, **7**:507, **7**:508
Hutchins, Thomas **10**:730
Huxley, Aldous, *Brave New World*
    7:528, **7**:530
Huxley, Thomas Henry **4**:267, **7**:488
Hwang Ho *see* Yellow River
hybrid remotely operated vehicle
    (HROV) **10**:727
Hydaspes River, Battle of the **1**:16
hydrographic survey **6**:451
hydrography **4**:313, **4**:319, **5**:371,
    6:452, **10**:733, **10**:760, **10**:799
hydrothermal vents **10**:727
hygrometer **10**:782
hypothermia **3**:173, **3**:239, **5**:366,
    5:370

Hythloday, Raphael **7**:531

Iberia *see* Spain
Iberian Peninsula **3**:175, **9**:704,
　9:719 *see also* Portugal; Spain
Ibn Battutah **5**:358–361, **8**:602
Ibn Juzay **5**:361
Ibn Khalaf, Ahmad **7**:500
Ibn Khordadhbeh, *The Book of
　Roads and Provinces* **5**:363
icebergs **7**:*517*, **7**:556, **7**:559, **9**:688
icebreakers **7**:512, **7**:*514*, **8**:612,
　8:614, **8**:615, **9**:650, **9**:655, **9**:*658*
ice floe **8**:614
Iceland **1**:70, **1**:71, **2**:106, **3**:184,
　4:246, **4**:247, **4**:248–250,
　4:316–318, **6**:404, **7**:491, **8**:624,
　8:625, **9**:717, **10**:743, **10**:747,
　10:773, **10**:774, **10**:775, **10**:781,
　10:785
ice sheet **4**:250, **7**:557
I-chang gorges **2**:93
Idaho **6**:412, **8**:616, **9**:667, **10**:737
Idrisi, al-Sharif al- **4**:298, **4**:301,
　5:*362–365*, **6**:428
iguana **3**:217, **3**:218
Iguazú Falls **2**:125
Île de France **4**:270
Ilkhanid dynasty of Mongols
　9:662
Illinois **2**:109, **8**:577
Illinois River **5**:372, **5**:384, **5**:386,
　6:436, **6**:438
illness and disease **5**:366–370
Ilminster **9**:707, **9**:709
immersion suits **3**:173
Imperial Trans-Antarctic
　Expedition **8**:636–637
Incan Empire **1**:72–73, **1**:75, **1**:79,
　9:682–683, **9**:687, **9**:705, **9**:706,
　9:719
Inca Road **1**:73, **1**:79, **9**:682, **9**:719
Incas **1**:72–73, **1**:74, **1**:*75*, **3**:177,
　4:*256*, **5**:356, **5**:*378*, **5**:379, **6**:440,
　6:478, **7**:521, **10**:752
Incense Trail **2**:139
India **1**:16, **2**:91, **2**:113, **2**:133, **2**:135,
　2:143, **3**:166, **3**:167, **3**:182, **3**:184,
　3:223, **3**:224, **4**:246, **4**:247, **4**:257,
　4:258, **4**:291, **4**:300, **5**:341, **5**:359,
　5:377, **6**:422, **6**:430, **6**:443, **6**:474,
　7:543, **8**:*574*, **8**:575, **8**:576, **9**:651,
　9:654, **9**:659, **9**:660, **9**:689, **9**:712,
　10:741, **10**:*748*, **10**:751, **10**:789,
　10:793, **10**:794
　ancient **5**:338
　British army in **9**:707, **9**:709
　British in **4**:313

Cabral's voyage to (1500–1501)
　2:*134*
and China **4**:259
Great Trigonometrical Survey of
　10:731, **10**:794
as the Holy Land **4**:259
Portuguese exploration of route
　to **8**:573, **8**:575–576
sea passage to **4**:247, **4**:298,
　10:749
southern **8**:567
Vasco da Gama's voyage to
　4:291–293, **4**:302, **8**:574, **8**:575
Indian agent **2**:144, **2**:147, **2**:159,
　6:411
Indian army **2**:113, **2**:115
Indian explorers **7**:491
Indian maps, ancient **6**:431
Indian Ocean **1**:17, **1**:67, **1**:68,
　2:133, **3**:164, **3**:175, **3**:218, **3**:232,
　4:292, **4**:302, **5**:336, **5**:338, **6**:416,
　6:422, **6**:428, **7**:489, **7**:*491*, **7**:504,
　7:505, **8**:575, **8**:593, **9**:688,
　10:732, **10**:733, **10**:743, **10**:761
Indians, beliefs about tides
　10:740
India rubber **3**:172
Indies **3**:184, **3**:185 *see also* East
　Indies; West Indies
indigenous people **1**:23, **1**:24,
　3:178
　rights of **6**:470, **6**:472
Indonesia **2**:98, **3**:184, **4**:259, **5**:347,
　5:349, **6**:475, **6**:477, **7**:503, **7**:533,
　8:573, **9**:653, **10**:732, **10**:750,
　10:779, **10**:780
Indonesians **1**:*22*
Indus River **1**:16–17, **4**:258
Industrial Revolution **6**:413
Indus valley **5**:358, **10**:741, **10**:747,
　10:797, **10**:798
influenza **3**:181, **5**:370
infrared rays **1**:47, **1**:48, **1**:65
Innocent IV, Pope **9**:662
Innsbruck **10**:783
Inquisition **1**:44
Institute of British Geographers
　4:254
Inter Caetera (papal bull)
　3:175–176
internal combustion engine
　5:376, **5**:378
International Boundary
　Commission **10**:736, **10**:738
international date line **5**:389
International Exchange Service
　9:673
International Geographical Union

4:253
International Geophysical Year
　(IGY) **2**:121
International Space Station (ISS)
　1:39, **6**:466, **6**:468, **6**:*469*, **8**:620,
　9:692, **9**:694
Internet **8**:604
　and SETI **8**:634
interrupted homosoline
　projection **6**:*435*
Inuit **1**:66, **3**:171, **4**:250, **4**:*275*,
　4:276–277, **4**:278, **4**:285, **4**:*286*,
　4:287, **4**:313, **5**:353, **5**:377, **5**:381,
　6:459, **6**:470, **6**:473, **7**:*510*, **7**:538,
　7:*557*, **7**:558, **7**:559
　drawings of **8**:603
　Frobisher and the **4**:285, **4**:287
　story of Franklin's expedition
　　4:276–277, **4**:278
　transport **8**:629
inventions **1**:71
　communications **3**:190–195
　the wheel **5**:376, **5**:377
Iran **1**:17, **1**:68, **1**:76, **9**:712
Iraq **1**:16, **1**:76, **1**:78, **5**:338, **6**:427,
　7:500, **7**:527, **10**:*728*, **10**:747,
　10:752, **10**:775, **10**:790, **10**:797
　National Museum **1**:78
Ireland **2**:104, **7**:491, **8**:599, **8**:624,
　8:636, **10**:775
Irkutsk **8**:585, **8**:586, **8**:588
iron firebox **8**:582
iron pyrite (fool's gold) **2**:154,
　2:159, **4**:285, **7**:515
Iroquois **2**:151, **2**:152, **3**:178, **4**:272,
　5:386, **6**:473
irrigation **10**:728
Irvine, Andrew **4**:315, **5**:341,
　10:795
Isabella, queen of Spain **3**:175,
　3:184, **3**:185, **3**:186, **3**:187, **3**:188,
　4:260–263, **4**:303, **9**:703, **9**:704
Isla Fernandina **3**:*218*
Islam **2**:114, **3**:175, **5**:358–361,
　5:362–365, **9**:660–661
　Christianity and **8**:573
Island Arawak **3**:186
Isleta Pueblo, New Mexico **3**:*176*
Israel **6**:476
Issus, Battle of **1**:15
Issyk-Kul **8**:586, **8**:588
al-Istakhri, map **6**:*429*
Istanbul (Constantinople) **2**:141,
　4:300, **10**:747, **10**:775
isthmus **7**:522, **7**:559, **10**:799
Isthmus of Panama **7**:*521*, **7**:522
Ita (abbess) **2**:105
Italia (airship) **1**:18, **1**:21, **3**:238

Italians
　explorers **4**:271, **10**:765–772
　mapmakers **7**:492
　missionaries **8**:608–611
　traders **10**:748–749
italic lettering **6**:447
Italy **2**:115, **2**:117, **2**:126–132, **3**:177,
　3:184, **3**:238, **4**:301, **5**:363, **5**:373,
　5:388, **6**:447, **6**:448, **6**:454–455,
　8:564, **8**:565, **8**:566, **8**:624,
　10:765, **10**:783
Ivan IV, Czar (Ivan the Terrible)
　2:132, **7**:512
Ivanov, Kurbat **8**:613
ivory **2**:143, **3**:222, **6**:477, **9**:662,
　10:747, **10**:749
Ivory Coast **6**:478
Iznik **5**:342

Jackson, Frederick **6**:458, **6**:461
Jackson, William H. **7**:543
jade **9**:662, **10**:748
Jaeder **4**:248
Jakarta (Batavia) **3**:214, **7**:504,
　10:732, **10**:733
Jamaica **2**:150, **3**:169, **3**:176, **3**:184,
　3:189, **3**:213, **6**:462
James I (James VI), king of
　England **3**:177, **8**:600, **9**:669,
　9:670
James IV, king of Scotland **4**:312
James, duke of York **7**:506
James, Thomas **4**:287, **7**:516, **7**:518
Jamestown **3**:177, **3**:182, **4**:313,
　9:668, **9**:670–671
James Webb Space Telescope
　1:48
Jane, John **5**:327
Jan Mayen Island **2**:103
Jansky, Karl **1**:46, **1**:51
Jansz, Willem **3**:198, **7**:504
Japan **2**:93, **3**:175, **3**:184, **3**:185,
　4:300, **4**:303, **8**:576, **8**:626,
　10:732, **10**:743, **10**:785, **10**:789
Jaramillo, Maria Josefa **2**:144,
　2:145, **2**:146, **2**:147
Jason and the Argonauts **7**:527,
　7:528, **9**:658
Java **2**:98, **4**:259, **5**:346, **5**:348, **7**:505
Jefferson, Thomas **6**:408, **6**:409,
　6:411, **6**:412
Jeffries, John **1**:62
Jemmy Button Sound **4**:*265*
Jenkins, Robert **6**:439
Jerez **7**:520
Jersey **2**:148
Jerusalem **2**:139, **4**:300, **6**:430,
　8:565

Jesuits **3**:179, **5**:371, **5**:373–375, **5**:383–387, **5**:399, **6**:436–438, **6**:450–451, **6**:452, **8**:608–609
jet aircraft **1**:59
jewels **6**:477–478, **9**:662
Johansen, Hjalmar **6**:458, **6**:460, **6**:*461*, **8**:627
John II, king of Castile **9**:703
John I, king of Portugal **5**:331, **8**:573, **8**:574
John II, king of Portugal **3**:184, **3**:185, **3**:222, **3**:223, **4**:261, **8**:575
Johnson, Donald **5**:351
Johnson Space Center, Houston, Texas **9**:*693*, **9**:697
Jolliet, Louis **4**:272, **4**:273, **5**:371–372, **6**:436–438
Juan Fernández Islands **3**:214
Juet, Robert **5**:353
Julianehåb **4**:250
Jungfrau **10**:791
junks **3**:*164*, **9**:647
Jupiter **5**:391, **6**:466, **8**:590, **8**:*619*, **9**:676, **9**:679, **9**:680, **9**:691, **9**:696, **9**:697, **9**:700–701
Great Red Spot **9**:680
moons **9**:*676*, **9**:679, **9**:680, **9**:700
Justinian, Emperor **9**:*659*

Kaaba **5**:359
Kagge, Erling **7**:555, **7**:558
Kalahari Desert **6**:414–415
Kamchatka **2**:87, **2**:88, **2**:89, **2**:*90*, **7**:514, **8**:614
Avachinsky inlet **2**:*90*
kangaroos **1**:70, **3**:198, **4**:*270*, **7**:486
Kansas **3**:202, **3**:203, **7**:525, **7**:526, **7**:546
Kapilavastu **4**:259
Karakol **8**:586, **8**:588
Karakoram Mountains **4**:258, **10**:793, **10**:794
Kara Sea **7**:513
Karlsefni, Thorfinn **4**:316, **4**:317, **4**:318, **6**:405, **6**:407, **10**:787
karst **10**:754, **10**:755
Kashgar **9**:661
Kashmir **10**:793, **10**:794, **10**:795
Kasia **4**:259
kayak **4**:285, **4**:287, **6**:460
Kazakhstan, Baikonur cosmodrome **1**:*37*
Keck I and II telescopes **1**:45, **1**:46
keelboat **6**:410, **6**:479
Kelsey, Henry **10**:751
Kelvin, Baron *see* Thomson,

William
Kelvingrove Museum, Glasgow **1**:23, **1**:26
Kendall, Larcum **3**:169
Kennedy, John F. **1**:28, **6**:466, **6**:467, **8**:621
Kennedy Space Center, Cape Canaveral **1**:27, **1**:28, **9**:692
Kennicott, Robert **9**:675
Kensington, West London **4**:*254*
Kensington Stone **8**:625
Kentucky **1**:56, **2**:95, **2**:96, **2**:144, **5**:384, **6**:448, **7**:547
Kenya **4**:294
Kepler, Johannes **1**:49, **1**:50, **3**:233, **7**:485, **9**:676
Kerguelen's Land **9**:*688*
Kerguélen-Trémarec, Yves-Joseph de **9**:*688*
Kevlar **3**:174
Kew, Royal Botanic Gardens **1**:70, **1**:71, **4**:314
Kezeh (Tabora) **2**:116, **9**:708
Khan-balik *see* Beijing
Khartoum **10**:744, **10**:745, **10**:746
Khotan **4**:258
Kikongo **5**:330
Kilkea, County Kildare, Ireland **8**:636
Killeedy, near Tralee **2**:105
King, Clarence **8**:580
King, John **2**:111, **6**:470, **6**:473
King, Philip Parker **4**:264
Kingsley, Mary Henrietta **4**:315, **10**:788, **10**:790
King's Lynn, Norfolk **10**:742, **10**:762
King William Island **4**:276, **4**:277
Kino, Eusebio Francisco **5**:373–375
Kiowa **2**:147
Kiro Shio current **10**:*742*
Klushino **4**:288
knarr **6**:407, **9**:648
knots (nautical miles per hour) **3**:221, **7**:492
Knutson, Paul **8**:624, **8**:625
Kodlurnan Island **4**:287
Kola Peninsula **7**:512
Kolobeng **6**:414
Kon-Tiki expedition **5**:336, **5**:337, **9**:658
Korea **2**:93, **10**:788
Kosina, Alaska **7**:538
Kotzebue, Otto von **8**:612
Krasnoyarsk **8**:612
Kremer, Gerhard *see* Mercator, Gerardus
Kremlin **4**:290
Krenitsyn, Petr **8**:613

Krenkel, Ernest **8**:614
Kristiania (Oslo) **6**:458, **6**:461
Kritøya Island **1**:61
Kronstadt, Saint Petersburg **2**:84, **2**:86
Kublai Khan **8**:564, **8**:566–568, **9**:660, **9**:662, **9**:663
Kunlun Mountains **4**:258
Kuruman **6**:414, **6**:452
Kusinagara **4**:259
Kwakiutl language **1**:24
Kyrgyzstan **2**:*140*, **8**:588

La Austrialia del Espíritu Santo *see* Vanuatu
Labrador **1**:56, **1**:57, **1**:69, **1**:71, **2**:151, **3**:236, **3**:238, **4**:318, **5**:372, **6**:407
Lachine Rapids, Saint Lawrence River **4**:271
Lac Saint-Jean **6**:450, **6**:451
Lagos **5**:335
Lagrée, Ernest Doudart de **4**:295, **4**:296
La Isabella **3**:188, **3**:189, **4**:262
Lake Athabasca **6**:418
Lake Baikal **8**:613
Lake Bangweulu **6**:414, **6**:417
Lake Chad **9**:658, **10**:746
Lake Champlain **2**:*158*
Lake Erie **5**:384, **5**:*385*, **9**:664, **9**:665
Lake Huron **4**:272, **6**:436
Lake Koko Nor (Tsing Hai) **8**:586
Lake Leopold II **9**:713
Lake Malawi **6**:417
Lake Manitoba **5**:395, **5**:398
Lake Michigan **2**:158, **5**:371, **6**:436, **6**:437, **6**:438
Lake Mistassini **5**:372
Lake Mweru **6**:414, **6**:417
Lake Ngami **6**:414
Lake Nyasa **6**:417
Lake of the Woods **5**:*394*, **5**:396, **5**:398
Lake Ontario **5**:384
Lake Piekouagami **6**:450
Lake Shirwa **6**:*414*
Lake Siecha **7**:526
Lake Superior **5**:394, **5**:396, **5**:*398*, **6**:436, **6**:*450*, **6**:451, **10**:737
Lake Tanganyika **2**:113, **2**:116–117, **4**:314, **6**:414, **6**:417, **9**:708, **9**:*709*, **9**:712, **9**:713, **9**:714
Lake Tumba **9**:713
Lake Ukerewe **2**:116
Lake Victoria **2**:117, **9**:707, **9**:708–710, **9**:713, **9**:714, **10**:746
Lake Winnipeg **5**:394, **5**:395, **5**:398

Lakota **1**:26
ghost shirt **1**:23, **1**:26
La Malinche **3**:204, **3**:206
Lambert conformal conic projection **6**:435
Lambeth, London **6**:455
La Navidad (fort) **3**:187
Lancaster Sound **1**:*66*, **1**:68, **4**:276, **7**:516, **7**:517, **7**:518
land **6**:474
establishing boundaries **10**:728, **10**:730
managing public in American West **8**:580
nationalization of **10**:780
native people's rights to **6**:472
surveying **10**:728–730
land claims,
in Australia **3**:180
and record keeping **8**:601
landmarks **7**:491
Landsat (Earth Resources Technology Satellites) **6**:432, **6**:468, **6**:469, **8**:606, **8**:607, **8**:622
land transport **2**:139–143, **5**:376–382
land vehicles, remote controlled on Mars **1**:65
Lane, Ralph **8**:598, **8**:599
L'Anse aux Meadows, Newfoundland **4**:317, **6**:407, **10**:776
Laos **4**:*295*, **8**:567
Laplace, Simon de **10**:742
Lapland **2**:132, **4**:254, **7**:487, **7**:512, **7**:553
La Pointe du Saint-Esprit **6**:436
Laputa **7**:530
Lartet, Edouard-Armand-Isidore-Hippolyte **10**:753, **10**:754
Larvik, Norway **5**:336
La Salle, René-Robert Cavelier de **5**:383–387, **6**:438
Lascaux cave painting **5**:*379*, **10**:754
La Trinidad **3**:188
lateen **4**:293, **9**:648, **9**:651, **9**:719
Latin **4**:298, **4**:302, **8**:591
latitude **1**:43, **3**:185, **3**:232, **4**:299, **4**:300, **4**:302, **4**:310, **5**:342, **5**:345, **5**:364, **5**:388–393, **5**:399, **6**:428, **6**:447, **7**:491, **7**:494, **7**:499, **8**:591, **8**:592
defined **5**:389
minutes and seconds **5**:389
latitude sailing **6**:406, **7**:492
La Vérendrye, François **5**:398
La Vérendrye, Jacques-René **5**:396

La Vérendrye, Jean-Baptiste 5:395, 5:397

La Vérendrye, Louis 5:398

La Vérendrye, Louis-Joseph 5:398

La Vérendrye, Pierre 5:395, 5:398

La Vérendrye, Pierre Gaultier de Varennes de 5:394–398, 8:625

Lawrence, Thomas 6:418

Lawson, John 8:599

Lazarev, Mikhail 2:84

lead and line 7:494, 7:497, 7:498

League of Nations 6:458, 6:461

Lebanon 1:15, 1:77, 6:476, 9:647, 10:747, 10:752, 10:789

Leeward Islands 3:187

Leif Eriksson 2:105, 3:231, 4:248, 4:301, 4:316, 4:317, 4:318, 6:404–407, 7:550, 8:624, 10:743, 10:775, 10:776

Le Maire, Jakob 7:504, 7:505, 10:734

Lemhi, Idaho 8:616

Lemoine, Auguste 2:152

Le Moyne, Jacques 6:470

Lenape Indians 7:506

Leonov, Alexei 1:38

Lescarbot, Marc 6:470

Lesser Antilles 10:767, 10:768

letter of safe conduct 8:568

letters of marque 3:213

Levant 6:476

Levashov, Mikhail 8:613

Leverrier, Urbain-Jean-Joseph 9:681

Lewis, Island of 6:418

Lewis, Meriwether 6:408–412, 8:616–618, 8:625, 9:654, 10:783, 10:787

Lewis and Clark expedition 2:96, 6:408–412, 8:616–618

Leyes Nuevas 3:205

Lhasa (Forbidden City) 4:314, 8:586, 8:588, 10:793, 10:794–795

libraries, Arabic 8:591

Libya 4:244, 10:746, 10:788

Lima 9:683, 9:704

Li Madou see Ricci, Matteo

Lincolnshire 1:69, 4:275, 9:668

Lind, James 8:584

Lindholm Hoje, Alborg, Denmark 10:776

Lindisfarne (Holy Island) 10:740

linen cloth 9:662

Linnaeus, Carolus (Carl von Linné) 1:71, 7:486, 7:487, 8:624, 8:626

Linnean Society of London 10:780

Linyanti 6:415, 6:416

Lippershey, Hans 1:44, 1:46

Lisbon 3:184, 5:346, 10:770
map 8:573

literature, utopias and dystopias in 7:530

Little America 1:62, 2:120, 2:121

Little Falls 7:545

Little Idrisi atlas 5:363, 5:365

Little Loretto, Kentucky 6:448

Liu Ch'e see Wu Ti

Livingstone, David 2:143, 4:253, 4:255, 4:299, 4:314, 5:366, 5:369, 6:413–417, 6:452, 6:472, 7:501, 9:652, 9:710, 9:711–712

Lofoten Islands 1:22, 1:23

logbooks 8:601, 10:767, 10:799

logline 3:220

London 1:33, 1:34, 3:214, 4:252, 4:254, 4:264, 4:267, 4:276, 4:278, 4:285, 4:299, 5:324, 5:350, 5:351, 5:391, 6:461, 10:735, 10:736, 10:762
first public aquarium 7:486, 7:488

Inuit in 4:285, 4:287

Natural History Museum 1:69, 4:314

Saint Paul's Cathedral 5:390

Saint Sepulchre's Church 9:669, 9:670

Tower of London 8:599, 8:600

London Bridge 10:742

London Company of Virginia 3:177

London Horticultural Society 1:71

London Missionary Society 4:314, 6:413, 6:415, 6:416

London Zoo 6:454, 6:455

Long Beach, California 5:324

longhouse 4:318

Long Island Sound 10:767

longitude 3:168, 3:197, 3:221, 3:232, 4:266, 4:299, 4:300, 4:302, 4:310, 5:342, 5:345, 5:364, 5:388–393, 5:399, 6:428, 6:447, 6:451, 7:496, 8:591
defined 5:389

lunar distance method 1:67
problem 1:43, 3:168–169, 7:494, 7:495

long ship 6:407, 8:624, 9:648

Lopes, Tomé 4:294

Lop Nor 8:586, 9:661

loran 7:495, 7:496

Lothal, tidal dock 10:741

Louisiana 4:273, 5:383, 5:386, 6:443, 7:548

Louisiana Purchase 6:408, 6:409

Louisiana Territory 1:34, 1:79, 7:545, 7:547, 7:559, 8:616, 8:639, 10:787, 10:788

Louis IX, king of France 9:663

Louis XIV, king of France 4:272, 5:383, 5:386, 6:442, 6:443

Louis XV, king of France 2:99, 2:100

Louisville 1:56, 5:384

Lounge, John 1:40

Louvain (Leuven) 6:444, 6:445

Louvre Museum, Paris 6:454, 6:456

Loyola, Ignatius 8:609

Lualaba River 6:414, 6:417, 9:713, 9:714

Luanda 6:415

Lucian of Samosata, True History 7:528, 7:532

Lucretia, Caroline 1:52

Lunae Montes 9:715

lunar distance method 1:67, 7:496

lunar eclipse 4:299, 6:451

lunar month 742, 5:344, 10:742

Lunar Rover 5:377, 5:382, 6:469

lunar roving vehicle (LRV) 9:696

luxury goods 2:143, 3:165, 6:474, 10:732, 10:748

Lysanias of Cyrene 4:244

Lysippos 1:14

Maas River 7:503

Mabotsa 6:414

Macao 3:175, 6:452, 8:576, 8:608, 8:609, 8:610, 10:751

McArthur, Ellen 10:789, 10:792

McCandless, Bruce 1:38

McClintock, Francis 4:277

McClure, Robert 7:518, 7:519

mace 6:475, 10:748, 10:750

Macedon 6:474

Macedonia 1:14, 1:16

Macedonian Empire 1:14

Macedonian Greeks 8:589

Macerata 8:608, 8:610

MacGillivray, William 1:58

Macguire, Thomas 4:276

Machu Picchu 4:256

Macie, James see Smithson, James Lewis

Macintosh, Charles 3:172

Mackenzie, Alexander 4:313, 6:408, 6:418–421, 9:654, 10:751

Mackenzie River 4:275, 6:420, 6:421, 9:654

mackintosh raincoat 3:172

McMurdo Station, Ross Ice Shelf 9:658

McNeish, Harry "Chips" 8:636

Macquarie Island 2:84, 2:86, 9:689

Mactan 6:424, 6:426

Madagascar 5:346, 5:347

Madeira 1:69, 2:105, 3:175, 5:332, 5:333, 5:335, 10:766

Madras 9:689

Madrid 6:456, 9:701

Maetsuyker, Joan 7:504

Magdalena Sonora 5:375

Magellan, Ferdinand 2:130–131, 3:231, 4:299, 4:302, 5:366, 6:422–426, 8:574, 9:650, 9:651, 9:653, 9:654, 9:687, 9:688, 9:704–705, 10:749, 10:751

Magellan Venus space probe 9:700

magnetic compass 3:220, 3:232, 4:302, 4:309, 6:428, 10:729

magnetic field 2:103

magnetic storms 5:354, 5:357, 5:399

magnetism
of the earth 4:253
and radio communication 2:103

magnetite 7:498, 7:559

magnetosphere 8:620, 8:639

Mahican Indians 7:506

Ma Huan 3:165

Maine 2:155, 2:156, 8:578, 10:768

Makarov, S. O. 8:612, 8:614

Makran 1:17

Malabar coast 8:574, 8:576

Malacca 3:166, 4:303, 8:574, 8:576, 10:751

malaria 1:17, 2:116, 5:356, 5:366, 5:368, 5:369, 5:399, 6:415, 7:559, 8:595, 10:771, 10:772, 10:779

Malay Archipelago 7:486, 10:779

Malay language 5:349

Malaysia 3:166, 3:175, 4:303, 8:574, 8:576, 10:755

Maldive Islands 5:336, 5:358, 5:359

Mali 2:143, 5:358, 5:359, 6:471, 6:472, 7:534, 8:602

Mali Empire 4:274

Malindi 4:292, 4:293, 4:294

Mallory, George 4:315, 5:341, 10:795

Malthus, Thomas Robert 7:488, 10:779

Mamluks 2:141, 2:142

Manchester House, North Saskatchewan River 10:735, 10:736

Manchuria 10:793, 10:794

Manchurian ponies 5:381, 8:629

Mandan people 5:397, 6:408, 6:410, 6:411, 8:625, 8:639

Mandeville, Sir John **5**:333, **7**:527, **7**:528

Mandingo **7**:534

Mandlakazi **1**:23

Manhattan **7**:519

Manhattan Island **7**:506

Manila **8**:595

manioc **3**:182, **3**:183

Manitoba **5**:394, **5**:*395*, **10**:738

manned maneuvering unit (MMU) **1**:*38*

Mannheim **1**:71

Mansa Musa **2**:143, **6**:*471*

Manso Indians **7**:524

mantle **3**:231, **3**:239

Manuel I, king of Portugal **2**:133, **2**:135, **4**:291, **6**:422

Manus people **1**:*25*

Maoris **3**:198, **4**:267, **10**:733

mapmaking **2**:102, **2**:130–131, **4**:299, **6**:427–432

Babylonian **3**:231

Dutch **7**:506

Italian **7**:492

medieval **5**:362, **5**:364–365

and surveying **10**:729

Mappa mundi, Hereford Cathedral **6**:428, **6**:430–431

mapping the seabed **10**:760

map projection **4**:247, **4**:299, **4**:319, **5**:345, **6**:427, **6**:428, **6**:429, **6**:433–435

conic projections **6**:*433*, **6**:435

cylindrical projections **6**:*433*, **6**:434–435

Eratosthenes' **4**:247

gnomonic projection **6**:434

Hipparchus's **5**:345

Mercator projection **4**:303, **6**:428, **6**:429, **6**:434–435, **6**:444, **6**:446–447, **7**:504, **7**:506

Peters projection **6**:434

plane projection **6**:433–434

pseudocylindrical **6**:435

Ptolemy's **8**:592

map referencing **5**:388–393

latitude and longitude **5**:388–393

maps **4**:298–299, **4**:303, **4**:303–304

al-Idrisi's map (1154) **5**:364, **5**:*365*

in the ancient world **6**:427–428, **6**:447

Bellingshausen's of Antarctica **2**:*86*

Bry's of the Caribbean Sea **8**:*570*

Byrd's of Antarctica **2**:120–121

Dias's **7**:*500*

dual function **6**:427

electronic **4**:311

Eratosthenes' map **5**:345, **5**:390

first world map printed in England **7**:*515*

Hakluyt's map **5**:*325*

humor in **6**:431

Kino's of California **5**:375

Marco Polo's of Asia **8**:568

Martellus's map **5**:*332*

medieval **5**:362, **6**:428, **7**:528–529

Mercator's map (1595) of *Terra Australis* **8**:595

Muslim **6**:431

names and claims **6**:432

Padrón Real **2**:131

pioneers **5**:390

Ptolemy's map **5**:363, **5**:*388*, **5**:390, **7**:494, **8**:591–593

as records **8**:601

Sebastian Cabot's world map (1544) **2**:*130*

standardized **5**:390

T and O renderings **6**:428

see also world maps

Marconi, Guglielmo **3**:190, **3**:193

Mare Humboldtianum **5**:355

Mariame Indians **2**:124

Marianas Trench **10**:725, **10**:726

marine archaeology **9**:656

marine biology **7**:488

marine conservation **3**:211

Mariner space probes **9**:678, **9**:691, **9**:696, **9**:698, **9**:700

marine science **9**:674, **10**:757–758

Marinus of Tyre **8**:591

maritime cultures **9**:647

Markham, Clement **4**:255

Markland **4**:318, **6**:407

Marquesas Islands **5**:336

Marquette, Jacques **4**:272, **4**:273, **5**:371, **6**:436–438

Mars **5**:377, **5**:382, **6**:466, **6**:469, **6**:475, **6**:*478*, **7**:498, **8**:590, **9**:674, **9**:676, **9**:678–679, **9**:691, **9**:696, **9**:698–699

Cydonia region **1**:*65*

from the air **1**:63, **1**:65

geology of **9**:674

moons of **9**:699

Marseilles **4**:247, **5**:355, **9**:717

Mars Global Surveyor (*MGS*) **1**:65, **6**:466, **9**:678, **9**:697, **9**:699

Marsili, Luigi Ferdinando **10**:756, **10**:760

Mars orbital laser altimeter (MOLA) **9**:699

Martel, Édouard-Alfred **10**:754, **10**:755

Martellus, Henricus, world map **5**:*332*

Martinique **6**:443

Marton, England **3**:196

Maryland **7**:547, **10**:760

Mary Rose **10**:*756*

Ma San-pao (Ma Ho) *see* Cheng Ho

Mas-a-Tierra **3**:214

Maslennikovo **10**:791

Massachusetts **1**:71, **3**:*178*, **3**:182, **10**:726, **10**:758

Massachusetts Bay **3**:178

Massalia **4**:246, **4**:247, **9**:717

Matagorda Bay **5**:386

mathematics **4**:265

Greek **4**:244–247, **4**:299, **5**:342–345

instrument making **6**:447

and map projection **6**:433–435, **6**:445

reasoning **7**:485

Matta, Jeronymo de **6**:452

Mauna Kea, Hawaii **1**:45

Mauritania **2**:*139*

Mauritius **2**:98, **3**:218, **4**:270, **7**:504, **10**:733

Mauro, Fra, 1400 world map **5**:333

Maury, Matthew Fontaine **10**:757

Mauvila, Battle of **9**:683, **9**:685

Mayan civilization **3**:206, **3**:239

Mayan language **3**:206

Mayday distress signal **3**:192

Mazocha Chasm **10**:753

Mead, Margaret **1**:23, **1**:25, **1**:26

measles **3**:181, **5**:370, **9**:706

Mecca **2**:114, **2**:126, **2**:139, **2**:140, **2**:143, **3**:166, **4**:294, **4**:314, **5**:358, **5**:359, **5**:361, **5**:363, **5**:365, **6**:431, **8**:602

Great Mosque **5**:359

Medal of Freedom **3**:211

Medici, Ferdinand II de' **10**:782

Medici, Lorenzo de **6**:453, **6**:*454*

Medici family **10**:769

Medina **2**:114, **5**:365

Mediterranean Sea **1**:17, **2**:126, **2**:142, **3**:176, **3**:210, **3**:211, **4**:299, **4**:300, **5**:363, **5**:377, **6**:428, **7**:492, **7**:498, **7**:527, **8**:571, **8**:624, **9**:647, **9**:648, **9**:649, **9**:659, **9**:709, **9**:716, **10**:747, **10**:750, **10**:753, **10**:756, **10**:757, **10**:761, **10**:765, **10**:775

tides **10**:739

Megasthenes **4**:246

Mekong River **4**:274, **4**:295, **4**:296, **10**:794

Melanesia **1**:26

Melbourne **2**:110

Méliès, Georges, *Le voyage dans la lune* **7**:528, **7**:532

Melqart **5**:330

meltwater **6**:411, **6**:479

Melville Bay **4**:276

Melville Island **7**:517

memory

Quintilian's method **8**:608

skills **8**:608, **8**:610

Mendaña de Neira, Alvaro **8**:594–595, **8**:596

Mendoza, Antonio de **2**:137, **3**:201, **3**:202–203

Mendoza, Luis de **6**:424

Menzies, Archibald **10**:764

mercantilism **6**:439–443, **7**:503, **10**:750

English **6**:441

and the nation-state **6**:441–442

in the Spanish Empire **6**:439–440

Mercator, Gerardus **6**:429, **6**:434–435, **6**:444–447

Atlas **6**:444, **6**:*445*, **6**:446, **6**:447

map (1595) of *Terra Australis* **8**:*595*

Mercator projection **4**:299, **4**:303, **6**:428, **6**:429, **6**:434–435, **6**:444, **6**:446–447, **7**:504, **7**:506

merchant companies **7**:515, **9**:659, **10**:747

merchant marine **8**:635, **8**:636, **8**:639

Mercury **4**:252, **7**:498, **8**:590, **9**:644–645, **9**:674, **9**:676, **9**:678, **9**:679, **9**:691, **9**:696, **9**:697

Mercury-Atlas 6 (MA-6) **4**:*306*

Mercury space program **3**:*174*, **6**:466–467, **9**:644–645, **9**:674, **9**:692, **9**:697

meridian **3**:168, **3**:197, **3**:239, **4**:266, **5**:389, **5**:390, **5**:399, **6**:434, **6**:435

Greenwich **5**:389, **5**:390–391, **5**:399

mermaids **2**:*104*, **5**:351

Mesopotamia **1**:16, **1**:76, **1**:*77*, **5**:338, **10**:747, **10**:752, **10**:797

Messenger (Mercury Surface, Space Environment, Geochemistry and Ranging) space probe **9**:678, **9**:697, **9**:700

Meta River **5**:356

meteorites **1**:53, **1**:54, **9**:678, **9**:681

meteoroids **1**:53, **9**:681

meteorology **3**:232–233, **3**:239, **4**:264, **4**:267, **8**:623, **8**:633, **8**:639, **10**:781–785

Meteosat **3**:229

Methodism **6:**452, **8:**577

Mexican War (1846–1848) **2:**146, **4:**282–283

Mexico **1:**54, **2:**123, **2:**125, **2:**136, **2:**137, **2:**145, **2:**155, **3:**176, **3:**181, **3:**182, **3:**201, **3:**204, **3:**205, **5:**355, **5:**373, **5:**374, **5:**375, **5:**386, **6:**455, **6:**462–465, **7:**523, **7:**547–548, **7:**551, **7:**552, **8:**597, **10:**752, **10:**791 see also New Spain

Mexico City **3:**203, **3:**208, **6:**463, **6:**464, **6:**465

Miami **3:**211

Michael, Czar **7:**512, **7:**513

Michiel, Giovanni **2:**132

Micmac Indians **2:**151, **4:**273, **6:**470

micrometeorite **8:**639

micrometeoroids **1:**38, **3:**174

Mid-Atlantic Ridge **7:**486, **7:**488, **10:**727

Middle Ages **1:**43, **3:**229, **10:**748
 geography in the **4:**300–301
 maps **6:**428

Middle East **1:**76, **1:**78, **2:**113, **2:**139, **2:**141, **4:**298, **4:**301, **4:**312, **6:**475, **8:**565, **9:**662, **10:**765, **10:**790, **10:**791

midshipman **4:**275, **4:**319

migration **3:**182, **10:**787
 and myth **7:**527

Milan **10:**783

military planning, aerial photography and **6:**432

militia **1:**30, **1:**79

Milky Way **1:**51, **1:**52, **1:**79

Miller, Alfred Jacob **10:**750

Mill Grove **1:**55, **1:**57

Milwaukee, Wisconsin **6:***436*

Mina **4:**284

Minden, Germany **1:**24

mineralogy **5:**354, **6:**452, **7:**507

mineral resources **6:**439, **6:**476–477

Ming dynasty **3:**164–167, **9:**660, **9:**663

mining **1:**30, **3:**231, **4:**284, **4:**286, **10:**728, **10:**752

Mini Remote-Operated Vehicle II (MR2) **10:***726*

Minnesota **5:**385, **7:**545, **8:**625, **10:**737

Minuit, Peter **7:**506

Miquelon **4:**273

Mir space station **1:**41, **8:**615, **9:**694

Mirza Abdullah see Burton, Richard Francis

missionaries **3:**178–179, **3:**182, **4:**301, **5:**373–375, **6:**405,

6:413–417, **6:**430, **6:**449–452, **6:**472, **9:**659, **10:**799
 British **4:**312, **4:**314
 as explorers **6:**448, **6:**449–452
 Italian **8:**608–611
 Jesuit **6:**436–438, **6:**450–451, **6:**452
 Norse **6:**404–405

missionary school **2:**159

mission hospitals **2:**91

missions **5:**375, **6:**436, **6:**448–452, **9:**706

Mississippi River **1:**56, **2:**123, **4:**272, **4:**273, **4:**279, **5:**371–372, **5:**383–387, **6:**408, **6:**436–438, **6:**465, **7:**545, **7:**547, **8:**577, **8:**578, **9:**683, **9:**684, **9:**685, **10:**736
 French map of **5:***372*

Mississippi River Valley **2:**158, **4:**273

Missouri **1:**30, **1:**32, **2:**94, **2:**95, **2:**96, **2:**107, **2:**109, **2:**145, **2:**146, **4:**279, **6:**411, **8:**616, **8:**618, **9:**665, **9:**667, **10:**787

Missouri River **1:**31, **1:**56, **1:**57, **4:**279, **4:**304, **5:**371, **5:**397, **6:**408, **6:**410–412, **6:**437, **9:**664, **10:**736
 Great Bend **8:**617
 Great Falls **6:**410, **6:**411

Mitchell, Edgar D. **9:***646*

Mitchell, Samuel **1:**58

Mobile, Alabama **9:**685

modules **4:**289, **4:**319

Moffat, Mary **6:**414, **6:**452

Moffat, Robert **6:**414, **6:**452

Mohenjo Daro **5:**377

Mojave Desert **9:**666, **9:**701
 Deep Space Communications Center **8:**632

Mojave people **9:**666

Mollard, Jean **3:**210

Moluccas see Spice Islands

Mombasa **4:**292

Mongol Empire **7:**528, **8:**564, **8:**565, **8:**566–568, **9:**660–661, **9:**662–663

Mongolia **8:**585–588, **8:**613, **10:**794

Mongol peace (*Pax Mongolica*) **9:**662

monopoly **2:**142, **2:**158, **2:**159, **5:**384, **5:**396, **5:**399, **6:**441, **7:**504, **8:**574, **10:**750

monsoon **4:**293, **5:**359, **5:**399, **7:**505, **9:**647, **9:**719

Montagnais **2:**156, **2:**158, **3:**178

Montaigne, Michel Eyquem de **6:**471

Montana **2:**109, **6:**410, **6:**411,

10:737

Monte Cristallo **10:**791

Monterey, California **9:**645

Monterey Bay **2:**137

Montezuma II **3:**206, **3:**207

Montgolfier, Jacques Étienne **1:**59, **1:***61*, **1:**62, **10:**784

Montgolfier, Joseph-Michel **1:**59, **1:***61*, **1:**62, **10:**784

Montreal **1:**35, **2:**152, **3:**194, **5:**372, **5:**383–384, **5:**385, **5:**394, **5:**395, **5:**397, **5:**398, **6:**418, **10:**736, **10:**738

moon **1:**28, **1:**46, **5:**355, **5:**393, **8:**619, **9:***676*
 distance from the earth **5:**344
 eclipses of the **4:**299, **6:**451
 exploration **6:**466, **6:**467, **6:**469
 first landing **1:**28–29, **3:**194, **7:**541, **7:***544*
 first spacecraft to reach the **9:**691
 first walk on the **1:**27–29, **1:**28, **1:**29, **1:**38, **1:**39
 gravitational pull of the **10:**739, **10:**742
 missions to the **9:**644, **9:**646, **9:**692, **9:**696
 radio-controlled lunar vehicles **5:**377
 in science fiction **7:**532
 space station on **9:**699
 and the tides **10:**740, **10:**742

moons **9:**676, **9:**679, **9:**701

Moors **3:**175, **4:**261, **4:**319, **8:**569, **8:**570, **8:**639, **9:**703

More, Thomas, *Utopia* **7:**528, **7:**530, **7:***531*

Mormons **2:**108–109, **2:**115, **6:**452

Morocco **2:**93, **3:**175, **5:**328, **5:**331, **5:**337, **5:**338, **5:**358, **5:**361, **5:**362, **5:**363, **6:**422, **10:**789

Morse, Samuel **3:**190, **3:**191, **3:**192

Morse Code **3:**190, **3:**191, **3:**192

Moscow **2:**90, **2:**132, **4:**288, **4:**290, **7:**512, **8:**615, **10:**791

Moskvitin, Ivan **8:**612, **8:**614

motion, Newton's laws of **1:**49, **1:**51, **3:**233, **9:**677

motor vehicles **5:**376, **5:**377, **5:**381
 extraterrestrial transport **5:**382

mountain men **9:**664, **9:**667, **9:**719

mountain transport **5:**382

Mount Baker **10:**763

Mount Cameroon **5:**330

Mount Cook **5:**339

Mounteney-Jephson, A. J. **9:***715*

Mount Erebus **7:**557

Mount Everest **1:**62–63, **3:**192, **4:**253, **4:**312, **4:**315, **5:**339, **5:***341*, **7:**541, **7:**543, **10:**794, **10:**795
 Hillary's expedition to **5:**339–340, **5:***341*
 surveying **10:**731

Mount Huascarán, Peru **10:**788, **10:**791

Mount Kakulima **5:**330, **8:**602

Mount McKinley **7:**539

Mount Meru **6:**431

Mount Saint Elias **2:**88, **2:**89

Mount Wutai **4:***257*

Moyano, Sebastián see Belalcázar, Sebastián de

Mozambique **1:**23, **4:**292, **4:**293

Mozambique Channel **3:**167

Muhammad ibn Tughluq, Sultan **5:**360

multispectral scanner **8:**606, **8:**639

mummification **1:**22

Munster, Sebastian, *Cosmographia Universalis* **10:***766*

Murree, Pakistan **10:**793

Muscovy Company of Merchants **1:**66, **5:**351

Muses **6:**453

museums **1:**23, **1:**24–26, **6:**453–457, **9:**672–675
 early collections **6:**453–454

Museum Tradescantium **6:**454, **6:**456

Muslims **2:**93, **3:**164, **3:**175, **3:**184, **4:**261, **4:**292, **4:**294, **4:**301, **5:**331, **5:**358–361, **5:**362–365, **6:**471, **7:**528, **9:**663, **9:***703*, **9:**704
 maps **6:**431
 Moors **3:**175, **4:**261, **4:**319, **8:**569, **8:**570, **8:**639, **9:***703*
 pilgrims **4:**294

mutiny **1:**66, **4:**313, **5:**350, **5:**353, **5:**386, **5:**399, **6:**424, **7:**516, **9:**656, **9:**670

Muybridge, Eadweard **7:**543

Muztagh Pass **10:**793, **10:**794

myths
 of ideal societies **7:**530
 and migration **7:**527

Nagel, J. A. **10:**753, **10:**754

Nagursky, Jan **1:**60, **1:**62

Nahuatl **3:**206, **3:**208

names for new botanical discoveries **7:**485, **7:**487

Namibia **3:**223, **3:**224, **8:**574

Nan-ch'ang **8:**610

Nanking **8:**610

Nansen, Fridtjof **1:**19, **6:**458–461,

7:510, 7:537, 7:554, 7:555, 8:624,
8:627
Nantes 1:55
Nantucket Sound 2:156, 10:768
naos 9:650, 9:653
Naples 6:463
Napoleon Bonaparte 2:100, 6:408,
6:409
Napo River 9:652
Narváez, Pánfilo de 2:122, 2:136,
3:207, 6:462–465, 6:477, 9:684
NASA (National Aeronautics and
Space Administration) 1:27,
1:28, 1:29, 4:308, 6:466–469,
6:478, 8:620, 9:645, 9:674, 9:677,
9:678, 9:692, 9:696, 9:699, 9:700
astronaut training 1:42
Deep Space Network 9:701
Earth Resources Technology
Satellite (ERTS) 6:469
John H. Glenn Research Center
4:306, 4:308
Project Mercury 3:174, 4:306
satellites 8:607, 8:620
Seasat satellite 8:607, 8:620,
10:760
SETI projects 8:632
space telescopes 8:622
Tektite project 10:761
worldwide weather observation
satellites 10:784–785
X-15 program 6:468
National Advisory Committee for
Aeronautics (NACA) 1:27
National Air and Space Museum
(U.S.) 9:675
National Audubon Society (U.S.)
1:55, 1:58
National Geographic Society
(U.S.) 4:253, 4:255, 4:256, 4:299,
4:305, 6:435
National Institute on Aging (U.S.)
4:308
National Museum of American
History 9:675
National Museum of Natural
History (U.S.) 9:675
nation-state, mercantilism and
the 6:441–442
Native Americans 2:96, 2:108,
2:137–138, 2:144, 2:147, 2:156,
2:157, 3:178, 5:350, 6:410,
6:411–412, 6:419, 6:420,
6:436–437, 6:451, 6:470, 6:472,
6:473, 7:546, 9:668–671, 10:767,
10:771
anthropology of 1:24, 1:26
artistic record of culture 8:603

canoes 9:653–654
conversion to Christianity 3:176,
3:187, 3:206, 5:375
and diseases brought by
explorers 3:181–182, 5:370
in Florida and Texas 2:123–125
fur trade 5:395
life and customs 10:738
mask 9:674
in North America 2:151, 2:152,
2:153, 2:155–156, 2:157
preservation of culture
8:577–580
Protestantism and 5:327
relations with 8:616–618
Spanish and 3:201, 3:202,
4:262–263, 9:684–685
transport 5:376, 5:379, 5:396
native peoples 6:470–473
conversion to Christianity
6:448–452
European first encounters with
6:470
explorers 6:473
Nattier, Marc 6:443
natural history 6:455, 7:485–486,
10:777–780
Natural History Museum, London
10:758
natural philosophy 7:485
natural resources 3:231, 6:474–478
food 6:474
land 6:474
minerals 6:476–478
spices 6:474–476
natural sciences 6:454, 7:484–488
natural selection 3:216, 3:219
nautical charts 6:428, 8:601
Navajo Indians 2:147
Naval Aviation Cadet Program
(U.S.) 4:306
navigation 3:168–169, 3:232,
7:489–496
celestial 1:43, 1:49, 1:67, 3:232,
5:343, 5:392, 7:484, 7:489–491,
7:496, 9:678, 9:695
dead reckoning 3:220–221
electronic 7:494–496
Global Positioning System
4:309–311
landmarks 7:491
mapmaking and 6:429, 6:447
and map referencing 5:388–393
Portuguese 7:498
radio-based 4:309
satellite-based 4:309–311
tides and currents 10:739–743
use of chronometer 4:266

Viking 7:491–492
winds in 7:489–491
Navigation Acts 6:440, 6:441, 6:442
navigational instruments
7:492–496, 7:497–502
chronometer 3:168–169, 4:266
Navstar 1 (GPS satellite) 4:309
Nearchus 1:17, 4:246
Nebraska 1:32, 1:56, 2:96
Neck, Jacob van 7:504
negative (photographic) 7:541,
7:559
dry-plate 7:541, 7:542, 7:543
Nelson, Horatio 8:601
Nelson, R. H. 9:715
Nelson River 8:625, 10:736
Neolithic period 9:647, 9:648
neoprene 3:173, 3:174
Nepal 5:339, 5:341, 10:731
Neptune 1:51, 5:391, 9:676, 9:679,
9:680–681, 9:697, 9:701
Netherlands 1:44, 5:346–349,
5:390, 6:447, 7:503–506,
7:512–513, 9:668, 9:706,
10:732–734, 10:744–746, 10:750
Golden Age 7:503–506
mapmaking 6:429, 7:506
neutron stars 1:52
New Amsterdam 7:504, 7:506
New Britain 2:149, 3:213, 3:214,
3:228
New Brunswick 2:156
New Caledonia 4:313
New Concord 4:306
New England 5:394, 6:432, 6:441,
7:526, 9:669, 9:670
Newfoundland 1:69, 1:71, 2:105,
2:106, 2:127, 2:128, 2:151, 2:154,
3:177, 3:184, 3:196, 3:213, 3:231,
4:271, 4:317, 4:318, 5:394, 6:407,
6:455, 6:474, 7:549, 9:652, 9:654,
10:739, 10:751, 10:765, 10:768,
10:776
cod fishing 2:128, 10:749
New France 2:156–157, 2:158,
4:271–273, 5:371, 5:383–384,
5:394, 6:436–438, 6:450–451
New Galicia 3:201, 3:203
New Guinea 1:25, 2:98, 3:214,
10:732, 10:733, 10:734
New Hampshire 9:644, 9:645
New Hebrides 2:98
New Holland 1:71, 3:198,
3:213–214, 4:268–270, 7:504,
9:687, 10:734 see also Australia
New Ireland 2:98
New Jersey 2:148, 7:545, 7:547
New Jerusalem 8:596, 8:597

New Mexico 1:46, 2:144, 2:145,
2:147, 3:176, 3:201, 3:202, 3:203,
7:523–526, 9:667
New Orleans 9:711, 9:712
Newport, Christopher 4:313
New Scotland 4:313
New Siberian Islands 6:460
New South France 9:688
New South Wales 3:198, 4:269
Parkes telescope 8:634
New Spain 2:155, 3:201, 3:203,
3:204, 3:208, 3:213, 5:374, 5:375,
7:523, 7:525, 8:594, 9:684, 9:685,
9:704
and South America 9:705–706
see also Mexico
New Stone Age see Neolithic
period
Newton, Isaac 1:45, 1:46, 1:49, 1:50,
1:51, 1:53, 3:233, 5:393, 8:620,
9:677
laws of motion 1:49, 1:51, 3:233,
9:677
theory of gravity 1:50, 10:742
New World 1:72, 3:179, 3:181,
3:230, 4:263, 4:271–272, 4:303,
4:313, 6:406–407, 6:428, 6:431,
6:440–441, 6:448, 6:462–465,
6:471–472, 7:520, 7:552,
8:569–572, 8:594, 9:668, 9:682,
9:703, 9:704, 10:752,
10:765–767, 10:769, 10:770–771
Columbus's voyage to the 3:186
Spanish colonization of
3:175–177, 3:205, 4:260, 4:263
New York 1:22, 1:34, 1:57, 2:158,
3:236, 4:252, 4:271, 4:279, 5:351,
7:504, 7:506, 8:578, 9:664, 9:665,
9:672, 9:673, 10:767
Waldorf-Astoria Hotel 1:36
New York Bay 10:765, 10:767
New Zealand 2:92, 3:218, 4:252,
4:264, 4:267, 4:303, 5:339, 9:687,
9:688, 10:732, 10:733, 10:734,
10:789
Cook's exploration of 3:196,
3:197, 3:198, 3:199, 3:200
the naming of 10:734
New Zealand High Commissioner
5:341
Nez Percé Indians 6:411, 6:412
Niagara Falls 5:384
Niagara River 5:384
Nicaea 5:342
Nicaragua 1:72, 1:74, 3:185, 3:189,
7:521, 9:683, 9:704
Nicholas of Cusa 10:782
Nicolet, Jean 2:158

Niepce, Joseph-Nicéfore **7**:541, **7**:542

Nigeria **2**:117, **2**:142, **7**:536

Niger River **4**:251, **4**:304, **4**:312, **7**:533, **7**:*534*, **7**:535, **7**:536, **9**:652

Nile River **1**:15, **1**:17, **4**:246, **4**:251, **4**:253, **4**:299, **4**:304, **4**:305, **4**:312, **4**:314, **5**:366, **5**:368, **6**:414, **6**:417, **6**:428, **7**:497, **9**:647, **9**:648, **9**:716, **10**:788

Ripon Falls **9**:709

search for the source of 746, **2**:113, **2**:115–117, **9**:707–710, **9**:711, **9**:714, **10**:744, **10**:746

nimbus **10**:785

Nimbus (weather satellite) **8**:607, **8**:620, **8**:623, **10**:*785*

nirvana **4**:259

Nobel Peace Prize **6**:458, **6**:461

Nobile, Umberto **1**:18, **1**:21, **2**:101, **3**:236, **3**:237, **3**:238

noche triste **3**:204, **3**:207

nomads **3**:180

Nombre de Dios **3**:227

Noonan, Fred **10**:789

Nootka Sound **10**:762, **10**:763, **10**:*764*

Nordenskiöld, Nils Adolf Erik **7**:507–510, **7**:511, **7**:512, **7**:514, **8**:624, **8**:627, **9**:655

Norfolk **10**:742, **10**:762

Norge (airship) **1**:18, **1**:21, **1**:60, **1**:62, **2**:119, **3**:236–237

Normans **8**:624, **10**:776

Norse **4**:300–301, **4**:319

explorers **4**:248–250, **4**:300, **4**:316–318

navigators **6**:405–407, **6**:474

sagas **4**:248, **4**:249, **4**:316, **4**:317, **4**:318, **4**:319, **6**:404–407, **7**:550

seafarers **4**:250, **4**:319

settlement in North America **4**:317

Norsemen *see* Vikings

North Africa **4**:244, **4**:292, **5**:331, **5**:359, **6**:432, **8**:573, **9**:668

North America **1**:24, **2**:87, **2**:126–128, **2**:129–130, **2**:151–154, **3**:196, **4**:248, **4**:272, **4**:284, **4**:303, **4**:304, **4**:316, **5**:377, **5**:394–398, **6**:430, **6**:446, **6**:448, **6**:450–451, **6**:478, **7**:491, **8**:612, **9**:652, **9**:658, **9**:682–685, **10**:743, **10**:747, **10**:749, **10**:750, **10**:751, **10**:762, **10**:765–768, **10**:773, **10**:781, **10**:787, **10**:789

British claims to **10**:763

British colonies in **3**:177–178, **3**:182, **3**:228, **4**:313, **5**:324–327, **8**:598–600, **9**:668–671

Cabrillo's exploration of the Pacific coast (1542–1543) **2**:137–138

Cartier's expeditions **2**:151–153

first overland crossing **6**:419–421

French colonies in **3**:178, **4**:271, **5**:371–372, **5**:383–387

Leif Eriksson's journey **6**:404–407

Norse settlement **4**:317, **8**:625

North Atlantic **7**:491, **9**:648, **9**:658, **10**:739, **10**:743, **10**:747, **10**:775, **10**:781

Viking exploration **8**:624–625

North Atlantic Drift *see* Gulf Stream

North Battleford **10**:735

North Carolina **2**:94, **8**:598, **8**:599, **8**:603, **10**:765, **10**:767

North Dakota **5**:395, **6**:410, **8**:617

Northeast Passage **2**:89, **2**:131, **2**:132, **5**:324, **5**:325, **5**:350, **5**:351, **6**:460, **6**:476, **7**:511–514, **7**:553, **9**:652–653, **9**:655, **10**:749

Amundsen's voyage **1**:18, **1**:21

Bering's voyage **8**:626–627

Dutch voyages **7**:503, **7**:504, **7**:512–513

English voyages **7**:511–512

Nordenskiöld's voyage **8**:624

northern routes **7**:511

Russian exploration **7**:*512*, **7**:514, **8**:614

Swedish exploration **7**:507, **7**:508–510, **7**:511, **7**:512

North Equatorial current **10**:743

Northern Lights *see* aurora borealis

Northern Sea Route **7**:512

North Pole **1**:18, **1**:19, **1**:21, **4**:313, **5**:351, **6**:458, **6**:459, **7**:491, **7**:492, **7**:498, **7**:508, **7**:517, **7**:553, **7**:554–556, **9**:648, **9**:655, **9**:674

Amundsen's voyage **1**:18, **1**:19

by balloon **1**:62

clothing for **3**:*171*

Cook's claim **4**:255

first aircraft at **8**:614, **8**:615

first flight over **3**:235–237

first woman to fly over **10**:790

first woman to reach **7**:555, **10**:792

flights over **2**:101, **2**:103, **2**:118–120, **7**:555

Nansen's voyage **8**:624, **8**:627

Peary's expedition **3**:231, **4**:253, **4**:255, **7**:538–540

Russian exploration **8**:614, **8**:615

Shepherd's expedition **3**:*190*

ski voyage to **8**:625, **8**:627

transport to **5**:381

North Pole 1 (drifting research station) **8**:614

North Saskatchewan River **10**:735

North Sea **3**:196, **4**:250, **7**:491, **10**:747

North Star **3**:185, **6**:406

Northumberland **10**:740–741

North West Company **1**:35, **1**:36, **5**:398, **6**:418, **6**:419, **6**:420, **6**:421, **10**:736–738, **10**:751

Northwest Passage **1**:18–19, **1**:21, **1**:66–68, **4**:275, **4**:276, **4**:284–285, **4**:286–287, **4**:305, **4**:313, **5**:324, **5**:326, **5**:351, **6**:476, **7**:*511*, **7**:515–519, **7**:553, **9**:652–653, **9**:654, **9**:655, **10**:749, **10**:757, **10**:762

Amundsen's voyage **1**:18–19, **8**:625, **8**:627

Baffin's voyages **1**:66, **1**:67–68

British explorers **4**:313

British naval expeditions **7**:517–518

Cook's voyage (1776–1780) **3**:196, **3**:200

Drake's search **3**:226–228

early English voyages **7**:515–516

Franklin's exploration **4**:275, **4**:276

French explorers **4**:271

Frobisher's exploration **4**:284–285, **4**:286–287

Greek belief in **4**:247

Hudson's voyage **1**:66–67

search for **2**:130, **2**:137–138, **2**:151–152, **2**:156–158

Northwest Passage Company **5**:324

Northwest Territories **6**:421, **10**:736, **10**:738

Norton, Edward **5**:341

Norway **1**:23, **2**:101, **2**:103, **4**:247, **4**:248, **4**:250, **4**:316, **4**:318, **5**:336, **6**:404–407, **6**:458–461, **7**:492, **7**:509, **8**:624, **9**:717, **10**:739, **10**:773

Norwegian explorers **1**:18–21, **3**:171, **5**:336–338, **10**:775

Nova Albion **3**:226, **3**:227, **3**:228

Nova Scotia **2**:156, **4**:272, **4**:313, **5**:351

Novaya Zemlya **1**:60, **3**:238, **5**:350,

5:351, **7**:512, **7**:513, **8**:612, **8**:614, **10**:745

Nubia **10**:*747*

nuclear powered ships **9**:650, **9**:651

Nuestra Señora de los Dolores **5**:374, **5**:375

Nugent, Jim (Rocky Mountain Jim) **2**:93

Núñez de Balboa, Vasco **6**:422, **7**:520–522, **9**:704

Nuptse Mountain **5**:*341*

nutmeg **5**:347, **6**:475, **7**:504, **10**:748, **10**:750

Nuuk (Godthåb) **4**:250, **6**:459

Nuxalk Indians **6**:420

oases **2**:139, **2**:140, **9**:661

Oates, Lawrence **5**:370, **8**:629, **8**:630, **8**:*631*

Oberth, Hermann **9**:690

observatories **5**:354, **5**:357, **5**:*390*, **5**:391, **9**:674

ocean drilling program **7**:486

oceanography **3**:234, **4**:311, **4**:319, **6**:461, **10**:743, **10**:756–761

remote-sensing studies **8**:605, **8**:607, **8**:620

ocean ridge systems **7**:486, **7**:488

oceans

depth sounding **10**:756–757

observing from space **10**:761

octant **7**:494, **7**:495, **7**:501

Ogooué River **4**:315

Ohio **1**:27, **4**:279, **4**:306, **6**:411, **10**:730

Ohio River **1**:56, **5**:371, **5**:384, **6**:437

Ohio River valley **4**:273

oil pipelines **10**:724

oil prospecting **6**:475, **6**:477, **10**:730–731

oil tanker **7**:519

Ojeda, Alonso de **2**:128, **6**:462, **10**:770, **10**:771

O'Keefe, Sean **1**:48

Okhotsk **2**:88

Okmok volcano **8**:607

Olaf Tryggvason **6**:404

Old World **3**:181, **3**:230

Oleson, Olaf **8**:625

Olmeda, Father **6**:465

Oman **5**:358

Ommanney, Erasmus **4**:276

Oñate, Juan de **7**:523–526

Ontario **4**:272, **10**:738

Operation Deep Freeze (1955) **2**:119, **2**:121

Operation Highjump
(1946–1947) **2:**119, **2:***120,* **2:**121
Opportunity space rover **9:**678,
9:697, **9:**699
Orange River **3:**224
orbit **6:**468, **8:**619, **8:**623, **9:**676,
9:679, **9:**681
Ordos Desert **8:**586
Oregon **1:**34, **1:**35, **2:**137, **2:**138,
4:280, **8:**618, **9:**665, **9:**666,
10:737, **10:**787, **10:**788
Oregon City **10:**787
Oregon Trail **1:**35, **1:**79, **2:**108,
2:109, **2:**146, **2:**159, **4:**280,
4:280–281, **9:**664, **9:**665
women on the **10:**787
Orellana, Francisco de **9:**652, **9:**654
Orinoco River **5:**355, **5:**356, **8:**599,
8:600
Orkney Islands **4:**250, **4:**313, **7:**491,
8:624
ornithology **1:**55–58, **10:**745
Ortelius, Abraham **6:**425, **6:**429, **7:**506
map (1570) **8:**610, **8:***611*
Ortiz, Juan **6:**464
Orwell, George, *Nineteen Eighty-
Four* **7:**530
Osage **7:**546, **7:***547,* **7:**559
Oscar II, king of Sweden and
Norway **7:**509
Oslo **1:**18, **3:***236,* **5:**337, **6:**458, **6:**459,
6:461
Fram Museum, Bygdøy **6:**459
Ostyak **8:***612*
Oswell, William **6:**414
otherworlds **7:527–532**
desert islands **7:**530
extraterrestrial **7:**532
of the future **7:**530
on medieval maps **7:**528–529
the moon **7:**532
utopias and dystopias **7:**530,
7:*531*
voyages by sea **7:**527
Ottawa Indians **5:**385
Ottoman Empire **1:**78, **2:**140,
2:141, **2:**142, **2:**159, **3:**175, **3:**178,
4:300, **9:**707
Ousland, Borge **8:**625, **8:**627
outback **2:**111, **2:**159
Outina **6:**470
Ovando, Nicolás de **8:**569, **8:**570
Owen, Robert **10:**780
Oxford, England **1:**23, **1:**24, **9:**669
debate on evolution **4:**264, **4:**267
Oxfordshire **10:**785
Oxford University, Ashmolean
Museum **6:**457

Paamiut **4:**250
Pacific Fur Company **1:**34
Pacific Islands **3:**212, **6:**471, **9:**658
Pacific Northwest **1:**33–36, **1:**79
Pacific Ocean **1:**27, **1:**28, **1:**29, **1:**41,
1:69, **2:**88, **2:**97, **2:**98, **2:**130,
2:149, **3:**226, **4:**266, **4:**271, **4:**275,
4:280, **4:**303, **4:**313, **5:**336, **5:**394,
6:408, **6:**410, **6:**412, **6:**418, **6:**422,
7:510, **7:**515, **7:**520, **7:**521–522,
7:530, **8:**596–597, **8:**612, **8:**615,
8:616, **9:**654, **9:**655, **9:**664, **9:**674,
9:687, **9:***692,* **9:**704–705, **10:**725,
10:727, **10:**732, **10:**733, **10:**737,
10:743, **10:**749, **10:**751, **10:**763,
10:765, **10:**789
Cook's first voyage **7:**486
discovery of the **7:**521–522
Mackenzie's search for
6:419–421
Magellan's crossing **6:**425–426
scientific exploration **3:**212,
3:213–214, **3:**216–219, **3:**234
see also South Pacific
Pacific Railway **9:**674
pack ice **8:**637
Padrón Real (Royal Map) **2:**131
Pakistan **4:**258, **10:**793
paleontology **10:**753
Palestine **1:**15, **5:**358, **7:**543
map **6:**444
Palmer, Nathaniel D. **2:**85, **7:**556,
9:689
Palmyra **10:**789
Palos **3:**184, **3:**186, **7:**549, **7:**551
Pamir Mountains **8:**566, **9:**663,
10:793, **10:**794
Pamlico Sound **10:**767
Panama **1:**72, **1:**73, **3:**185, **3:**189,
3:213, **3:**226, **3:**227, **3:**228, **4:**287,
6:422, **7:**520, **7:**521, **8:**597, **9:**704,
9:705
Panama City **7:**521
Papanin, Ivan **8:**614
Papua New Guinea **1:***25*
papyrus reeds **5:**337, **5:***338,* **9:**647,
9:709
papyrus rolls **4:**245
Pará (Belém) **10:**779
Paraguay **2:**117, **2:**123, **2:**125
Paraguay River **2:**125
parallels **4:**247, **5:**389, **5:**390, **5:**399,
6:434
Paris **1:**55, **2:**97, **3:**211, **5:**324, **5:**354,
5:390, **7:**541, **10:**783
Paris, Treaty of (1763) **1:**33, **4:**273
Parkes telescope, New South
Wales **8:**634

Parke, Thomas Heazle **9:***715*
Parkinson, Sydney **1:**69
Parkman, Francis **5:**372
Park, Mungo **1:**70, **4:**251, **7:533–536**
Parma, duke of **9:**706
Parry, William **7:**517, **7:**518, **7:**554,
7:555
Parthians **9:**659
Patagonia **4:**264, **4:**266
Patanou **6:**470
patent **1:**79
Pathfinder space probe **6:**469,
6:*478,* **9:**678, **9:**699
Paul III, Pope, *Sublimis Deus Sic
Dilexit* **6:**470, **6:**472
Pawnee Indians **3:**202, **3:**239,
7:546, **7:**559
PDAs (personal digital assistants)
8:604
Peace River **6:**419
pearls **7:**520, **9:**662, **9:**684
Peary, Robert E. **1:**19, **1:**60, **3:**231,
3:237, **4:**253, **4:**255, **5:**366, **5:**370,
5:381, **7:**502, **7:537–540,** **7:**554
Pedrarias *see* Dávila, Pedro Arias
Peel Sound **4:**276
Pella, Macedonia **1:**16
peninsula **4:**313, **4:**319
Pennsylvania **1:**57, **2:**94, **7:**538,
9:664, **10:**782
Penny, William **4:**276
Pensacola, Florida **2:**94
pepper **5:**347, **5:**349, **6:**476, **10:**748,
10:749
Peralta, Don Pedro de **7:**524
Père Marquette River **6:**436
Perestello e Moniz, Felipa **3:**184
Periplus (Hanno of Carthage)
5:330, **8:**602
Perkiomen River **1:**57
Persepolis **1:**16
Persia **1:**14, **1:**68, **1:**76, **1:**77, **5:**358,
5:359, **8:**565, **9:**659, **9:**712, **10:**798
Persian Empire **1:**14–16, **1:**22
Persian Gulf **1:**17, **1:**67, **1:**68, **3:**166,
3:167, **5:**338
Perthshire **6:**420, **6:**421
Peru **1:**72–73, **3:**177, **3:**213, **4:**256,
5:336, **5:**337, **5:**355, **5:**356, **5:**357,
5:379, **6:**475, **6:**478, **7:**521, **8:**595,
8:596, **8:**597, **9:**658, **9:**682, **9:**683,
9:687, **9:**704, **9:**705, **10:**752,
10:788, **10:**791
Peru Current **5:**357
Peruvian Indians **5:***369*
Peshawar **4:**259
Peter the Great, Czar **2:**87, **2:**89,
7:514, **8:**612

Peter I Island **2:**84, **2:**86
Peters, Arno **6:**434
Peters Projection **6:**434
Petropavlovsk **2:**88, **2:**89, **2:**90
Petropavlovsk Kamchatsky **2:**90
Philadelphia **1:**55, **4:**253, **5:**390
Philip II, king of Macedonia **1:**14
Philip II, king of Spain and
Portugal **5:**388, **8:**594, **8:***597,*
9:704
Philip III, king of Spain **8:**595
Philip of Bourbon **5:**394
Philip of Macedonia **10:**753
Philippines **1:**26, **3:**213, **3:**227,
6:424, **6:**426, **8:**594, **8:**595, **8:**596
philology **4:**244, **4:**319
Philopater **4:**244
philosophy, Greek **4:**244, **4:**299,
9:686
Phoenicia **10:**752
Phoenicians **5:**329, **5:**330
colonies **3:**176
exploration **8:**602
navigation **5:**329
shipbuilding **9:**647
trade **10:**747
photogrammetry **10:**729
photography **1:**23, **1:**62–63, **1:**65,
2:92, **2:***93,* **2:**101, **2:**102,
7:541–544, **8:**604
aerial **1:**62–63, **8:**605, **8:**606
digital **7:**544
dry-plate glass negatives **1:**22
flexible film strip **7:**541, **7:**542
and printing **7:**542
satellite **1:**63, **1:**65, **3:***229,* **3:**230
wet collodion process **7:**541,
7:542
photointerpretation **8:**605
physical anthropology **1:**22
physical geography **4:**305
phytoplankton **10:**761
Piccard, Auguste **1:**61, **10:**725,
10:726
Piccard, Jacques **10:**725
Piccard, Jean **1:**61
Piegen Blackfeet **6:**411
Pigafetta, Antonio **6:**425, **6:**426
Pike, Zebulon Montgomery
7:545–548
Pike's Peak **7:**547, **7:***548*
pilgrimage **2:**143, **2:**159, **3:**166,
4:257, **4:**258, **4:**294, **4:**318, **5:**358,
5:361, **5:**363
Pilgrim Fathers **3:***178,* **7:**526
pilgrims **2:**139, **9:**660
Buddhist **8:**588
massacre of **4:**294, **4:**319

pillage 6:453, 6:479
Pillars of Hercules 5:328
Pima people 5:373, 5:374
Pimeria Alta 5:374, 5:375
pinnace 3:227, 4:285, 4:319
Pinzón, Francisco 7:550
Pinzón, Martín Alonso 7:549–550, 7:551
Pinzón, Vicente Yáñez 7:550, 7:551–552
pioneers 6:479, 7:559
Pioneer space probes 6:466, 9:696, 9:700, 9:701, 9:702
piracy 3:166, 3:213, 4:284
pirogue 4:296, 6:410, 6:479
Pisa 1:44, 10:783
Pisania 7:534, 7:536
Pitcairn, Robert 2:150
Pitcairn Island 2:149, 2:150
Pitt Rivers, Augustus Henry Lane-Fox 1:24
Pitt Rivers Museum, Oxford 1:23, 1:24
Piura 1:73
Pizarro, Francisco 1:72–73, 1:74, 3:176–177, 5:379, 6:439, 6:475, 6:478, 7:521, 9:682, 9:683, 9:704, 9:705
Pizarro, Gonzalo 9:652
Plains Indians 2:151, 3:183
plane projections 6:433–434
plane table 10:*728*, 10:729
Planetary Society 8:632
planets 1:51, 4:252, 5:391, 6:468, 7:485, 9:676, 9:678, 9:680–681, 9:698–702
  far 9:680–681
  giant 9:680
  gravitational pull 9:691
  hot 9:678
  movement of 3:233
  orbits 1:50
  red 9:678–679
  supporting life 9:678
planisphere 5:364, 5:399
plantations 1:55, 1:70, 3:176, 3:182, 6:472
plants 6:455, 8:599, 8:617, 8:624, 8:626
  classification of 7:486, 7:487
Plate River (Río de la Plata) 2:125, 2:131, 3:217, 7:552, 10:772
Plato 7:529
Platte River 2:146
Pliny the Elder 5:329, 5:330
plumb line 3:185
Pluto 1:51, 9:676, 9:679, 9:680–681
Plymouth, England 3:197, 3:199,

4:285, 8:598
Plymouth, Massachusetts 3:*178*
Pocahontas 6:464, 9:668, 9:669
Pocock, Frank 9:714
polar bears 7:513, 7:556, 7:*557*
polar controversy 4:255
polar exploration 1:18–21, 1:60–62, 4:315, 6:458–461, 7:553–558, 8:614, 8:624, 8:627, 8:628–631
  British 8:629–630, 8:635–637
  by air 1:60–62, 3:235–238
  drifting research stations 8:614
  early 7:553
  English and Dutch voyages 7:553
  Norwegian 1:18–21
  Peary's expedition 7:537–540
  provisioning 8:*581*, 8:583
  Russian 8:613–614
  Scandinavian 8:624, 8:627
  Swedish expedition 7:507–510
  transport 5:381, 8:629
  by women 7:555, 7:558
  see also North Pole; South Pole
Polaris expedition 9:674
Pole Star 7:489, 7:491, 7:493, 7:499
Polk, James 4:283
Polo, Maffeo 8:564, 8:565, 8:566
Polo, Marco 1:22, 2:126, 4:301, 5:361, 6:478, 8:564–568, 8:586, 8:603, 9:647, 9:660, 9:663, 10:748, 10:749, 10:751, 10:798
Polo, Niccolò 8:564, 8:565, 8:566, 8:*568*
Polyakov, Valeri V. 8:615, 9:*694*
Polynesia 1:69, 3:198, 9:658
Polynesians, navigation 10:743
Ponce de León, Juan 8:569–572, 9:704, 10:765
Ponce de León, Luis 3:204, 3:208
Pond, Peter 6:418
Ponting, Herbert 7:558, 8:604, 8:*630*
Popayán, Colombia 1:74
population 3:182
  growth 6:443, 6:474
  Malthus's theory 7:488, 10:779
  world 3:182
porcelain 3:*166*, 5:360, 5:361
Port Adelaide 3:*180*
portage 5:371, 5:399, 6:438, 6:479
Port Conclusion 10:763, 10:764
Port Discovery 10:763
Port Jackson 4:268, 4:269
portolan charts 6:*423*, 7:492
Port Royal, Nova Scotia 2:156
Portsmouth 2:85, 4:264, 7:534

Portugal 2:133–135, 2:143, 3:184, 4:271, 4:291–294, 4:302, 5:390, 6:422–426, 6:429, 6:448, 6:452, 6:471, 7:503, 7:510, 8:573–576, 9:652–653, 9:686, 9:703, 9:704, 10:750, 10:770
  and Spain 3:175–176, 4:261, 4:263, 4:272, 8:594
Portuguese 3:177, 4:284, 5:331–335, 5:346, 5:348, 9:663
  in Africa and Asia 3:175
  in Brazil 2:133
  cartographers 8:574
  colonization in Africa and Asia 2:131, 3:175
  explorers 4:291–294, 7:511, 7:528, 8:594–597
  navigators 3:222–225, 4:298, 4:302, 5:346, 7:498, 10:743
  shipbuilders 9:650
  traders 10:749
Portuguese Empire 4:294, 8:573–576
Portus Novae Albionis (Drake's Harbour) 3:228
postal service
  Chinese system 8:568
  first transatlantic 2:121
postcards 7:543
Potala, Palace of 8:588
potatoes 3:182, 3:226, 3:228, 8:599
Potomac River 9:670, 9:671
Powell, John Wesley 8:577–580
Powhatan, Chief 9:668, 9:669
Prado, Madrid 6:454, 6:456
precession of the equinoxes 5:343
prehistory 10:752, 10:753–754, 10:781
  migration 5:377
  transport 5:377
Prescott, William H. 6:465
pressure ridge 6:479
Prester John 5:332, 5:333, 7:528
prevailing wind 9:650, 9:703, 9:719, 10:743
priest-kings 5:332, 5:333, 7:528
priests 6:443, 6:448, 6:449
prime meridian 5:388, 5:390–391, 5:399
primitive societies 6:470–471
Prince of Wales Island 4:277
Prince William Sound 3:200
printing,
  invention of 6:429
  and photography 7:542
privateer 1:55, 3:212, 3:213, 3:239, 4:284, 6:441

Project FAMOUS (French-American Mid-Ocean Undersea Study) 10:727
projection *see* map projection
Project Mercury *see* Mercury space program
Project Ozma (SETI) 8:632
Project Phoenix (SETI) 8:633, 8:634
Promontory, Utah 5:380
propeller 9:648, 9:650, 9:719
Protestantism 5:326, 5:327, 6:446, 6:451, 6:452, 8:609
Provins, Guy de 7:493
provisioning 8:581–584
Proxima Centauri (star) 1:43
Przhevalsky, Nikolay 8:585–588, 8:613
Przhevalsky's horse 8:587
Ptahhotep 9:647
Ptolemy, Claudius 4:300, 4:302, 5:345, 5:363, 7:484, 8:589–593, 9:676, 9:680, 9:686, 9:688, 9:715, 9:718
  as astronomer 1:49, 3:233, 8:589–591
  atlas of 5:390
  as geographer 8:591–593
  map of 4:301, 5:363, 5:*388*, 5:390, 6:428, 6:429, 6:445, 6:447, 7:494, 9:686
Ptolemy III 4:244, 4:245
pueblos 3:202, 3:*203*
Puerto Rico 3:176, 3:187, 6:440, 7:551, 7:552, 8:569, 8:570, 8:571, 8:572, 9:704
  Arecibo radio telescope 1:46, 1:*54*, 8:632, 8:*633*, 8:634
Puget Sound 10:763
pulsars 1:52, 9:702
Punt 6:477
Purchas, Samuel 1:68, 5:327
Puritans 3:178, 7:526
pygmies 6:431
pyramids 6:*542*, 10:730
Pythagoras 4:246, 6:428, 9:686
Pytheas of Massalia 4:246, 4:247, 9:717, 9:718

Qassiarsuk 4:250
Qeshm 1:68
Qing dynasty 5:361
quadrant 1:43, 3:185, 7:494, 7:499–500
  Davis 1:*67*
Quakers 10:785, 10:799
quasars 1:53
Quast, Matthijs 10:732
Qubbet ed Duris, Lebanon 1:*77*

Quebec 2:151, 2:152, 2:156, 2:*157*, 2:158, 3:179, 3:196, 4:271, 5:372, 5:394, 6:419, 6:451, 9:655
  founded 4:272
Queen Charlotte Islands 2:149, 9:674
Quelimane 6:416
Quen, Jean de 6:450, 6:451
Querini, Pietro 1:22, 1:23
Quetzalcoatl 3:207
Quicheberg, Samuel van, *Teatrum sapientiae* 6:454
quinine 5:366, 5:369
Quintilian 8:608
Quirós, Pedro Fernández de 8:594–597, 9:655, 9:687, 9:688
Quito 1:73, 1:74, 9:652
Quivira 3:202, 3:203, 7:524, 7:529
  treasure 7:525

radar 1:43, 1:63, 1:64, 1:65, 7:495, 7:*496*, 10:728, 10:784, 10:799
radar mapping 3:230, 3:231, 3:239
radiation 8:607, 8:620, 8:639
radio 3:*190*, 3:192, 3:193, 3:194, 4:289
radio astronomy 1:46
radio communication 2:103, 3:190, 3:192, 3:193, 3:194, 4:289, 7:496
radio waves 4:309, 4:310
Rae, Dr. John 4:276, 4:313
Rae Strait 4:313
rafts 9:647, 9:648, 9:651, 9:658
Ra II expedition 5:336, 5:337, 5:*338*
railroads 4:283, 5:380, 10:728
Rainy Lake 5:396
Raleigh, Walter 3:228, 4:285, 4:287, 4:313, 5:324, 5:325, 5:326, 8:598–600, 8:603
  map of El Dorado 7:524
Raleigh Travellers' Club 4:254
Rand'l He-dow Teton 8:618
Rapa Nui *see* Easter Island
Raroia 5:337
Rasmussen, Knud, *Across Arctic America* 8:627
Real, Gaspar Corte 2:128
Reber, Grote 1:46
Recife 7:551
Recollect order 3:179, 5:385
reconnaisance 1:59, 1:79, 5:399, 8:605
Reconquista 3:175, 4:260, 4:261, 4:263, 4:319, 9:704
record keeping 8:601–604
  classic visual records 8:603
  classic written accounts

8:602–603
  in early civilizations 8:602
  modern 8:604
  purpose of 8:601
Red River 4:296–297, 5:394, 7:546, 10:736
Red Sea 3:210, 6:474, 6:477, 10:757, 10:761
  map 5:*365*
reflecting telescopes 1:45, 1:46, 1:50
refracting telescopes 1:44–45, 1:46, 1:50
refractor 1:44–45, 1:79
Reindeer Lake 10:736
Reindeer River 10:736
relativity theories 1:50–51, 1:79, 9:677
relay system 3:191
religion, and science 7:485
remotely operated vehicle (ROV) 1:65, 10:726–727
  hybrid (HROV) 10:727
Remote Manipulator System 1:*47*
remote sensing 6:432, 6:468–469, 6:*478*, 6:479, 8:605–607, 9:675
  aerial photography 8:605
  early developments 8:605
  electromagnetic spectrum 8:605–606
  mapping the earth 8:606–607
  satellites 8:605–607
Renaissance 6:447, 6:453, 6:479, 8:591
Renwick, James, Jr. 9:672
Republican Party (U.S.) 4:283
research centers 9:672
Reykjavik 2:106
Rhine 7:503
Rhode Island 3:178, 10:767
Rhodes 5:342, 5:343, 10:767
rhododendron 6:455
rhumb lines 6:447
Rica de Oro 10:732
Rica de Plata 10:732
Ricci, Matteo 8:608–611
Richards, Emma 8:*604*
Richardson, John 4:275
Richelieu, Cardinal 2:158, 6:450
Richelieu River 2:155
Ride, Sally 1:42, 10:789, 10:791
rights, native people's 6:470, 6:472
Rio Charna 7:525
Rio de Janeiro 1:69, 3:197, 4:252
Río de la Plata *see* Plate River
Río de Oro 3:175
Rio Grande 5:375, 6:464, 7:524–526, 7:547

Río Negro 7:552
Ripon Falls, Nile River 9:709, 10:746
Ritter, Carl 4:*252*, 4:253, 4:254, 4:305
Roanoke 3:226, 3:228
Roanoke Island 5:326, 5:*327*, 8:598–599, 8:603
Roaring Forties 7:505
Roberval, Jean-François de la Roque, sieur de 2:152, 2:153, 2:154
Robinson, Bradley 5:370
Robinson projection 6:435
Robledo, Jorge 1:75
robotics 10:760
Rochefort 1:55
Rockefeller, John D. 2:118
rocket power 9:690, 9:695
rocket science 1:37
Rocky Mountain Fur Company 2:107
Rocky Mountain House 10:736
Rocky Mountain Jim *see* Nugent, Jim
Rocky Mountains 1:30–32, 1:34–36, 2:92, 2:93, 2:107–109, 2:144–147, 4:280, 4:313, 6:410, 6:412, 6:421, 7:543, 8:577, 8:616, 8:618, 9:664–667, 10:736, 10:737, 10:750
  South Pass 1:35, 2:146, 9:664, 9:665
Roebuck Bay 3:214
Roger II, king of Sicily 4:301, 5:362, 5:363–364
Rolfe, John 9:669
Roman Catholic Church 4:271, 8:609, 9:662
  missions 6:448–449, 6:452, 6:471
  Vatican collections 6:456
Roman Empire 4:300, 5:379, 6:428, 8:592, 10:798
  collapse of Western 8:591
  missionaries 6:448
Romans 8:589, 9:659
  geography 4:300
  mapmakers 6:428
Rome 3:176, 4:316, 4:318, 5:390, 9:716, 9:717, 10:797
  Jesuit college 8:608
Roosa, Stuart A. 9:*646*
Roosevelt, Theodore 9:674
Ross, James Clark 7:554, 7:556–557
Ross, John 8:583
Rosselli, Francesco 6:428
Ross Ice Shelf 2:120, 5:340, 7:554, 7:557, 8:628, 9:658
Ross Sea 8:627

Rotz, Jean 2:154
Rouen 5:384
Rousseau, Jean Jacques 2:99
Rowlands, John *see* Stanley, Henry Morton
Royal Astronomical Society, London 1:51
Royal Botanic Gardens, Kew 1:70, 1:71
Royal Canadian Geographical Society 4:253
Royal Canadian Mounted Police 7:519
Royal Geographical Society, London 2:91, 2:93, 4:252, 4:253, 4:254–255, 4:266, 4:299, 4:305, 6:414, 6:417, 7:507, 8:628, 9:708, 9:709, 9:713, 10:779, 10:791, 10:795
Royal Greenwich Observatory 5:*390*, 5:391
Royal Institution of Great Britain 1:71
Royal Society for Asian Affairs 10:794
Royal Society of London 1:69, 1:71, 2:85, 2:98, 3:197, 4:251, 4:252, 7:486, 8:628, 9:689, 10:756
Royal Society of Victoria 2:110
Rozier, Ferdinand 1:56
Ruggieri, Michel 8:609, 8:610
Rumford, Count 1:71
Rush, Richard 9:672
Russia 2:115, 2:132, 4:288, 5:359, 5:377, 6:455, 6:476, 6:478, 7:507, 7:508, 7:512, 8:612–615, 9:668, 10:747, 10:774, 10:775
  Napoleon's invasion of 2:100
  naval expeditions 2:84–86, 2:87–90
  treaty with Chinese 10:794
  war with Sweden 2:87
  war with Turkey (1828–1829) 2:86
Russian Empire 8:585
  and the British 10:793–795
Russian exploration 7:514, 8:585–588, 8:612–614, 10:749
  polar 8:612–614
  space 1:37–38, 1:41, 4:288–290, 8:612, 8:615
Russian Geographical Society 4:252
Russian navy 2:84–86, 2:87–90, 8:613
Russians, in America 8:613
Russian steppes 8:602
Rusticello of Pisa 8:568

Ruwenzori Mountains **9:**713, **9:**715
Ruxton, George F. **1:**31

Saaremaa Island **2:**84
Sabarmati River **10:**741
Sacagawea **6:**409, **6:**410, **8:616–618,** **10:**787, **10:**788
sacrifice
  human **3:**206, **6:**470
  ritual **7:***526*
Saga of Erik the Red **4:**249, **4:**317, **6:**404, **6:**405, **6:**407, **10:**787
Saga of the Greenlanders **6:**404, **6:**406, **6:**407, **10:**787
Sagan, Carl **1:**54, **8:**632
Sagarmatha **5:**341
sagas **4:**248, **4:**249, **4:**316, **4:**317, **4:**318, **4:**319, **6:**404–407, **7:**550, **10:**776, **10:**787, **10:**799
Sagres **4:**302, **5:**331, **8:**574
Saguenay **2:**152, **2:**153, **5:**372
Saguenay (Ottawa) River **2:**152, **2:**153, **2:**155
Sahara Desert **2:***142,* **2:**143, **4:**273, **5:**332, **5:**358, **5:**359, **5:**361, **7:**536, **8:**573, **10:**746
Saigon **4:**295, **4:**296
Saint-André-de-Cubzac **3:**209
Saint Augustine, Florida **3:***179,* **8:**571, **8:***572*
Saint Brendan's Island **2:**105
Saint Croix River **2:**156
Saint-Etienne **4:**295
Saint Francis Xavier **5:**373, **5:**375, **6:**438
Saint Helena **1:**53, **2:**100
Saint Ignace **6:**436, **6:**437, **6:**438
Saint Lawrence colony **6:**419
Saint Lawrence Island **8:**612
Saint Lawrence River **2:**155, **2:**156, **2:**158, **3:**178, **3:**196, **4:**271, **5:**372, **6:**475
  Lachine Rapids **2:**152, **2:**153
Saint Lawrence valley **3:**178, **4:**273
Saint Louis **1:**30, **1:**36, **1:**56, **1:**57, **4:**280, **4:**281, **6:**408, **6:**409, **6:**410, **6:**412, **7:**545, **7:**547, **8:**616, **9:**664, **9:**665, **9:**667
Saint-Lusson, Daumont de **5:**372
Saint Malo **2:**99, **2:**151
Saint Petersburg **2:**84, **2:**86, **2:**87, **2:**88, **2:**89, **4:**252, **5:**390, **7:**493
Salamanca **3:**204
Salas, Juan de **3:**176
Salazar, Eugenio de **7:**500
Salinas, Battle of **1:**73
Salt Lake City **2:***109,* **2:**115
saltpeter **1:**30

Salt River **5:**374
Salt Road **2:**139, **2:**142
Salyut 1 space station **1:**38, **8:**620, **9:**692, **9:**694
Samarkand **8:**565, **9:**660, **9:**661
  Gur-I-Amir Mausoleum **9:***661*
Samoa **1:**25, **2:**98
samurai **2:**93, **2:**159
Sanderson, William **1:**68
Sanderson's Hope **1:***68*
sandglass **3:**220, **7:***492*
San Diego Bay **2:**137, **2:**138, **10:**763
Sandwich, Lord **4:***314*
Sandwich Islands *see* Hawaii
San Francisco **2:**102, **2:**103, **4:**281, **10:**764
San Francisco Bay **3:**228
San Gabriel **7:**524, **7:**525
San Jacinto, California **8:**615
San Joaquin valley **9:**666
San Juan **8:**569
San Juan de los Caballeros **7:**524, **7:**525
San Juan Mountain **4:**283
San Julián **6:**424
Sanlucar **3:**185
San Miguel (San Diego) **2:**137
San Salvador Island (Santa Catalina Island) **2:**137, **3:**186
Sansandig **7:**536
San Sebastián de la Gomera **3:**186
San Servas, Campos **8:**570
Sanskrit **4:**259, **4:**319
Santa Barbara **7:**524
Santa Catalina Island **2:**136
Santa Cruz Islands **2:**150, **8:**595, **8:**596
Santa Fe **7:**548, **9:**665, **9:**667
Santa Fe Trail **2:**145
Santa Hermandad **4:**262
Santa Lucie River, Uruguay **2:***99*
Santa María la Antigua del Darién **7:**520
Santiago **6:**462
Santiago River **9:**683
Santo Domingo **1:**55, **3:**205
Sapin **5:**373
Saqqara **6:**455
Sarawak **10:**755
Saskatchewan River **5:**397, **5:**398, **10:**736
satellite communication **3:**191, **3:**194, **3:**195, **4:**311, **6:**468, **8:**620, **8:**621
satellite photography **1:**63, **1:**65, **3:***229,* **3:**230
satellites **1:**41, **1:**63, **1:**79,

4:309–311, **4:**319, **5:**393, **6:**432, **6:**466, **6:**468, **6:**469, **7:**496, **8:619–623**
  communication **4:**311, **8:**604, **8:**620, **8:**621
  exploring the universe **8:**622
  the first **8:**620
  geostationary **4:**311, **8:**623, **10:***785*
  mapping the earth **8:**606–607, **10:**729
  natural **5:**391, **8:**619
  navigation **4:**309–311
  networks of **8:**623
  observation from space **8:**622, **10:**761
  orbiting **4:**309–311, **8:**619, **8:**623, **9:**690, **9:**695
  remote-sensing **8:**605–607
  in sea mapping **3:**234
  weather **8:**606, **8:**620, **8:**623, **10:**781, **10:**784–785
satire **7:**530
Saturn **6:**466, **8:**590, **9:**676, **9:**679, **9:**680, **9:**691, **9:**692, **9:**696, **9:**697, **9:**701
  ring system **9:**680, **9:**701
Saturn rockets **9:***691,* **9:**692
Saudi Arabia **2:**114, **5:**358, **8:**602
Sault Sainte Marie **5:**372, **10:**737
Sautuola, Marcellino de **10:**754
savages **6:**470, **6:**471
Savannah **4:**281
Savannah River **9:**684
Scandinavia **8:624–627,** **10:**747, **10:**773–776 *see also* Denmark; Faeroe Islands; Finland; Iceland; Norway; Sweden
Schelde River **7:**503
Schelleken, Barbara **6:**444
Schirra, Walter M., Jr. **9:**645
Schouten, Willem **7:**504, **7:**505, **10:**734
science **5:**354
  and religion **7:**485
science fiction **3:**195, **7:**530–532
scientific collections **9:**672–675
scientific exploration **4:**305, **6:**452, **6:**454, **8:**577–580
scientific revolution **4:**251, **7:**484–485
Scilly Isles **3:**168, **5:**393
Scotland **1:**23, **1:**26, **2:**91, **2:**105, **4:**314, **6:**413, **6:**418, **6:**421, **6:**452, **7:**533, **8:**624, **10:**739, **10:**775, **10:**781
Scott, David R. **1:**27
Scott, Robert Falcon **1:**19, **1:**21,

1:*62,* **3:**170, **3:**171, **3:**190, **4:**253, **4:**255, **4:**315, **5:**339, **5:**340, **5:**366, **5:**370, **5:**381, **7:**502, **7:**537, **7:**543, **7:**553, **7:**554, **7:**555, **7:**557, **7:**558, **8:***602,* **8:**604, **8:628–631,** **8:**635, **8:**636, **9:**657
  Antarctic expedition (1911) **8:***581,* **8:**629–630
  journals and letters **8:**630–631
Scott-Amundsen Base, South Pole **1:**62
Scottish explorers **9:**689, **9:**711, **9:**712–713
Scottish inventions **3:**172
screw propeller **9:**648, **9:**650
scuba **3:**209–210, **10:**758
scurvy **1:**18, **2:**89, **2:**98, **2:**111, **2:**112, **2:**149, **2:**152, **2:**153, **2:**156, **2:**159, **3:**197, **3:**217, **4:**269, **4:**278, **4:**292, **4:**293, **5:**347, **5:**352, **5:**366–368, **5:**370, **5:**399, **6:**425, **7:**512, **7:**513, **7:**557, **7:**558, **8:**629, **8:**635, **8:**639, **9:**655
  remedies for **8:**584, **10:**763, **10:**764
Scythia **6:**471
Scythians **1:**22
sea
  clocks at **3:**168–169, **5:**392–393
  clothing for exploration at **3:**172–173
  communication signals **3:**192
  time at **7:**492, **7:**495, **7:**559
seabed **7:**497
  mapping the **3:**234, **10:**760
seals **2:**86, **3:**200, **7:**518, **9:**689
seamarks **7:**491
Sea of Okhotsk **8:**612, **8:**614
Sea of the West **5:**394, **5:**396
Sea of Tranquillity (Moon) **1:**28, **1:**79
Sea of Ujiji *see* Lake Tanganyika
seaplanes **1:**60, **3:**237
Seasat **8:**607, **8:**620, **10:**760
Segno **5:**373
Ségou **7:**535
seismic measurement **1:**65, **3:**231, **3:**239
seismic test **10:**731
Selenites **7:**532
Seleucus of Babylon **10:**740
Selkirk, Alexander **3:**213, **3:**214, **3:**215, **7:**530
semaphore **3:**190, **3:**191
Semliki River **9:**713, **9:**715
Seneca **10:**753
Seneca Indians **2:**157
Senegal River **5:**329, **5:**332, **5:**335,

7:535, 8:574
Sennacherib, King 5:329
SETI (Search for Extraterrestrial
    Intelligence) 1:54, 8:632–634
    history 8:632
    instruments 8:634
    projects 8:633, 8:634
    radio waves and interference
        8:633
settlers 3:175, 3:176
    European in North America
        3:182–183
Seven Years' War (1756–1763)
    3:196, 4:313 see also French
    and Indian War
Severin, Tim 2:106, 9:658
Seville 2:125, 2:130, 3:189, 3:205,
    3:208, 6:424, 6:441, 9:653,
    10:769, 10:771
    Casa de las Indias 10:772
sextant 1:43, 1:46, 2:121, 2:159,
    3:232, 3:239, 4:309, 5:345, 5:392,
    5:399, 7:494, 7:495, 7:496, 7:501,
    7:502, 10:735, 10:737
Shackleton, Ernest Henry 4:315,
    5:381, 7:542, 7:543, 7:554, 7:555,
    7:557, 8:604, 8:628, 8:635–637,
    9:656
Shahhat 4:244
Shantung 4:259
Shanxi Province 4:257
Shawnees 2:94, 2:96
Shendu (Sind) 2:113, 10:798
Shepard, Alan B., Jr. 1:37, 1:38,
    4:306, 9:644–646
Shepherd, Ollie 3:190
Sherpa 5:339, 5:399
Shetland Islands 4:249, 4:250,
    4:285, 7:491, 8:624
shipbuilding 9:647–650
    Chinese 3:167
    design 6:429, 6:459
    Dutch 7:503
    early 9:647
    in the East 2:90
    European 2:86
    French 6:443
    materials 9:648, 9:650
    New England 6:441
ships 9:651–658
    reconstructing ancient 9:658
    and speed 3:220, 7:492
    Sumerian 5:338
Shirshov, Peter 8:614
shoran 7:495, 7:496
Shoshone Indians 2:108, 6:410,
    6:411, 6:412, 8:616–618, 8:639,
    10:787

Lemhi branch 8:616
Shrewsbury 3:216, 3:218
Siam 3:166
Sian (Chang'an) 4:258
Siberia 2:87–90, 6:459, 7:508, 7:514,
    7:555, 8:585, 8:586, 8:612, 8:614,
    8:624, 8:627
Sicily 5:362, 10:775
Sierra Leone 3:184, 5:327, 5:328,
    5:332, 8:574, 8:602
Sierra Madre 2:146
Sierra Nevada 2:146, 2:147, 4:280,
    9:666, 9:667
signal fires 3:191
sign language 4:287
Sikdhar, Radhanath 10:731
Sikkim 10:731
silk 3:175, 4:296, 6:478, 9:659,
    10:748, 10:797, 10:798
Silk Road 1:17, 2:139, 4:300, 5:376,
    5:378–379, 8:565, 9:659–663,
    10:748, 10:751, 10:797, 10:798
silt 7:497, 10:741
silver 3:175, 3:182, 5:386,
    6:439–440, 6:477–478, 7:523,
    7:526, 9:684, 9:706, 10:747,
    10:750, 10:752, 10:753
Simpson, Thomas 7:519
Sinai Mountains 6:427
Sinbad the Sailor 7:527, 7:528
Sind (Shendu) 2:113, 10:798
Sintra, Pedro de 5:332
Sioux 1:23, 1:26, 5:385, 5:395, 5:397,
    5:399, 6:411, 6:436, 6:473, 7:546,
    7:559
Skraelings 4:318, 4:319
Skylab space station 1:38, 6:466,
    6:468, 8:623, 9:691, 9:692, 9:694
SLAR (side-looking airborne
    radar) technology 1:63, 1:64
slavery 1:55, 4:265, 4:283, 8:577,
    9:668
slaves
    African 3:176, 3:182, 3:226, 5:332,
        5:335
    Indian 4:263
    on plantations 3:176
    West Indian 3:205
slave trade 2:143, 4:314, 6:413,
    6:414–415, 6:440–441,
    6:472–473, 9:682, 10:744,
    10:749
    abolished 6:470, 6:473
    African 4:252, 4:284–287
    Portuguese 3:175
Slayton, Donald "Deke" 9:645
sled boat 7:517, 7:518
sleds 1:20, 5:376, 5:381, 7:519,

7:538, 7:554, 7:555, 7:557, 7:558,
    7:559, 8:629
sleeping sickness 5:368
Slessor, Mary 4:314
Sloane, Sir Hans 6:456
sloop 2:149, 2:159
Small, Charlotte 10:736, 10:737
smallpox 3:176, 3:180, 3:181, 3:182,
    3:208, 5:366, 5:370, 9:669, 9:706
Smith, Adam 6:442, 6:443
Smith, Annie Peck 10:788, 10:791
Smith, Jedediah Strong 1:31, 1:32,
    1:35, 9:664–667
Smith, John 6:432, 9:668–671
Smith, Joseph 2:109
Smith, Thomas 1:66
Smith, William 9:689
Smithsonian Astrophysical
    Observatory 9:674, 9:675
Smithsonian Contributions to
    Knowledge 9:673
Smithsonian Environmental
    Research Center, Chesapeake
    Bay 9:675
Smithsonian Institution 6:454,
    6:456, 6:457, 9:672–675, 10:783
Smithsonite 9:672
Smithson, James Lewis
    9:672–673, 9:675
Smolensk 8:586
Snake River 6:412
SnoCats 5:381
Snorri Thorfinnsson 4:316, 4:318,
    10:787
Sobat River 10:744, 10:745
Société de Géographie de Paris
    4:252
Society for the Abolition of
    Slavery 4:252
Society of Jesus see Jesuits
Socotra 10:745
Soderini, Pier 10:771
Solander, Daniel 1:69, 7:486, 8:626
solar eclipse 1:51, 1:59, 3:197,
    5:344
solar flares 9:677, 9:719
Solar and Heliospheric
    Observatory (SOHO) 9:677,
    9:702
solar system 1:49, 1:52, 3:233,
    6:468, 8:590, 8:591, 8:619, 8:632,
    8:639, 9:676–681
    origins of the 9:677
solar wind 9:702, 9:719
solar year 5:342, 5:344
Solomon Islands 2:98, 8:594
solstice 4:245, 4:319
Somalia 6:477, 9:707

Somaliland 2:114–115, 9:707,
    9:709
Somervell, Howard 5:341
sonar 1:65, 3:234, 3:239, 7:494,
    7:495, 7:559, 10:728, 10:760
sonic device 2:103
Sonora Desert 5:375
Sorocco, New Mexico 1:46, 1:47
SOS signal 3:192
Soto, Hernando de 3:182,
    9:682–685
South Africa 3:214, 3:224, 4:291,
    6:452, 6:477, 6:478, 8:626
South America 1:60, 1:70, 1:72–75,
    2:98, 2:113, 2:115, 2:117,
    2:130–132, 2:137, 2:155, 3:176,
    3:182, 3:188, 3:204, 3:212, 3:213,
    3:216, 4:253, 4:264, 4:303, 5:336,
    5:377, 5:378, 6:430, 6:446, 6:462,
    6:476, 6:477, 6:478, 7:487, 7:488,
    7:505, 7:552, 8:574, 8:600, 9:652,
    9:653, 9:658, 9:682–685, 9:687,
    9:703, 9:704, 9:705–706, 10:734,
    10:769–772, 10:777, 10:778
    1550 French map of 7:552
    Fitzroy's voyage to 4:264–265
    Humboldt's voyage 5:355–356
    medieval maps of 7:528
    Sebastian Cabot's expedition
        2:131
South Asia 4:258, 9:647
South Atlantic 1:53, 2:84–86, 2:97,
    2:100, 2:134, 9:689
South Atlantic wind system 3:224,
    4:293
South Australia 2:110
South Carolina 1:57, 4:279, 6:432
South Dakota 1:26, 5:398, 6:411
Southeast Asia 3:166, 3:184, 4:258,
    6:474, 7:487, 10:732, 10:748,
    10:777
    Portuguese settlements in 8:576
southern Africa 4:299, 7:504, 9:650,
    10:763
southern continent 3:197, 4:303,
    7:529, 9:654, 9:656, 9:686–689,
    10:733, 10:734 see also Terra
    Australis
Southern Hemisphere 1:53, 4:265,
    4:267, 7:556
Southern Ocean 7:504
South Georgia 2:85, 4:315, 8:636,
    8:637–638, 9:688, 9:689
South Orkney Islands 9:689
South Pacific 1:25, 1:70–71, 2:84,
    2:85, 2:148–150, 3:196–200,
    7:529, 8:596, 8:613, 8:626, 9:687,
    10:762

South Pass, Rocky Mountains **1**:35, **2**:146, **9**:664, **9**:665
South Pole **1**:18, **1**:19, **1**:20–21, **2**:84, **3**:171, **3**:231, **4**:255, **4**:315, **7**:502, **7**:553, **7**:554, **7**:557–558, **8**:595, **10**:762, **10**:792
  Amundsen's voyage **1**:18, **1**:20–21, **3**:231, **8**:625, **8**:627, **8**:629
  first flight to **2**:*118,* **2**:120
  Hillary's expedition to **5**:339
  Scott-Amundsen Base **1**:62
  Scott's 1911–1912 expedition **3**:171, **8**:602, **8**:629–630
  ski voyage to **8**:627
  transport to **5**:381
South Sandwich Islands **2**:85, **2**:86, **9**:689
South Shetland Islands **1**:61, **8**:637, **9**:689
Soviet Union **4**:288–290, **5**:382, **6**:466, **6**:468
  cold war with United States **8**:620
  launch of *Sputnik 1* **4**:310, **6**:466, **8**:614, **8**:615, **8**:620, **9**:690, **9**:692, **9**:695
  search for extraterrestrial intelligence **8**:632
  spacecraft **9**:690–694
  space exploration **1**:37, **1**:38, **1**:40, **1**:41, **4**:306, **9**:695–702
  and United States in space race **1**:37–42
  see also Russia
space
  observing the oceans from **10**:761
  pictures of the earth from **6**:428, **6**:432, **6**:435, **6**:469
space capsule **4**:307
spacecraft **4**:288, **4**:289, **9**:690–694
  first manned **1**:28–29, **4**:306, **9**:692
  Russian **8**:614, **8**:615
space exploration **1**:27–29, **1**:37–42, **4**:288–290, **4**:306–308, **6**:466–469, **6**:477, **7**:531, **7**:544, **9**:644–646, **9**:695–702
  clothing **3**:173–174
  docking in space **1**:27, **1**:39
  first American journey **9**:644, **9**:645
  first explorers **1**:37, **4**:288, **8**:615
  first woman in **1**:37, **1**:38, **8**:615, **10**:789, **10**:791
  international projects **1**:39
  living and working in space

1:40–41
  manned spaceflight programs **6**:466–467
  remote control **6**:432, **6**:468–469, **6**:*478,* **6**:479
  Russian **1**:37, **1**:38, **1**:40, **1**:41, **4**:306, **8**:612, **8**:615, **9**:695–702
  satellites **6**:432, **6**:466, **6**:468, **6**:469
  walking in space **1**:38–39
Spacelab mission **9**:697
space oblique Mercator (SOM) projection **6**:435
space probes **6**:468–469, **6**:479, **9**:678, **9**:691, **9**:692, **9**:695, **9**:700
space race **1**:37–42, **6**:466, **6**:467, **8**:620, **8**:621, **9**:696
space shuttles **1**:29, **1**:39, **1**:41, **4**:308, **6**:466, **6**:468, **8**:620, **8**:622, **9**:692–694
space sickness **1**:41
space stations **1**:38–39, **1**:39, **1**:41, **6**:468, **8**:615, **8**:620, **8**:*623,* **9**:691, **9**:692, **9**:694, **9**:699
space suits **1**:38, **3**:173–174, **4**:*306*
space telescopes **1**:47–48, **8**:620, **8**:622
Spain **2**:97, **2**:122–125, **2**:130, **2**:131, **3**:186, **4**:247, **4**:271, **5**:363, **5**:390, **5**:394, **6**:423, **6**:426, **6**:442, **6**:448, **6**:462–465, **6**:471, **6**:474, **7**:503, **7**:504, **7**:511, **8**:565, **8**:597, **8**:602, **9**:652–653, **9**:654, **9**:703–706, **10**:750, **10**:752, **10**:754, **10**:769, **10**:772, **10**:775
  colonization **2**:131, **3**:175–177, **3**:205
  control in America **7**:546, **7**:547
  and Portugal **3**:175–176, **4**:261, **4**:263, **4**:272, **8**:594
Spanish **10**:762, **10**:763
  navigators **10**:743
  traders **10**:749
Spanish Armada **4**:284, **4**:285, **4**:287, **9**:706
  defeat (1587) **3**:226, **3**:228
Spanish Empire **3**:204, **4**:260–263, **6**:463
  mercantilism in **6**:439–441
Spanish explorers **1**:72–75, **3**:181, **3**:201–208, **5**:373–375, **7**:511, **7**:520–522, **7**:523–526, **7**:549–552, **8**:569–572, **9**:663, **9**:682–685, **9**:687
species **7**:486, **7**:487, **7**:488
Speke, John Hanning **2**:114–117, **4**:253, **4**:255, **4**:314, **5**:366, **5**:368, **6**:417, **9**:707–710, **9**:714, **10**:745,

10:746
speleology **10**:755
Sperry, Elmer **7**:502
Sphinx, Giza **7**:*542*
Spice Islands (Moluccas) **2**:130, **2**:131, **2**:142, **3**:213, **5**:347, **5**:349, **6**:422–423, **6**:426, **6**:475, **7**:515, **7**:551, **7**:552, **8**:574, **8**:576, **9**:704
Spice Route **2**:139
spices **6**:422–423, **6**:474–476, **8**:574, **9**:662
spice trade **1**:66, **2**:126, **2**:133, **2**:135, **2**:142, **3**:175, **4**:291, **4**:293, **5**:346–349, **7**:503, **7**:504, **9**:655, **10**:747, **10**:748–749, **10**:750
Spirit space rover **6**:469, **9**:678, **9**:697, **9**:699
Spitsbergen **1**:66, **1**:67, **2**:101, **2**:102, **3**:235, **3**:236, **3**:237, **4**:254, **6**:461, **7**:507, **7**:508, **7**:509, **7**:510, **7**:513, **7**:518, **7**:554, **8**:612, **8**:614, **8**:627, **10**:745, **10**:751
  King's Bay **2**:119
sponsorship **8**:601, **9**:672, **10**:747, **10**:748, **10**:790
SPOT satellite **8**:606
spruce beer **10**:763, **10**:764, **10**:799
Sputnik 1 **4**:310, **6**:466, **8**:614, **8**:615, **8**:620, **9**:690, **9**:692, **9**:695
Sri Lanka (Ceylon) **3**:167, **4**:257, **5**:347, **5**:359, **10**:750
Ssuma Ch'ien **10**:798
Stadacona **2**:152, **2**:153, **2**:154, **4**:272
Stadaconans **2**:151
Stafford, Edward **5**:324
Stairs, William G. **9**:*715*
Stanhope, Hester **10**:*788,* **10**:789
Stanley, Henry Hope **9**:711
Stanley, Henry Morton **6**:414, **6**:417, **9**:708, **9**:710, **9**:711–715, **10**:746
Stark, Freya **10**:790–791
stars **1**:49, **1**:52–53, **5**:342–343, **5**:393, **7**:484, **7**:489, **8**:634
  Hipparchus's catalog **1**:50, **5**:342, **5**:343
  Ptolemy's catalog **8**:589
  shooting or falling **9**:681
Staten Landt **10**:734
steam-powered locomotives **5**:378
steamships **9**:648, **9**:650, **10**:743
Steele, Richard **3**:214
Steengracht-Capellan, Henrietta van **10**:744
Stein, Marc Aurel **9**:660, **9**:663
steppes **5**:379, **8**:602

Steudner, Hermann **10**:745, **10**:746
Stine Ingstad, Helge and Ann **4**:317
Stokes, Pringle **4**:264
Stone Age, cave paintings **10**:754
Stornoway **6**:418
Strabo **4**:247, **4**:298, **4**:300, **4**:301, **9**:716–718
Stradling, Captain **3**:214
Strait of Belle Isle **2**:151
Strait of Gibraltar **5**:328
Strait of Magellan **2**:98, **2**:148, **3**:217, **3**:227, **4**:266, **6**:424, **6**:425, **6**:*426,* **7**:505, **9**:687, **9**:705
Straits of Mackinac **6**:436, **6**:437
stratosphere **1**:61, **1**:79
Stromness **8**:638
Stuart, John McDouall **2**:110
Stuart, Robert **1**:35
Sublimis Deus Sic Dilexit (papal bull) **6**:470, **6**:472
submarines **3**:195, **9**:648
  nuclear-powered **9**:650, **9**:651
submersibles **3**:234, **10**:724–727
  autonomous **10**:727
  unmanned **10**:726–727
Su-chou **8**:610
Sudan **9**:709, **9**:710, **9**:715, **10**:745
Sudd **9**:709
Suez Canal **9**:712
Suffolk **4**:264
sugar plantations **3**:176, **3**:182
Süleyman I, Sultan **4**:300
Sumatra **3**:166, **3**:167, **5**:346, **5**:348, **5**:349, **5**:358, **7**:533, **8**:*574*
Sumer **5**:377
Sumerians **10**:730
  ships **5**:338
sun **1**:43, **1**:46, **1**:49, **3**:233, **8**:590, **8**:591, **9**:676, **9**:677, **9**:702
  and celestial navigation **7**:489, **7**:491
  as center of the universe **7**:484, **7**:486
  eclipse of the **1**:51, **1**:59, **3**:197, **5**:344
  measuring height of **7**:499
sunblock **3**:172
Sunda Strait **7**:504
sundials **4**:*298,* **7**:491, **10**:799
sunspots **1**:44, **1**:49, **5**:357, **9**:677, **9**:719
supernovas **1**:52
superpowers **6**:466
Surveying Corps **4**:265
surveyor's chain *see* Gunter's chain
surveys **4**:311, **10**:728–731
  aerial **1**:65, **4**:305

in the ancient world **10:**730
geological **3:**231
instruments **10:**735
methods **6:**419, **6:**452
for oil **10:**730–731
purpose of **10:**728–729
technology **10:**729
underwater **10:**729
of the United States **10:**730, **10:**735–738
survival of the fittest **3:**219, **7:**487–488, **10:**779
Sutter's Fort **2:**146
Svalbard archipelago **2:**101, **7:**507, **7:**513
Sverdrup, Otto Neumann **8:**627
Swan, Captain **3:**213
Sweden **4:**250, **6:**461, **7:**507–510, **10:**773
Russian war with **2:**87
Swedes **10:**775
Swedish North Polar Expedition **7:**507–508
sweet potato (*batata*) **3:**182, **3:**183, **3:**186
Swift, Jonathan **6:**429, **7:**528, **7:**529, **7:**530
Sydney **2:**84, **2:**85, **2:**86, **4:**268
Syene **4:**245
synoptic chart **4:**267
Syria **1:**76, **1:**77, **2:**115, **2:**117, **5:**358, **5:**359, **5:**360, **9:**647
Syrian Desert **1:**76, **10:**788, **10:**789
Szechwan **2:**93

Tabascans **3:**206, **3:**239
Tabasco **3:**204, **3:**206
Tabora (Kezeh) **2:**116, **9:**708
tacking **2:**149, **2:**159, **9:**648, **9:**719
Tadoussac, Treaty of **3:**178
Tagus River **3:**223
Tahiti **1:**69, **2:**98, **2:**99, **3:**197, **3:**198, **3:**199, **3:**200, **3:**218, **4:**252, **6:**471
Taino **3:**186, **3:**187, **8:**569, **8:**570, **8:**572, **8:**639
Taiwan **4:**300
Tajikistan **9:**663, **10:**793
Takla Makan Desert **5:**379, **8:**586, **9:**661, **9:**663
Talon, Jean-Baptiste **5:**371
Tampa Bay **6:**464
Tang dynasty **9:**660, **9:**662
Tangier **5:**358
Tanit **5:**330
Tanki **6:**455
Tanner, Joseph **1:***47*
Tanzania **4:**314, **9:**708, **9:**712
Taos **2:**145

Tashkent **9:**661
Tasman, Abel **3:**198, **4:**303, **7:**504, **9:**687, **9:**688, **10:**732–734
Tasmania **4:**268, **4:**303, **9:**687, **9:**688, **10:**733, **10:**734 *see also* Van Diemen's Land
Tavistock **3:**226
Taxila **4:**259
taxonomy **7:**559
Taylor, Annie Royle **4:**314
Taylor, E. G. R. **7:**493
Tchou Yu **7:**498
tectonic plates **10:**779
Teflon **3:**174
Tehran **2:**93
Teixeira, Tristão Vaz **5:**332, **5:**333
Tektite project (NASA) **10:**761
telegram **3:**190, **3:**192, **3:**193
telegraph **4:**267, **5:**380
electric **3:**190, **3:**192, **3:**193
transatlantic cable route **10:**743, **10:**757, **10:**760
telegraphy, wireless **3:**190, **3:**193
telemetry **3:**190, **3:**195
telephone **3:**190, **3:**192, **3:**194
cellular **3:**194
mobile system **3:**191
underwater **3:**234
video service **3:**191
telescopes **1:**44–45, **1:**46, **1:**47–48, **1:**49, **1:**50, **1:**54, **3:**191, **5:**342, **5:**343, **9:**695, **10:**735
arrays **1:**47
Galileo's **7:**484, **7:**532
radio **1:**46, **1:**47, **1:***54*, **8:**632–634
reflecting **1:**45, **1:**50
refracting **1:**44–45, **1:**50
space **1:**47–48, **8:**620, **8:**622
television **3:**194
underwater cameras **3:**210
Telstar **3:**191, **3:**194, **6:**468, **8:**620, **8:**621
Tenochtitlán **3:**204, **6:**464, **9:**706
conquest of **3:**206–208
Tenzing Norgay **4:**253, **4:**315, **5:**339, **5:**340
Tereshkova, Valentina **1:**37, **1:**38, **8:**615, **10:**789, **10:**791
termination shock **9:**702
Ternate **6:**475
Teroahauté, Michel **4:**275
Terra Australis **3:**197, **6:***425*, **7:**529, **7:**556, **8:**593, **8:**594, **8:**595, **9:**654, **9:**656, **10:**734 *see also* Australia; southern continent
Terra da Vera Cruz **2:**134
Terra Incognita **9:**656, **9:**686
Terra Nova **8:***630*

Terrebonne **10:**738
test pilots **4:**288, **4:**306, **9:**644, **9:**645
Teton Sioux **6:**411
Texas **2:**122–125, **2:**147, **3:**201, **3:**202, **5:**384, **5:**386, **6:**410, **7:**547, **7:**548, **9:**684, **9:***693*
Texas Surgical Society **2:**124
Thailand **3:**166, **8:***574*
Thales of Miletus **6:**434
Thanksgiving **7:**526
thermal imaging **1:**63, **1:**79
Thomas, Pascoe **5:**367
Thompson, Almon **8:**579
Thompson, Benjamin **1:**71
Thompson, David **4:**313, **10:**735–738
Thomson, Charles Wyville **10:**758
Thomson, George Malcolm **1:**68
Thomson, William (Baron Kelvin) **10:**741, **10:**757
Thorbjarn Vifilsson **4:**316
Thorfinn Thordarsson *see* Karlsefni, Thorfinn
Thorne, Robert **7:**511
Thorstein Eriksson **4:**248, **4:**316
Thorvald Aswaldsson **4:**248
Thorvald Eriksson **4:**248, **4:**316, **6:**407
Thousand and One Nights **7:**527, **7:**528
Thule **4:**246, **4:***247*, **8:**627, **9:**717, **9:**718
Thunberg, Carl Peter **8:**626
Thunder Bay **5:**396
Tiberius, Emperor **10:**798
Tibet **2:**91, **4:**314, **5:**341, **8:**585, **8:**586, **8:**588, **8:**613, **9:**707, **9:**709, **10:**731, **10:**789, **10:**793, **10:**794–795
tidal bore **10:**741, **10:**799
tidal dock, at Lothal **10:**741
tide clocks **10:**742
tide predictors **10:***740*, **10:***741*
tides **10:**739–743
defined **10:**739
measuring **10:**741–742
Tidore **6:**475
Tien Shan Mountains **4:**258, **8:**586
Tierra del Fuego **1:**69, **3:**216, **3:**217, **3:**226, **3:**227, **4:**264, **4:***265*, **4:***266*, **6:***426*, **9:**687
Tigris River **1:**16, **5:**338, **6:***429*
Timbuktu **2:**143, **4:**252, **4:**273, **4:**274, **5:**361, **7:**533–534, **7:**536, **8:**602
time at sea **3:**168–169, **5:**392–393, **7:**492, **7:**495, **7:**559

Timia **2:**142
Timocharis **5:**343
Timor **3:**214
Timucuan Indians **3:**179, **6:***470*
Timur (Tamerlane) **9:**661
Tinné, Alexandrine-Pieternella-Françoise **10:**744–746, **10:***786*, **10:**788
Tinn, Philip F. **10:**744
Tirol **5:**373
TIROS (weather satellite) **8:**606, **8:**620, **8:**623, **10:**784
Titanic, HMS **1:**36, **3:**234, **4:**311, **7:**542, **7:**544, **9:**651, **10:**724, **10:**726, **10:**727
Tlaxcala **3:**208
Tlaxcalans **3:**207, **3:**239
Tlingit language **1:**24
tobacco **3:**182, **3:**186, **3:**226, **3:**228, **6:**440, **6:**441, **8:**599
Todd, Sarah **1:**34
Tombaugh, Clyde W. **9:**680
Tombouctou *see* Timbuktu
Tomsk **8:**612
Tonga **10:**734
Tonty, Henri de **5:**383, **5:**384–386, **5:**387
topography **3:**239, **4:**279, **4:**319, **8:**591, **8:**605, **8:**639
Tordesillas, Treaty of (1494) **2:**131, **3:**176, **4:**261, **4:**263, **4:**272, **6:**423, **6:**448, **9:**704
Torell, Otto **7:**507, **7:**508
T and O renderings **6:**428
Torquay **2:**113
Torres Strait **10:**734
Torricelli, Evangelista **10:**782
total ozone mapping spectrometer (TOMS) **8:**607
Totonacs **3:**207, **3:**239
Toulon **3:**209
Toulouse **8:**605
tourism **9:**660, **9:**661
space **9:**694
Tower of the Winds **10:**783
trade **3:**165, **3:**182, **9:**659–663, **10:**740, **10:**747–751
beginnings of **3:**231
between Europe and Asia **10:**748
caravan routes **2:**139–143
Chinese **3:**165–167
control of **6:**476
early 747, **10:**747
England-Russia **2:**132
luxury goods **2:**143, **3:**165, **6:**474, **10:**732, **10:**748
new routes **10:**749

trade (cont.)
  Portuguese routes **8**:573–576
  rivalry 750, **10**:750
  silent **2**:142
  Silk Road **5**:378–379
  see also fur trade; slave trade;
    spice trade
Tradescant, John **6**:455, **6**:457
Tradescant, John, Jr. **6**:454, **6**:456,
  6:457
Tradescant's Ark **6**:455–456
trading post **3**:176, **7**:546, **7**:559,
  8:639, **9**:659, **10**:735
Tralee **2**:104, **2**:105
Trana, Kristian **6**:458
Trans-Africa Hovercraft
  (1969–1970) **9**:658
transit **1**:69, **1**:79, **4**:252, **5**:380
transport **3**:179
  animals **5**:378
  extraterrestrial **5**:382
  land **5**:376–382
  land survey for **10**:728
  in the mountains **5**:382
travel books **8**:603
Traversay Islands **2**:85
traverse board **3**:220, **3**:221
Trent, Council of **6**:448–449
Treschler, Christoph **7**:499
tribute **5**:375, **6**:411
trigonometry **5**:344, **5**:345, **6**:435,
  6:479
Tripoli **10**:746
trireme **5**:329
Tristão, Nuno **5**:332, **5**:335
Triton **10**:783
Trois-Rivières, Quebec **5**:394, **5**:396
Tromsø **7**:509
Tropic of Cancer **5**:389
Tropic of Capricorn **5**:389
Tsangpo River **10**:794
tsetse flies **5**:368
Tsien Tang River **10**:741
Tsing Hai (Lake Koko Nor) **8**:586
Tsiolkovsky, Konstantin **1**:37, **9**:690
Tswana language **6**:452
Tuamoto atolls **2**:85
Tuaregs **2**:142, **10**:746, **10**:799
Tuckey, James **5**:366
Túcume **5**:336, **5**:338
Tupinamba **2**:134
Turkey **1**:15, **1**:76, **1**:77, **5**:342, **5**:358,
  8:565, **9**:716, **10**:747, **10**:752,
  10:775, **10**:791
  Russia's war with (1828–1829)
    2:86
  see also Asia Minor
Turkistan **8**:585, **8**:586, **8**:588

Turnor, Philip **10**:735
Tuscany **9**:716, **10**:782
typhoid **4**:296, **4**:319, **5**:368, **9**:670,
  9:706
Tyre **1**:15, **1**:16
Tyrkir **6**:404
UAVs (unmanned aerial vehicles)
  1:63, **1**:65
Udyana **4**:259
Uganda **9**:710, **9**:715
Ujiji **6**:414, **6**:417, **9**:712
Ukerewe **9**:708
Ukraine **9**:707, **9**:712
Ulan Bator **8**:586
Ulm, Germany **8**:589
ultraviolet rays **1**:47, **1**:65, **3**:172,
  3:239
Unanga people **8**:613
underground exploration **10**:728,
  10:752–755
undersea observatories **10**:724,
  10:761
undersea telegraph cable **10**:757
underwater exploration **3**:234,
  4:274, **10**:724–727, **10**:756–761
  breathing **10**:759
  clothing **3**:173
  communication devices **3**:195,
    3:234
  Cousteau's **3**:210–211
Union Pacific Railroad **2**:109, **5**:380
United East Indies Company
  7:504, **7**:505
United Kingdom see Great Britain
United Nations, International
  Environment Prize **3**:211
United States **1**:30–32, **1**:33–36,
  2:91, **3**:191, **5**:355, **6**:408–412,
  6:466, **7**:495, **7**:496, **8**:577–580,
  9:664–667, **9**:692–702
  in Alaska **2**:90, **8**:613
  border with Canada **10**:736,
    10:737, **10**:738
  and Britain **1**:33
  cold war with U.S.S.R. **6**:466,
    8:620
  Coronado's route through
    southern **3**:202
  frontier exploration **4**:279–283
  geographical societies **4**:256
  independence **6**:408
  land claims in Antarctica **2**:120
  railroads **5**:380, **10**:728
  settlement of western
    9:664–667
  southwestern **7**:523–526
  spacecraft **9**:690–694
  space exploration **1**:27–29,

  1:37–42, **9**:695–702
  surveys of **10**:730, **10**:735–738
  and U.S.S.R. in space race
    1:37–42
  war with Mexico **4**:282–283
universe **3**:230
  big bang theory **1**:54, **9**:677
  extraterrestrial life **1**:54
  geocentric theories **1**:49, **3**:233,
    8:590
  heliocentric theory **1**:49, **8**:591
  Newton's laws of motion **1**:51
Ural Mountains **2**:87, **7**:507, **8**:612
Uranus **1**:50, **1**:52, **5**:391, **9**:676,
  9:679, **9**:680–681, **9**:697, **9**:701
Urga **8**:586
Uruguay River **7**:552
U.S. Army **6**:408
  Corps of Topographical
    Engineers **4**:279, **4**:281
U.S. Congress **1**:30, **1**:32, **1**:36,
  4:280, **9**:673, **9**:675
U.S. Corps of Discovery **6**:408
U.S. Exploring Expedition **9**:674
U.S. Geological Survey **8**:580
Usk, Wales **10**:777
U.S. Marine Corps **4**:306
U.S.-Mexican Boundary
  Commission **9**:674
U.S. Mint **8**:618
U.S. National Oceanic and
  Atmospheric Administration
  (NOAA) **10**:761
U.S. Naval Experimental Station,
  Annapolis, Maryland **10**:760
U.S. Navy **2**:118, **7**:519, **7**:537,
  10:725, **10**:726
  aerial photography **8**:606
  Polaris expedition **9**:674
Usodimare, Antonio di **5**:332,
  5:335
U.S. Senate **4**:283
U.S.S.R. see Soviet Union
Ussuri **8**:586, **8**:613
Ussuri River **8**:585
Utah **2**:109, **2**:145, **5**:380
Utah Desert **7**:543
Ute Indians **2**:108, **2**:147
utopias **7**:530, **7**:531
Uzbekistan **8**:564, **8**:565, **9**:661

Valenzuela, Maria de **6**:462
Valignano, Alessandro **8**:609
Valladolid **3**:185, **3**:189, **6**:462
Vallseca, Gabriel **6**:471
Van Allen radiation belt **8**:620
Vancouver, British Columbia **1**:24,
  4:313

Vancouver, George **4**:313,
  10:762–764
Vancouver, Washington **8**:615
Vancouver Island **3**:227, **10**:762,
  10:763, **10**:764
Vandenberg Air Force Base,
  California **10**:785
Van der Grinten projection **6**:435
van Diemen, Anthony **7**:504,
  10:733, **10**:734
Van Diemen's Land **4**:268, **10**:733
  see also Tasmania
Vanguard **8**:601
Vanuatu **1**:71, **8**:596, **9**:687, **9**:688
Varagian Guard **10**:775
Varanasi **4**:259
Varenius **4**:304, **4**:305
Vasquez, Louis **2**:108
Vatican collections **6**:456
Veer, Gerrit de **7**:513, **7**:556
vehicles
  four-wheel drive **5**:382
  lightweight tracked **5**:381
  radio-controlled lunar **5**:377
  remote-controlled land **5**:382
  wheeled **5**:376, **5**:377
  wind-powered **5**:381
Velázquez, Diego **3**:204, **3**:205,
  3:207, **3**:208, **6**:462, **6**:464, **9**:704
Venetians
  cogs **9**:649
  traders **4**:301
Venezuela **3**:188, **5**:355, **8**:599,
  8:600, **10**:770
Venice **2**:126, **2**:129, **6**:476, **8**:564,
  8:565, **8**:566, **8**:568, **9**:663,
  10:748–749
  war with Genoa **8**:566, **8**:568
Venus **1**:46, **1**:69, **4**:252, **7**:498,
  8:590, **9**:676, **9**:678, **9**:679, **9**:691,
  9:696, **9**:700
Veracruz **3**:204, **3**:206, **5**:374
Vergil, Polydore **2**:128
Verina **5**:356
Vermeer, Jan, The Geographer
  4:304
Verne, Jules **7**:528, **7**:530
  Around the Moon **7**:532
  From the Earth to the Moon **7**:530
  Journey to the Center of the
    Earth, A **7**:530
  Twenty Thousand Leagues under
    the Sea **7**:530
Verrazzano, Giovanni da **4**:271,
  4:272, **5**:324, **10**:765–768
Verrazzano, Girolamo da **10**:766,
  10:767
Verre Company **5**:347, **5**:349

Versailles **1:***61*

Very Large Array (VLA) radio telescope, Sorocco, New Mexico **1:***46*, **1:***47*

Vespucci, Amerigo **2:**129, **2:**135, **6:**431, **7:***497*, **7:**530, **7:**531, **10:769–772**

Victoria, Queen **2:**115, **2:**117, **3:**190, **3:**193, **9:**713, **9:**715

Victoria, South Australia **2:**110

Victoria Falls **6:**414, **6:**416

Victoria Land **7:**554, **7:**557

Victory Point, King William Island **4:**277

videophone **3:**191, **3:**194

Vieira, Antonio **8:**576

Vietnam **3:**166, **3:**167, **4:**274, **4:**295, **4:**296–297

South **8:**567

Vignau, Nicolas de **5:**353

Vikings **3:**184, **4:**250, **4:**300–301, **4:**319, **6:**404–407, **8:**624–625, **10:**747, **10:773–776**

explorers **10:**743

migrations **10:**775–776

navigation **4:**250, **7:**491–492, **7:**494, **7:**559, **10:**776, **10:**781

shipbuilding **9:**648

ships **10:***774*, **10:**775

traders **10:**751

Viking space mission **9:**691, **9:**696, **9:**698–699

Vilgerdarsen, Floki **7:**491, **7:**494

Villagra, Gasper Perez de **7:**526

Vine, Allyn **10:**727

Vineyard Sound **10:**768

Vinland **4:**317–318, **6:**407, **7:**549, **7:**550

Virginia **1:**30, **2:**94, **2:**118, **3:**177, **3:**182, **3:**213, **4:**281, **4:***312*, **4:**313, **5:**326, **6:**454, **6:**455, **6:**456, **8:**598, **8:**599, **9:**668–671, **9:**669

Virginia Company **9:**668, **9:**669

Virgin Islands **3:**187

Visscher, Frans Jacobszoon **10:**733

vitamin deficiency **8:**583, **8:**584, **10:**763

volcanoes **2:**92, **2:**106, **3:**217, **3:**218, **3:**231, **5:**329, **7:**557, **8:**602, **8:**606, **10:**785

on Jupiter **9:**700

thermal monitoring **8:**607

underwater **10:**727, **10:**761

Vostock Island **2:**86

Vostok (spacecraft) **1:**37, **4:**288, **4:**289, **4:**290, **8:**615, **9:**692, **10:**791

Voyager (spacecraft) **8:**619, **9:***676*,

9:697, **9:**700, **9:**701, **9:**702

vulcanized rubber **3:**172, **3:**239

Wadi Hammamat **6:**427

Waldseemüller, Martin **4:**303, **6:**428, **6:**431, **10:**771, **10:**772

Wales **2:**105, **9:**711, **9:**712, **10:**777, **10:**779

Walker, John **3:**196

Wallace, Alfred Russel **7:**486, **7:**487, **7:**488, **10:777–780**

Wallace's Line **10:**779

Wallis, Samuel **2:**148, **2:**150

Walsh, Don **10:**725, **10:**726

Wang-P'an **8:**610

Ward Hunt Island **8:**627

War of Jenkins's Ear **6:**439

War of the Spanish Succession **5:**394

Warwick, Ambrose Dudley, earl of **4:**285

Warwijck, Wijbrandt van **7:**504

Washington (state) **1:**33, **1:**34, **4:**279, **4:**280, **8:**615, **10:**737, **10:**788

Washington, George **2:**94, **6:**430

Washington, DC **3:**193, **4:**253, **4:**256, **5:**390, **6:**411, **6:**454, **6:**457, **9:**671, **9:**672, **9:**673, **10:**789

water clock **10:**783, **10:**799

Waterloo Place, London **4:***278*

Watson-Watt, Robert Alexander **7:**495

weapons, Portuguese **8:**576

weather **3:**232–233

charts **9:**673

the science of **10:**782–783

weather forecasting **4:**267, **8:**623, **10:781–785**

in the air **10:**784

by satellites and computers **3:**229, **8:**606, **8:**620, **8:**623, **10:**781, **10:**784–785

early **10:**781–782

weather observation network **10:**782–783

Webber, John **9:**688

Webb, James **1:**48

Weddell Sea **8:**627

Wedgwood, Josiah **3:**216

weightlessness **1:**40, **1:**42, **4:**289, **4:**307, **4:**308

Wellington Channel **4:**276

Wells, H. G., *The Island of Dr Moreau* **7:**528, **7:**530

Wen Wang **6:**455

West Africa **1:**70, **2:**115, **2:**117, **2:**143, **3:**183, **3:**213, **3:**222, **4:**252,

4:273, **4:**274, **4:**284, **4:**302, **4:**314, **5:**328–330, **5:**332, **6:**431, **6:**470, **7:**533–536, **8:**602, **9:**650, **9:**651, **9:**654, **10:**788, **10:**790

West Australia current **10:***742*

West Indies **1:**70, **2:**126, **2:**155, **3:**187, **3:**205, **3:**226, **4:**247, **4:**287, **4:**298, **6:**443

Westminster Abbey, London **3:**219, **5:**324, **6:**417

wet collodion process **7:**541, **7:**542

Wetheringsett, Suffolk **5:**324

wet suits **3:**173

whaling **4:**276, **7:**513, **7:**517, **9:**689, **10:**749, **10:**751

whaling ships **9:**655

wheel, invention of the **5:**376, **5:**377

Whitby **3:**196

White, Edward **1:**38, **6:***468*

White, John **6:**473, **8:**598, **8:**599, **8:**603

White Nile **10:**745

White Sea **2:**89

Wichita Indians **3:**202, **3:**239

Wilderness Road **2:**94, **2:**95

Wilkes, Charles **6:**430, **7:**556

Wilkes Land **7:**556

Wilkins, George Hubert **1:**61, **1:**62

Wilkinson, James **7:**545, **7:**546, **7:**547

Willamette River valley **9:**665

William I, king of Sicily **5:**365

William of Rubruck **9:**662

Williamstown, Ontario **10:**738

Willoughby, Lincolnshire **9:**668

Willoughby, Hugh **2:**132, **7:**511–512, **7:**553

Wills, William John **2:**111–112, **4:**299, **4:**314, **6:**470, **6:**473

Wilson, Edward **8:**628, **8:**629

Wilson, William **5:**353

Winchester, Virginia **2:**118

wind drift instrument **2:**121, **2:**159

wind power vehicles **5:**381

Wind River Mountains **4:**280

winds

measurements **2:**121, **2:**159, **4:**266, **4:**267

in navigation **7:**489–491, **7:**505

southwest **7:**491

wind vane **10:**781, **10:**783, **10:**799

Winkel Tripel projection **6:**435

Winnipeg River **5:**397

wireless communication **3:**190, **3:**192–193

Wisconsin River **5:**371, **6:**437

Wisting, Oskar **1:**21

women

around-the-world yachtswomen **8:***604*, **10:**789, **10:**792

aviators **2:**103

early explorers of America **10:**787–788

explorers **1:**76–78, **2:**91–93, **2:**101–103, **10:**744–746, **10:786–792**

first in space **1:**37, **1:**42, **8:**615, **10:**789, **10:**791

heiresses **10:**788–790

in society **10:**786–787

suffrage **10:**780

travel writers **10:**790–791

Woodman, David C. **4:**278

Woods Hole Marine Biology Laboratory, Massachusetts **10:**758

Woods Hole Oceanographic Institution (WHOI) **10:**726

Deep Sea Submergence Laboratory **10:**727

World Air Sports Federation **4:**289

World Congress of Faiths **10:**794, **10:**795

world maps **6:**430–431, **6:**435, **6:**444, **6:**446

of Eratosthenes of Cyrene **4:**245, **4:**246–247, **4:**299, **5:**345

Garcia's (1076) **3:***230*

of Henricus Martellus **5:***332*

World Ocean Circulation Experiment **10:**760

World's Columbian Exposition (1893), Chicago **1:**26

World War I (1914–1918) **1:**78, **2:**118, **6:**432, **10:**784

aviation in **1:**60

reconnaissance missions **8:**605, **8:**606

World War II (1939–1945) **2:**103, **2:**121, **4:**306, **6:**432, **8:**605, **8:**606, **10:**784

World Wide Web **10:**727

Worsley, Frank **8:**638

Wrangel, Ferdinand Petrovich von **8:**612

Wren, Christopher **5:**390

Wright, Orville and Wilbur **1:**59, **1:**62, **8:**606

Wu Ti, emperor of China **10:**796, **10:**797

Wu Tsu-Hsu **10:**741

Wyoming **1:**32, **2:**108, **5:**398, **8:**578, **8:***618*, **9:**664

X-15 program (NASA) **6:**468
Xanadu **8:**567
Xeres, Francisco de **6:**478
X Prize Foundation **9:**694

yachtswomen **8:**604, **10:**789,
    10:792
Yakutsk **2:**88, **2:**90, **8:**612
Yang-chou **8:**567
Yangtze River **2:**93, **3:**166, **8:**567,
    8:586
Yanov, Colonel **10:**793
Yasshüyük **1:**15
Yellow River **4:**257, **4:**258, **8:**586
Yellowstone National Park **2:**107,
    2:109
  map **8:***580*
Yellowstone River **1:**57, **6:**408,
    6:412
Yemen **5:**358
Yenisei River **7:**508
Yermak **8:**612
Yiyang **8:**567
York, Canada **7:**548
Yorkshire, England **2:**91, **4:**284,
    4:287
Young, Brigham **2:**109
Younghusband, Francis Edward
    10:793–795
Young, John W. **9:***695*, **9:**697
Yucatán **3:**204, **3:**205, **6:**462
Yucatán Peninsula **7:**551
Yüeh-chih **10:**796, **10:**797
Yukon **9:**675
Yumurtalik **8:**565
Yunnan Province **3:**164, **3:**167,
    4:296, **4:**297, **8:**567

Zacatecas **7:**523
Zambezi River **6:**414, **6:**416, **9:***652*
Zanzibar **6:**417, **9:**712
Zarco, João Gonçalves **5:**332,
    5:333
Zayton **5:**361
Zeeland **10:**734
Zhang Qian (Chang Chi'en) **4:**300,
    9:659, **9:**660, **10:796–798**
Zhaoqing **8:**610
Zheng He *see* Cheng Ho
zoology **6:**455, **6:**461, **7:**484, **8:**587,
    10:745
zoos **6:**455
Zubayda **2:**140
Zurara, Gomes Eanes de **5:**335